China's Poor Regions

Despite recent economic advances, a significant proportion of people in China are still poor. This book investigates the problem of poverty in China's regions, discussing in particular the role of rural–urban migration in reducing rural poverty. It surveys the distribution and characteristics of poverty, examines anti-poverty initiatives by the Chinese government, and includes the results of an original case study conducted in Shanxi, a typical province in central China.

Mei Zhang holds a Ph.D. degree from the University of Cambridge. Her main areas of work are women's labour, rural–urban migration and poverty, urbanisation, and quantitative analyses of urban environments.

RoutledgeCurzon Studies on the Chinese Economy
Series Editors
Peter Nolan, University of Cambridge
Dong Fureng, Beijing University

The aim of this series is to publish original, high-quality, research-level work by both new and established scholars in the West and the East, on all aspects of the Chinese economy, including studies of business and economic history.

China's Poor Regions

Rural–urban migration, poverty,
economic reform, and urbanisation

Mei Zhang

RoutledgeCurzon
Taylor & Francis Group

LONDON AND NEW YORK

First published 2003
by RoutledgeCurzon
11 New Fetter Lane, London EC4P 4EE

Simultaneously published in the USA and Canada
by RoutledgeCurzon
29 West 35th Street, New York, NY 10001

RoutledgeCurzon is an imprint of the Taylor & Francis Group

© 2003 Mei Zhang

Typeset in Times by Wearset Ltd, Boldon, Tyne and Wear
Printed and bound in Great Britain by Biddles Ltd, Guildford and
King's Lynn

British Library Cataloguing in Publication Data
A catalogue record for this book is available from the British Library

Library of Congress Cataloging in Publication Data
Zhang, Mei, 1963–
  China's poor regions : rural-urban migration, poverty, economic
reform, and urbanisation / Mei Zhang.
    p.cm. – (RoutledgeCurzon studies on the Chinese economy)
Includes bibliographical references and index.
  1. Rural-urban migration–China. 2. Rural poor–China.
I. Title. II. Series.
  HB2114.A3Z478 2003
  339.4'6'0951091734–dc21   2003001974

ISBN 0–415–32145–X

Contents

Illustrations

Figures

Tables

Foreword

As China enters the twenty-first century, it faces a series of deep challenges that threaten the entire social, economic and political system. China is in a period of high-speed economic and social change. It has long been pointed out by political analysts that the potential for political instability is especially acute during such periods. The Chinese government is working extremely hard to try to increase its risk management capabilities to meet these challenges. These include the challenge that large firms in China must face within the World Trade Organization (WTO) from the global business revolution that has taken place since the 1980s; the environmental challenge – there already are deep threats to the prospect for ecologically sustainable development in China; the challenge to raise the capability of, and identify the appropriate development role for, the state; the international relations challenge that faces the country, especially in its relationship with the United States; the financial challenge, which was vividly illuminated by the Asian financial crisis; and the challenges within the Chinese Communist Party, especially the drive to eliminate corruption.

Dr Zhang's study of the internal migration process in China addresses one of the most important issues in its political economy in the early twenty-first century, perhaps the most important of all. Behind almost every aspect of China's development lies the harsh reality of the 'Lewis model' of economic development with unlimited supplies of labour. China has a huge population, totalling almost 1.3 billion. The population growth rate is still quite fast, adding an extra 15–16 million people each year to the total. From 1990 to 1999, China's working-age population rose from 679 million to 829 million, an increase of no fewer than 150 million in less than a decade. Almost 70 per cent of the Chinese population still lives in rural areas. Employment in the farm sector is stagnant, at around 330 million. It is estimated that there are around 150 million 'surplus' farm workers. This places a powerful constraint on the rate of growth of real incomes for low-skilled occupations in the non-farm sector.

As the impact of the WTO increases, pressures on rural employment will intensify. The main alternative source of rural labour absorption, the 'township and village enterprises' (TVEs), stagnated in terms of employment creation (at around 127 million employees) after the mid-1990s. The rapid growth of the TVEs in the 1980s and early 1990s was based mainly on the rapid growth of small businesses in labour-intensive activities using simple technologies. In order to compete within the global value chain, the TVEs are being forced to increase labour productivity fast, and the thousands of new entrants to various industries in the early 1990s faced increasing challenges from greater market integration and pressures to consolidate. The unavoidable reality is that the level of rural under-employment will continue to rise in the early years of the twenty-first century.

The farm sector is continuing to grow at around 5–6 per cent per annum, and investing on a large scale. However, the rate of growth of farm incomes has reduced to, at best, slow progress. Many analysts estimate that rural incomes have stagnated, and some argue that they have even declined since the mid-1990s. For example, Chen Xiwen, deputy director of the State Development Research Centre, estimates that average real income of China's farmers 'suffered an average decline in income in 1998, 1999, 2000 and 2001' (reported in the *Financial Times*, 31 October 2002). The farm sector will face severe challenges in the face of the rise in imports within the WTO, and possible deterioration in the terms of trade for farm products. One recent study believes that within the WTO in the years ahead, 'the prospects for most rural households are grim'.

All analysts are agreed that the early years of China's rural reforms in the late 1970s and early 1980s saw a massive decline in absolute poverty. However, there still are huge numbers of people who are absolutely poor in terms of international poverty lines. Moreover, recent estimates suggest that in eight out of 29 provinces, the incidence of poverty rose significantly from 1985 to 1996. Official Chinese data for 2001 show that the average per capita income of China's 800 million rural residents is just $290 (RMB 2366), or 80 cents per day.

The growth of massive amounts of rural underemployment deeply affects the character of development in the non-farm sector. It provides intense incentives for rural–urban migration, and great downward pressure on non-farm wages in unskilled occupations. It is estimated that by 2002, there were around 150 million rural residents who worked in the urban areas without permanent urban residence qualifications. These were predominantly 'lumpen' labour, with very limited skills. The rate of pay is simple to estimate, namely, the equivalent of roughly US$1–2 per day, which is the price of 'lumpen' migrant labour throughout human history. Even in the fastest-growing region of China, the Pearl River Delta, there was no increase in the real wages of unskilled labour during the whole of the 1990s. There is intense social tension in China's urban areas, with relatively large numbers of rural migrants at subsistence wages struggling for survival alongside the rising Chinese middle class and high income earners working mainly in the foreign sector and in Chinese businesses within the value chain of the global giants.

The basic mechanism through which wages and conditions of work are determined for 'lumpen' unskilled labour is exactly that described by John Steinbeck on the Californian fruit farms during the Depression:

> And the migrants streamed in on the highways and their hunger was in their eyes. They had no argument, no system, nothing but their numbers and their needs. When there was work for a man, ten men fought for it – fought with a low wage – If that fella'll work for thirty cents, I'll work for twenty-five. If he'll do it for twenty-five, I'll do it for twenty. No me, I'm hungry. I'll work for fifteen. I'll work for food.
> (John Steinbeck, *The Grapes of Wrath*, 1939, Penguin edition: 298)

Steinbeck graphically portrays the threat to social stability posed by huge numbers of migrants:

> In the West there was panic when the migrants multiplied on the highways. Men of property were terrified for their property. Men who had never been hungry saw the eyes of the hungry. Men who had never wanted anything very much saw the flare of want in the eyes of migrants. And the men of the towns and the soft suburban country gathered to defend themselves; and they reassured themselves that they were good and the invaders bad, as a man must do before he fights. They said, These goddamed Okies are dirty and ignorant. They're degenerate, sexual maniacs. These goddamed Okies are thieves. They'll steal anything. They've got no sense of property rights.
> (ibid.: 296).

Dr Mei Zhang's study is one of the few that is based on in-depth fieldwork among the poor migrant communities in China. There is wide concern among Chinese policy makers about the implication of the massive internal migration for the country's social stability. However, 'migration' does not simply mean going to work in one of China's giant coastal urban areas. Dr Zhang's study is unique in its focus on the coal-mining area of north-west China, and in its analysis of the process of internal migration within a single poor region. Her fieldwork demanded high-level interviewing skills and great determination, as well as a deep understanding of the broader analytical framework necessary to comprehend the forces shaping the migration process.

Many analysts believe that the Chinese reform process has entered a period in which there is an increased possibility for social instability compared with the past twenty years of reform. There has been extensive discussion among policy makers about how it will be possible to ensure that during this tense period, China is sustained as a 'steady and harmonious society'. China's leaders have a declared vision of an 'everlasting and peaceful nation'. There has been intense debate about how to build a dynamic economy while 'laying the groundwork for a market that is moral and fair'. Internal migration presents a huge challenge for the leadership in the years ahead. Dr Mei Zhang's study is of great value in illuminating the nature of this challenge within one of the country's poorest regions.

Peter Nolan

Preface

The economic reform in China has energetically promoted the growth of the Chinese economy, particularly in rural areas. However, the number of poor people in China is still significant, about 30 million at the end of 2000.

Migration is the oldest course of action against poverty. This tendency, starting from some provinces in south China, has now extended to other parts of China. Internal migration in China has been, and still is, a feature of the changes accompanying the economic reforms. The number of labour migrants from rural to urban areas in China today is enormous; it is estimated that at any one time, there are about 121 million permanent and temporary migrants in China. By 2000, 88 million rural people were living in urban areas. Rural–urban mobility is advocated as a means of alleviating poverty because little capital investment is required.

Clearly, it is important to study the mutual effects between internal migration and poverty in China after the economic reform. In the past few years I have carried out extensive research in this field, including a series of case studies. This book is mainly based on that research.

The main objective of this book is to investigate the effects of internal migration on economic and social developments in China, particularly on reducing poverty. The book is in six chapters. In Chapter 1, theories on rural poverty and rural–urban migration, especially the effects of internal migration on economic and social development, are reviewed generally. In Chapter 2, the characteristics of rural–urban migrants in China today and their economic and social activities in their areas of origin and their destinations are analysed. The distribution and characteristics of poverty in China and some anti-poverty public works by the Chinese government are also briefly reviewed. The major part of the book is the presentation of a case study in a poor region, Shanxi, a typical province in central China. The methodology and results of the case study are described in Chapters 3, 4 and 5. In three sampled counties, 200 households, 100 with migrants and 100 without, were extensively interviewed. Correspondingly, a two-ended approach was made in several cities. A number of interviews were also carried out with local officials. On the basis of the case study, various aspects of internal migration in this region are analysed, including reasons for migration, differences between households with and without migrant members, difference between migrants and city residents, and the socio-economic impact of migration on the sending areas and destinations. Attention has been paid to the differences and similarities between the studied region and the situation elsewhere in China. In Chapter 6, some conclusions are drawn on the basis of all the analyses above. I suggest from my research that rural–urban migration has played, and will continue to play, a positive role in economic and social developments in China, particularly in resolving rural poverty.

It is expected that this book can help us to understand the cause and consequences of these movements. Indeed, the theme consistently running through the chapters is that imbalance in the access to resources – between regions, between villages and between families – is at the core of under-standing the phenomenon of migration. This theme applies also to famine migration or recruited labour migration. It is because the regions of origin have neither the resources nor the infrastructure to withstand such climatic shock, nor the social and economic structures to diffuse, share and hence soften them, that such catastrophes occur.

Acknowledgements

This book is mainly based on my Ph.D. work carried out at the University of Cambridge Faculty of Social and Political Sciences.

First of all, I wish to thank my Ph.D. supervisor, Professor Peter Nolan at the University of Cambridge Judge Institute of Management, for his unflagging help and encouragement throughout this work.

I am indebted to Mr Z. B. Shang, director of the Anti-Poverty Office of Shanxi province, Professor N. S. Bai at the Research Centre for Rural Economy, my former colleagues at the National Bureau of Statistics of China, and my former teachers at Beijing University, especially Professor H. S. Wang, for their continuous support and for providing useful information during the course of my research, and to many people who helped me in various aspects during the case studies. Without their sincere help it would have been impossible for me to complete such a long-term case study – this was the longest time I have ever lived in a rural area.

I am especially thankful to Ms J. Fleming for proofreading my manuscript and for many useful discussions; to Professors G. Hawthorn and J. Dunn for their useful guidance; to Dr D. Lehmann, my Faculty adviser, for his invaluable advice; to Dr L. Reade for proofreading my first-year report; to Drs R. Murphy and G. Yeung for useful discussion, and to Dr N. Emerton, my former college tutor, for her help on many non-academic matters.

The completion of this work was made possible by substantial financial support from the Cambridge Overseas Trust, the Cambridge Political Economy Society Trust, the Suzy Paine Foundation, the Cambridge University Board of Graduate Studies, the Great Britain–China Centre, the BWF Foundation and Wolfson College.

Finally, and most profoundly, I wish to thank my family for their unceasing support and patience, as regards both my Ph.D. dissertation and this book. My husband, Dr J. Kang, has helped me with the data analysis, and our son, Zhengyu Joe, has helped me with inputting some numbers for the database and with proofreading Chapters 3 and 4.

Introduction

Poverty

The economic reform in China, which started in the late 1970s or early 1980s, has energetically promoted the growth of the Chinese economy, particularly in rural areas. It was estimated by the World Bank (1992) that those suffering rural poverty had declined from about one-third of the rural population – 250 million in 1978 – to roughly one-tenth by 1985–90. The World Bank indicated that, while the number of poor people world-wide fell by 8 million between 1987 and 1998, the number of poor outside China actually increased by 82 million (World Bank, 2000). The poverty line adopted by the World Bank was based on the monetary value of a calorie intake of 2,150 kilocalories (kcal) per day and included a measurement of average expenditure of the poor on non-food goods and services. The poverty line for 1990 stood at 275 yuan (US$35)[1] per year.[2] Currently, one common international standard for determining absolute poverty is an income of US$1.00 or less per day (World Bank, 2000).

However, substantial challenges remain for the rural poor. According to the Chinese government, by the end of 1995, 65 million people and 592 counties were still classed as poor (Jiang, 1997). They reported that the number of poor people was about 42 million (*Beijing Youth Daily*, 21 April 1999). At the end of 2000, the number of poor people was about 30 million, mainly disabled people or those living in areas where the natural environment is poor, often without access to clean water, or adequate health and education services. Although the poor in these poorest areas have land-use rights, in most cases the land itself is of such low quality that it is not possible to achieve even a subsistence level of crop production. Consequently, most of the poor are net consumers of grain and other subsistence foods, and are negatively affected by price increases for these commodities.

Migration

Migration is the oldest course of action against poverty (Galbraith, 1979). Internal migration in China has been, and still is, a feature of the changes accompanying the economic reforms. The number of labour migrants from rural to urban areas is enormous in China today. Although it is difficult to give an exact figure, it is estimated that at any one time there are about 120 million permanent and temporary migrants in China (Croll and Huang, 1996). This figure has been confirmed as 121,070,000 by the fifth national census, which was conducted by the National Bureau of Statistics of China in 2000 (NBSC, 2002a).[3] According to the census, 88.4 million rural people were living in urban areas (NBSC, 2002a).

People living outside the place where their residence records are maintained are known as China's 'floating population'. It is estimated that at least one-third of the long-term floating population is living in urban areas (World Bank, 1992). It has been suggested that the seasonal floating population[4] is at least equal to the long-term floating population and may in fact be larger (Wang Gin, 1996).

Clearly, the main reason for internal migration is the intention to raise one's income. This motive is particularly important when a household's land is limited in its capacity to absorb labour and to generate income, and when there are limited opportunities for earning income in non-agricultural activities within the village.

In addition to raising income, urban demographic changes show that the growth of the total working-age population was predicted to decline by more than half from 3.1 per cent per annum during 1978–90 to 1.1 per cent per annum during 1995–2000 (World Bank, 1992)[5] and expected to decline by 768,000 annually during 2005–10 (Ministry of Agriculture, 2000).

The early success of family planning measures in urban areas in the 1970s also resulted in a sharp reduction in the number of urban-born entrants to the urban workforce. A steady stream of migration from rural areas will therefore be needed from the 1990s to offset the declining numbers of urban-born workforce entrants and replace large numbers of retiring urban workers.

Another important reason for internal migration is the differences in peasants' net income between different regions, as shown in Table I.1.

In comparison with rural–urban migration, a greater potential for the absorption of surplus rural workers might lie in the multitude of small and medium-sized cities and urban towns, following the development of these cities and towns. Construction and service-sector jobs in these places often do not require a certain level of school education. These jobs and pre-

Table I.1 Difference in peasants' net income between various regions of China

Region	1983	1993	1996	2000
East	144	166	257	300
Central	126	115	140	192
West	100	100	100	100

urban agriculture provide employment opportunities to the poor. Thus, efforts to facilitate the out-migration of excess labour from the poor areas could play a key role in translating this potential into reality.

Clearly, rural enterprises are also important sources of employment in the rural economy. Rural–urban migration can be diminished by the development of rural enterprises. However, in poor areas the rural enterprises have developed very slowly. Not only are fewer employed, but also wages and profits in rural enterprises are lower in poor areas than in more developed areas. Rural enterprise growth will continue to be concentrated in wealthier areas with inexpensive access to national and international markets. If the poor are to share in that growth, it will be largely through migration to take advantage of employment opportunities where they occur (World Bank, 1992).

This research

From the above analyses it can be seen that:

1   Rural poverty is still an important issue after the economic reform.
2   The stream of migration in China flows from rural to urban, and from poor areas to rich areas.
3   Rural–urban mobility is advocated as a means of alleviating poverty because little capital investment is required. It is therefore useful to investigate the mutual effects between internal migration and poverty in China after the economic reform.

There have been some investigations into migration, poverty and development in many areas in China, such as the World Bank's (1988) study in Gansu Province, Davin's (1996a, b) study in Sichuan Province, Knight and Song's (1993) study in Hebei Province, the Labour Bureau's (1997) survey based on 4,000 households and 3,000 migrants in eight provinces, Huang's (1997) investigation in eight villages in four provinces (Jiangsu, Anhui, Sichuan and Gansu), and Du and Bai's (1997) study of 2,820 households in Anhui and Sichuan Provinces. Investigations of the origins, characteristics, motivation and welfare of migrants have been carried out. These studies, however, have mainly focused on either provinces of southern China, which typically reflect the Chinese economic reform since 1979, or some of the provinces which are regarded as the poorest by certain international programmes, such as Anhui, Sichuan and Gansu. In contrast, the investigation of migration has been limited in China's central provinces where economic reform development has been slow and consequently rural poverty is significant.

The objective of this book is therefore to investigate the effects of internal migration on economic and social developments in central China, particularly on reducing poverty. A case study in a poor region, Shanxi Province, has been carried out to investigate:

1   The social and economic characteristics of the rural–urban migrants, such as sex, education, life cycle, type of village, income, remittances.
2   The relationship between rural labourers' socio-economic characteristics and migrants' economic activities in their destinations, such as occupation, income, lifestyle.
3   The contribution made by migrants to social and economic development, especially on reducing poverty in sending areas.
4   The necessity of introducing rural–urban migration into the Chinese government's anti-poverty policies. This study focuses on those who come from rural areas, and who are looking for a job or already hold a job in urban areas. They are called peasant workers, migrant workers, migrants or rural–urban migrants.

Thus, this book focuses on working migrants, and migrants' households in villages, rather than certain types of large-scale migration like that resulting from the Three Gorges migration project or the migration programme in the Yellow River areas. Such movements have not been properly studied by village-level microanalysis, nor would analysis of such migration yield specific policy recommendations for generating employment.

Most existing studies of migration in rural areas have focused on people not living there at the time of study, and thus, many of their characteristics are undermined. Also, the migrants have seldom been followed up at their destination, hence the possibilities of return migration as well as the details of 'pull' factors are often unknown. In this research, these aspects have been paid particular attention.

1 Poverty and migration

A theoretical overview

To study internal migration and poverty in China, it is useful briefly to review the general theories and existing investigations regarding rural poverty and migration from the viewpoint of both sociology and economics.

Poverty

This section first discusses the concept and definition of poverty. It then reviews some theoretical studies relating to poverty.

General definition

Poverty refers to economic, social and cultural disadvantages; that is, a lack of the basic necessities of life and essential services, and an absence of opportunities or means for development as a result of having a low income.

There are two types of poverty: absolute and relative poverty (Tong and Lin, 1995). Absolute poverty refers to living conditions in which there is no guarantee of subsistence, people lack adequate clothing and food, and simple production is difficult or impossible to maintain. Relative poverty refers to a situation in which people have just adequate food and clothing but their living standard is below the recognised basic level, and simple production can be maintained but there is very little or no ability to extend production. Absolute poverty may be subdivided into subsistence poverty and living poverty. The former, also referred to as abject poverty, is the lowest living standard, a standard at which people can survive but find it difficult to satisfy their basic physiological requirements.

Rural households may be classified as follows (Tong and Lin, 1995):

1   Basic survival – abject poverty. The average annual income of rural households within this bracket is barely enough to cover expenditure on the minimum physiological requirements.
2   Relative poverty. Average annual income is sufficient to maintain

simple production and to cover the minimum expenditure for food, clothing and services.
3   Eliminating poverty (the development line) – becoming better off. Average annual income is more than enough to cover expenditure for sufficient food and clothing, and part of it can be used for investment to expand production and increase the family's wealth. Poor rural households aspire to cross this line, and if they do, their economy changes from a self-sufficient or semi-self-sufficient type to a commodity type.
4   Fairly well off.
5   Prosperous.

The biological approach

Rowntree (1941, 1980), in his famous study of poverty in York, defined families as being in 'primary poverty' if their 'total earnings are insufficient to obtain the minimum necessities for the maintenance of merely physical efficiency'. It is not surprising that biological considerations related to the requirements of survival or work efficiency have often been used in defining the poverty line. Starvation, clearly, is the most telling aspect of poverty.

The biological approach has come under rather intense fire. There are indeed several problems with its use. First, there are significant variations related to physical features, climatic conditions and work habits. Second, the translation of minimum nutritional requirements into minimum food requirements depends on the choice of commodities. Third, for non-food items, such minimum requirements are not easy to specify, and the problem is usually solved by assuming that a specified proportion of total income will be spent on food.

The inequality approach

Miller and Roby (1971) have concluded that casting the issues of poverty in terms of stratification leads poverty to be regarded as an issue of inequality. In the study, they moved away from efforts to measure a poverty line with pseudo-scientific accuracy. Instead, they looked at the nature and size of differences between the bottom 20 per cent or 10 per cent and the rest of the society. Their concern became one of narrowing the differences between those at the bottom and the better off in each stratification dimension.

Sen (1981) indicated that inequality and poverty are not unrelated, but that neither concept subsumes the other. It is a different matter to recognise that inequality and poverty are associated with each other, and to note that a different distribution system may cure poverty even without an expansion of the country's productive capabilities. Recognising the distinct nature of poverty as a concept permits one to treat it as a matter of intrinsic interest. The role of inequality in the prevalence of poverty can then figure in analysis of poverty without making the two conceptually equivalent.

A cycle of deprivation

The 'subculture of poverty' thesis has been considered in Britain as a 'cycle of deprivation' when Sir Keith Joseph drew attention in 1972 to the persistence of deprivation and the problem of maladjustment despite improvements in living standards (Townsend, 1979, p. 70):

> Perhaps there is at work here a process, apparent in many situations but imperfectly understood, by which problems reproduce themselves from generation to generation ... Do we not know only too certainly that among the children of this generation there are some doomed to an uphill struggle against the disadvantages of a deprived family background? Do we not know that many of them will not be able to overcome the disadvantages and will become in their turn the parents of deprived families?

The concept attracted critical attention by Hawthorn and Carter (Townsend, 1979). Theoretically, deprivation is treated as being a residual personal or family phenomenon rather than a large-scale structural phenomenon. It is difficult, as the critics have pointed out, to reconcile this treatment with the allocative outcome of market economy as well as its inputs, whether production processes or determination of consumer preferences and lifestyles.

The poor-peasant economy in China

The research on the poor-peasant economy in China has seen significant contributions by Tawney (1932), Fei (1939) and Huang (1985). Tawney published his famous book *Land and Labour in China* in 1932, and made an original contribution to the study of China's economic organisation and social problem. Regarding rural progress, he pointed out that the problems presented by the economic conditions of rural life in China were of two principal types (Tawney, 1932, p. 78):

> There are those, in the first place, which spring from natural or inherited disadvantages, such as poverty or exhaustion of soil, a deficient or irregular rainfall, the destruction of forests, rivers liable to flood, the physical limitation of the cultivable area and the immense number of human beings, which, as a result of past history, that area must support. There are those, in the second place, which have their source in defects of economic organisation or in social habit: the absence, for example, of a tolerable system of communications.

It appears that some of Tawney's descriptions about the poor rural areas in China (Tawney, 1932, p. 77) still hold true today: 'the position of the rural population is that of a man standing permanently up to the neck in water, so that even a ripple is sufficient to drown him.'

Fei (1939) carried out a field study in the Yangtze valley. Two main motives dominated his study: the exploitation of the soil, and the reproductive processes within the household and the family. He introduced a fundamental aspect of peasant life in China, especially in his use of the concept of social ties to explain chain migration.

As to the poverty in rural areas in China, Huang's description appears to be rather typical. From a study on the peasant economy and social changes in northern China, Huang (1985, p. 299) indicated:

> These characteristics of the poor-peasant economy caution against a simple equation of modern China's agrarian crisis with natural or man-made calamities. In an economy in which peasants enjoyed more of a margin above subsistence and worked under less harsh production relations, short-term disruption would not have been nearly as devastating. It was the combination of long-term semi-proletarianization with short-term disasters that made the condition of the poor peasants in China so desperate. A poor peasant already at the margins of subsistence was easily forced into debt or even into pawning part of his land when he lost his crop on account of drought or flood. Once he did so, his already meagre prospective income was further reduced by new interest and rent obligations. Under those conditions, few could hope to recover and redeem their land.

Migration

There have been an enormous number of studies of migration and rural labour. These have been from various viewpoints, as indicated by Berliner (1977, p. 443):

> Most people who write about migration are not interested in migration at all. They are interested in its consequences. Economists study migration because they are interested in income and employment, and migration of labour influences the spatial distribution of income and employment. Anthropologists study migration because they are interested in culture, and migrants act as 'culture brokers' in the process of culture diffusion. Sociologists study migration because they are interested in all aspects of social relations, and migration affects virtually all aspects – from stratification and mobility patterns to the stability of such basic social institutions as the family.

Theories of rural–urban migration can be broadly classified as macro and micro in their level. In the former category are those which focus on the migration stream, identifying those conditions under which large-scale movements occur and describing the demographic, economic and social characteristics of the migration in aggregate terms. The macro level also includes most theories concerning the rural–urban migration adaptation process: economic and social integration, assimilation, etc. when regarded from a structural or cultural perspective. The micro level includes studies of social psychological factors differentiating migrants from non-migrants, together with theories concerning motivation, decision making, satisfaction and identification.

Space does not permit a comprehensive review of all theories concerning rural–urban migration. However, a brief summary of the most relevant contributions is appropriate.

The review in this section is focused on

1   demands for labour and levels of remuneration;
2   social influence of migration; and
3   factors determining the decision to migrate, such as the role of women.

Although some of the studies reviewed below are based on international migration, some of their conclusions are also applicable to internal migration.

Macro theories

The main macro theories are the seven laws of migration, the systems model, the Lewis–Fei–Ranis model and the Todaro-Harris models.

The seven laws of migration

The main objectives of descriptive theories of migration are to define the characteristics of migration, or to predict the amount and size of the migration stream or to estimate under what circumstances it is probable that certain types of people will move. The earliest and simplest example of this type of theory is Ravenstein's 'seven laws of migration'. Ravenstein (1885, 1889) put forward his so-called law of migration on the basis of empirical observation of internal migration in the nineteenth century. Some of his generalisations have stood the test of time, such as the fact that most migrations are over short distances, that they generate counter-streams and that they are related to technological development. Others have been contradicted, including the suggestion that urban populations are less migratory than rural, that females predominate among short-distance movers or that migration proceeds by stages from rural areas to small towns, and from the latter to larger cities and the metropolis.

According to this theory, migrants move from areas of low opportunity to areas of high opportunity, and the choice of destination is regulated by distance.

Lee (1966), building on Ravenstein's observations, offered a series of hypotheses about the volume of migration under varying conditions, the development of stream and counter-stream, and the characteristics of migrants. These hypotheses have been used extensively as a framework for investigating the spatial, temporal and causal factors in migration. The significance of Lee's work is that he has restated Ravenstein's 'laws' in a more precise fashion and therefore made them more amenable to testing. In other words, Lee has helped to shift the emphasis in migration research from a purely descriptive to a more analytical approach. Similar developments of this way of looking at population movement are the interaction theory proposed by Haddon (1919), Young (1928), Stouffer (1940) and others.

The systems model

Mabogunje (1970) developed a 'systems model', recognising an interdependence between sending and receiving areas. He identified four components in rural–urban migration movements: economic, social, technological and environmental. He described rural–urban migration as a circular, interdependent and self-modifying system in which the effects of changes in one part have a ripple effect throughout the whole system. By conceptualising migration as a system, it becomes possible to identify the interacting elements, their attributes and their relationships.

In order to reveal the components of such a migration system, a brief summary is presented below of the arguments contained in Mabogunje's paper 'System approach to a theory of rural–urban migration'. Although Mabogunje was concerned with rural–urban migration in Africa, his conceptualisation of the process in system language has wider relevance.

A migration system is made up of three basic elements. First, there is the potential migrant who is encouraged to leave the rural village by stimuli from the environment. Second, there are the various institutions, or control sub-systems, which determine the level of flow within the system. In a rural–urban migration system, the two most important subsystems are the rural and urban control systems. In the rural system, the nuclear and extended family, and the local community, by means of the various activities which it sponsors, can act in both a positive and a negative way in determining the volume of migration. On the other hand, the urban control system determines, by means of occupational and residential opportunities, the degree of assimilation into the urban environment. Third, there are the various social, economic and political forces, or adjustment mechanisms, which play a significant role in the process of a migrant's transformation. The act of migration sets in motion a series of adjustments in both the village and the city. Within the rural areas it involves a loss of one productive unit as well as one member of the family and community life, while in the city the migrant is incorporated into a new situation more relevant to his or her needs.

Lewis–Fei–Ranis models

The Lewis (1954) and Fei and Ranis (1961) models developed in the 1950s and 1960s showed the positive effects of the shift of labour force from a rural surplus-labour agricultural sector to the urban industrial sector. Rapid internal migration was thought to be a desirable process by which surplus rural labour was withdrawn from traditional agriculture to provide cheap human resources to fuel a growing modern industrial complex. Rural–urban migration also contributes to the urban economy by supplying the unmet demand for labour in certain employment sectors. A related consequence is the role migration plays in determining wage levels.

Lewis (1954) has pointed out that the main sources from which workers come as economic development proceeds are subsistence agriculture, casual labour, petty trade, domestic service, wives and daughters in the household, and the increase of population. In most but not all of these sectors, if the country is overpopulated relative to its natural resources, the marginal productivity of labour is negligible, zero or even negative. Moreover, the subsistence wage at which this surplus labour is available for employment may be determined by a conventional view of the minimum required for subsistence; or it may be equal to the value of the average produced per capita in subsistence agriculture, plus a margin. The most important point is that mass immigration of unskilled labour does sometimes even raise output per head, but its effect can be to keep unskilled wages in all areas near the subsistence level of the poorest areas.

The above model has been criticised for failing to explain where the demand for goods produced by the capitalist sector will come from and for assuming the existence of entrepreneurs who act in the way specified (Elkan, 1973; Hirschman, 1957; Meier, 1975). Todaro (1976) also questioned this model, querying how it could explain the rising tide of migration to cities of Africa, Asia and Latin America in the face of growing urban unemployment. If urban wages were not adjusting to equate supply and demand as in the traditional equilibrium model, then surely one must be dealing with a disequilibrium process – one in which wages were sticky; expected incomes rather than nominal wage differentials were guiding rural migration, and the urban unemployment rate was in fact acting as the equilibrating mechanism between rural and urban expected incomes. However, if this were true, it would mean that if urban unemployment became high enough to offset the rising urban–rural wage gap, then it would slow down migration until eventually migration, in theory, would cease. But at what social and economic cost?

The basic message of the above models was: invest in modern industry and let the traditional surplus labour, cheap food and forced saving (through terms of trade manipulation) allow an urban, modern economy to grow. Bias investments towards the urban, modern industrial economy and, eventually, the needed structural transformation will be realised.

Todaro and Harris's models

Contrary to the Lewis–Fei–Ranis model, Todaro and Harris's (1970) migration model, developed in the 1960s, represented a break with the traditional, neoclassical equilibrium model of labour markets and a demonstration of how conventional Western theory needed to be adjusted to fit the realities of developing nations. It emphasised the negative impact of migration in terms of increasing unemployment, underemployment and urban poverty in the destination. This is still an accepted view despite criticism of the model by dissenters who view internal migration favourably, such as Galbraith (1979). This migration model and its extensions viewed the urban labour force as distributed between the relatively small modern sector and a large traditional sector (Harris and Todaro, 1970). Todaro has pointed out that migration is stimulated primarily by rational economic considerations of relative benefits and costs, mostly financial, but also psychological. Two factors are important for migration decisions: the actual urban–rural wage difference and the probability of successfully obtaining employment in the modern urban sector. The probability of obtaining an urban job is inversely related to the urban unemployment rate. Migration rates in excess of urban job opportunity growth rates are not only possible but rational and likely in the face of continued positive expected income differences between urban and rural areas. High rates of urban unemployment are therefore inevitable outcomes of the serious imbalances of economic opportunities between the urban and rural areas of most underdeveloped countries.

Clearly, the focus of Todaro's attention was on migrants rather than on productivity. In the model, rural–urban migration is viewed as the major contributing factor to the ubiquitous phenomenon of urban surplus labour and as a force that continues to exacerbate already serious urban unemployment problems caused by growing economic and structural imbalances between urban and rural areas. Moreover, rural–urban migration itself must act as the ultimate equilibrating force. With urban wages assumed to be inflexible in a downward direction, rural and urban 'expected' income can be equalised only by falling urban job possibilities resulting from rising urban unemployment. According to Todaro, there is a relationship between education and wages. More highly educated migrants have higher expected urban incomes owing both to higher wages and to greater chances of obtaining employment.

The Todaro–Harris model had a major impact not only on theoretical

and empirical but also on policy-oriented debate about urban unemployment and development. Relating to this model, Connell *et al.* (1976)
addressed two central questions based on studies of 40 Indian villages in
the 1970s. One question is, what sort of villages produce what sort of
migration? The other is, what are the effects of absence, contact and
return upon the villages of origin? Connell *et al.* suggested that:

1   Rural poverty is a cause of migration – the converse of Todaro's
    hypothesis, which works better in explaining differences among vil-
    lages than among villagers.
2   The rural-end evidence regarding the Todaro hypothesis is mixed.
3   Migration remittances are unlikely to increase villagers' prosperity
    unless ample investment opportunities exist in the village.
4   Patterns of migration from a rural community may well change in
    stages, following the integration and development of the community.
5   Increasing distance is in general associated with declining propensity
    to migrate.

Micro theories

Corresponding to macro theory is a micro theory of individual choice.
Most micro-level studies of migration decision making have found that the
main motives are economic or family-related reasons. An assumption of
'rational choice', following a considered evaluation of the options available, is implicit in most theories of motivation. A distinction is generally
made between 'push' and 'pull' factors, which must be taken into account
and weighed in the balance.

Push and pull theory

Herberle (1938) argued that migration is caused by a series of factors
which encourage an individual to leave one place (push) and attract him or
her to another (pull). In other words, if an individual's needs cannot be
satisfied in his or her present location, then a move elsewhere may be considered. On the other hand, even for individuals satisfied with their
present situation, information about greater opportunities elsewhere may
persuade them to move. For each migration, several push and pull forces
may be operating and interacting, so that the move cannot be attributed
wholly to either force. However, by examining large migration flows, the
common stimulants to movement may be established.

Bogue (1969) has succinctly summarised these 'push–pull' forces as
follows:

PUSH FACTORS

1   Decline in a nation's natural resources or in the prices paid for them; decreased demand for a particular product or the services of a particular industry; exhaustion of mines, timber or agricultural resources.
2   Loss of employment resulting from being discharged for incompetence, from a decline in need for a particular activity, or from mechanisation or automation of tasks previously performed by more labour-intensive procedures.
3   Oppressive or repressive discriminatory treatment because of political, religious or ethnic origins or membership.
4   Alienation from a community because one no longer subscribes to prevailing beliefs, actions or mode of behaviour – either within one's family or within the community.
5   Retreat from a community because it offers few or no opportunities for personal development, employment or marriage.
6   Retreat from a community because of catastrophe – floods, fire, drought, earthquake or epidemic.

PULL FACTORS

1   Superior opportunities for employment in one's occupation or opportunities to enter a preferred occupation.
2   Opportunities for employment to earn a larger income.
3   Opportunities to obtain a desired specialised education or training such as a college education.
4   Preferable environment and living conditions – climate, housing, school, or other community and facility.
5   Dependency – movement of other persons to whom one is related or betrothed, such as the movement of dependants with a breadwinner or migration of a bride to join her husband.
6   For rural and small-town residents, attraction of new or different activities, environments or people, such as the cultural, intellectual or recreational activities of a large metropolis.

Despite the push–pull theory's elegant abstraction of the specific forces generating migration, a number of researchers, such as Lee (1966) and Thomas (1954), have criticised it as an oversimplification of a highly complex process. Thomas has cogently argued that all sorts of prompting may lie behind the decision of an individual or family to leave one country in order to live in another. It is not by making a catalogue of such 'reasons' that one can hope to understand the phenomenon of migration, any more than an attempt to describe the manifold motives leading people to want to buy a commodity would constitute analysis of demand. Nothing is easier than drawing up a list of factors labelled 'push' and 'pull' and then writing a descriptive account in terms of these two sets of influences.

Social aspects of migration

Like Todaro, Lipton also emphasised the negative impact of rural–urban migration on the migrants' area of origin. He wrote (1977, p. 86):

> Migration saddles the rural environment with one of those avoidable features that, to the casual observer, seem the marks of inherited or chosen individual poverty. First, it is the bright young men who migrate to urban jobs, leaving behind the less bright, the children, the elderly and female.

According to Lipton, rural–urban migration does, however, have some social benefits. The marginal product of labour at the destination is higher than at the place of origin. Migrant remittances can also overcome credit constraints and so increase investment in farming. In addition, migration can have a direct effect on social welfare by altering the pattern of rural income distribution.

Cost–benefit analyses

Those who adopt a cost–benefit procedure provide another economic interpretation of migration. A pioneer working along these lines was Sjaastad (1962). He recognised that some other important factors should be considered in migration besides economics, and produced a cost–benefit model for assessing their relative importance. He regarded migration as an investment activity involving resources, requiring costs to be incurred and producing returns. Costs include financial costs – both 'opportunities forgone' and direct costs of movement, such as those incurred in moving belongings and family – and psychological costs, which, although difficult to measure, estimate the loss in leaving a known environment, friends and relations. In other words, cost is perceived more concretely and positively than most other indices of general economic development as far as the individual migrant is concerned (Todaro, 1969). When the benefits are greater than the costs, migration is most likely to occur. This is a much more fruitful approach than other kinds of economic theories.

Sjastaad developed a migration equation:

$$M_{ij} = \frac{(Y_{dj} - Y_i) - T}{N(1 + r)}$$

where M_{ij} is the migration from area i to j, Y_{dj} is the earnings in the Nth year at the destination, Y_i is the earnings in the Nth year at origin, T is the cost of moving, N is the number of years in which earnings are expected, and r is the discount rate on future earnings. This formulation has been tested not only by Diehl (1966) and Shaw (1974) in a variety of different situations but also by Todaro and associates (Harris and Todaro, 1970; Todaro and Rempel, 1972; Todaro, 1976) in their attempts to explain the increasing rural to urban migration rates in Third World countries.

Speare (1971) included an information factor as well as a non-pecuniary one in the form of the location of the migrant's parents relative to the path of migration. By transforming the cost–benefit equation into multiple regression form and by using data derived from a personal migration survey in his analysis of rural–urban migration in Taiwan, he attempted to estimate the significance of the components involved. His results indicated the order of the factors to be (a) cost of moving, (b) parents of respondent living at place of destination, (c) unemployment level in place of origin, and (d) home ownership at place of origin. Despite the success of the study, Speare concluded that it should not be interpreted to mean that the costs and benefits of migration are actually calculated – in fact, limited data suggest that people have only vague concepts of costs and benefits.

Three types of migration in developing countries

Bogue (1969) tentatively suggested that internal migration in developing countries was of three basic types. Although the theory was first intro-duced over thirty years ago, it appears that it is still useful for the current situation in China. The three types are:

1   In most developing nations, the principal political, commercial and industrial centres are enjoying moderate to rapid population growth, as a result of both high fertility and net in-migration. However, whole-sale exodus from rural areas to principal urban centres has not materi-alised.
2   An amazingly high proportion of the rapidly accumulating 'surplus population' in the developing nations appears to be staying in rural village areas and struggling to exist through more intensive cultivation of the land.
3   Whenever significant industrial and commercial expansion does take place, an immediate stream of migration ensues. But much of this migration results in failure and in return to the place of origin.

The decision to migrate

Herbst (1964) indicated that the conscious decision to leave a place of origin involves transposing indecision into a resolution of commitment to the organisation (or social and economic environment) of which the migrant is a part. Usually, in such a situation the decision-making unit is the household. Within this unit, some of its members are more directly involved in the decision-making process than others. Rochin (1972) noted that family males make the economic decision in a Pakistani household and determine the destiny of the family. Dahya (1973) also observed how the family head plans and finances the migration of young members in order to fulfil his socio-economic goals. It must be emphasised that not all individuals have complete freedom of choice (Bassett and Short, 1980; Wiseman and Roseman, 1979). In many poor rural areas of both the developed and the developing world, households may perceive no choice but to move to the cities, or to emigrate.

Wolpert (1964, 1965, 1966) introduced the concept of 'place utility'. This may be a positive or negative quality, expressing respectively the individual's satisfaction or dissatisfaction with respect to that place. Where migration is intended and not forced, the argument is reasonable. The migrant will tend to resettle at a destination which offers a relatively higher level of utility than both the place of origin and any alternative places of destination. Also, individuals tend to choose locations of relative certainty, either by postponing the move or by acquiring more information by greater search and feedback.

Women

The structure of employment mostly requires men to work in coal mining, industry, commerce or mechanised transportation. Thus, men tend to migrate alone, leaving their wives behind. The cultural factors that initially favoured the education of males over females have had the effect of confining women to the lower ranks of formal employment, given that employment in the originated labour market is highly correlated with education (Adepoju, 1983; Stamp, 1989).

A case study in Tanzania shows that in Lushoto District, the ratio of men to women in the district has fallen since the Second World War because of out-migration (Sender and Smith, 1990). In the district, there were 87 males per 100 females in both 1967 and 1978, compared with virtual equality in numbers recorded in the 1931 census. This ratio was significantly below the ratio for Tanzania as a whole.

It appears, however, that female migration is changing. There is a shift from women who accompany or join their husbands to women as autonomous migrants in their own right (Findley and Williams, 1990). Women may migrate in search of better opportunities, in response to natural disasters or in flight from penury, war and internal strife. On the other hand, migration may for women be associated with serious vulnerability and exposure to economic and sexual exploitation. It is associated with profound changes in their role.

Tienda and Booth (1988) noted that male absenteeism, cash cropping and declining land quality are pushing many more women out of rural areas. However, it is not just the poor quality of the land but the lack of access to it that is pushing rural women out of traditional agriculture – so far the major sector of employment. In Kenya, for instance, the land reform legislation denies independent access to land to women who are single heads of household and married women without a son (Selassie, 1986).

The 1960, 1970 and 1980 rounds of censuses confirmed that women in Africa were migrating to urban areas in greater numbers in search of wage employment (Tienda and Booth, 1988). Two reasons have been advanced for this phenomenon: the deteriorating living and working conditions of women in rural areas and the instability of marriage. Thus, women in East Africa often migrate to urban areas in the expectation of greater autonomy. Single women in Uganda are able to improve their social position by increasing their autonomy through urban employment; migration *per se* provides an alternative to their subordination in the villages.

Generally the remittances sent by migrants are irregular, and inadequate either to maintain household members or to hire labourers in sufficient numbers at peak periods to maintain output. The lack of family labour, and the uncertain and inadequate remittances, have pushed women to seek employment in the urban formal and informal sectors. In some cases, such as in Lesotho and Botswana (Adepoju, 1988), this has resulted in more women than men undertaking rural–urban migration.

Female migration is not directed to urban areas alone. Women sometimes accompany their husbands when they migrate to other rural areas (Adepoju, 1984). Whatever the direction, recent empirical evidence tends to suggest that the fact of migration tends to increase women's recorded participation in economic activities, and in particular the occupational mix among these migrants (Pittin, 1984).

Return of migrants

One important migration issue to consider is the return of migrants. Berg (1965) indicated that labour migration has been an economic benefit not only to the recipient areas but also to the labour-exporting villages. Also, it has been shown that migration can significantly affect agricultural practices, such as in a case study in Upper Volta by Skinner (1965).

Cerase (1974) has suggested that returning migrants may be differentiated into three types on the basis of their level of assimilation into a host community. First, there are those who fail to adjust in the host community and return to their homeland as 'failed' migrants. These migrants are reabsorbed quickly into their home community and therefore their impact is a 'return of conservatism'. The second group is composed of those who do not return until they have retired and their age precludes them from making any significant social or economic impact. Third, there are those who return after some success in the host country and therefore are full of ambition and drive and ready to innovate within their home community. According to Cerase, this is the 'return of innovation'. Overall, Cerase's work provides a means of assessing whether the 'return of innovation' is myth or a reality.

It has been argued that the high rates of natural increase in rural areas and high rates of return migration reduce the equilibrium function of migration. In other words, the reduction in excess rural population through mobility to urban areas has been less than dramatic (Caldwell, 1969).

Inkeles' modern man theory

Although not directly related to poverty and migration, Inkeles' modern man theory (Inkeles, 1983; Inkeles and Smith, 1974) is very useful for such research. The theory states that people become modern through undergoing particular life experiences. More specifically, it emphasises the contribution of people's work experience in making them modern. He believed that employment in complex, rationalised, technocratic and even bureaucratic organisations has a particular propensity to change people so that they move from the more traditional to the more modern in their attitudes, values and behaviour (Inkeles and Smith, 1974, pp. 9–10):

> We have very little scientific knowledge as to how far the qualities of a nation's people are important in fostering development. Our concern in this study is to bring people back in. We feel that an essential element in the development process is the individual, and that a nation is not modern unless its people are modern. . . . We believe that at any stage of life, and particularly in the early and middle years of adulthood, people may experience quite substantial personal change, some deep enough to qualify for the designation of a personality 'transformation'.

According to Inkeles, the following personal qualities can be used to define modern man within the framework of his analytic perspective:

1 openness to new experience;
2 readiness for social change;
3 the realm of the growth of opinion;
4 information;
5 time;
6 efficacy;
7 planning;
8 calculability or trust;
9 valuing technical skill;
10 aspirations, education and occupation;
11 awareness of, and respect for, the dignity of others; and
12 understanding production.

The theoretical framework outlined above has been worded into the questionnaires. As described in Chapters 4 and 5, interviews with migrants and households with and without migrant members were structured to examine the extent to which the experiences of migration affected personal viewpoint.

Summary

It is difficult to explain all aspects of rural–urban migration within a single theoretical framework. The theories outlined above bring together certain key elements in order to explain broad features of contemporary migration, particularly those of rural–urban migration. It is useful to consider these theories and investigations in relation to the present study, as they are very relevant to the situation in China. The analysis in the next chapter focuses particularly on poverty and migration in the Chinese context.

2 Poverty and internal migration in China

This chapter first describes poverty and anti-poverty work in China. It then analyses the current situation with regard to rural–urban migration, and migrants' activities in both sending areas and their destinations.

Poverty and anti-poverty works

Poverty is an essential push factor for current rural–urban migration in China, and anti-poverty work has played an important role in creating an adjustment system of rural–urban migration. In this section, these two aspects are briefly discussed.

Characteristics of poverty

Many characteristics of the poor in China are similar to those in other developing countries, such as ill health, a high illiteracy rate, poor sanitary conditions, and lack of skills and spirit of enterprise. These factors result from poverty, while they also form part of the reasons that the poor have become poorer. The main features of poverty in China can be summarised as rural poverty concentrated in certain regions and particularly affecting the agricultural sector.

China's worst remaining poverty is concentrated in remote and mountainous areas where, in most instances, the arable land is particularly infertile, and limited transport, power and other rural infrastructure constrain development. Minority people and members of households disadvantaged by illiteracy, ill heath or other disabilities constitute a disproportionate share of these poor (World Bank, 1992).

After the founding of new China in 1949, for almost thirty years the Chinese government spared no effort to develop production and eliminate poverty. However, the poverty relief programme was put forward and implemented on a large scale only after the initiation of the economic reform.

In 1978, it was reported that the number of people without enough to eat and wear in the rural areas of China was 250 million (World Bank,

1992). There were many causes giving rise to such a large number of poverty-stricken people, of which the main one was that the operation system in agriculture did not suit the needs of the development of the productive forces, so that peasants lacked enthusiasm for production. Seven years later, the number of poor people who lived in absolute poverty had been halved to 125 million, mainly owing to the successful rural reform policies of Deng Xiaoping.

Consistent with the post-1984 pattern of slow growth of rural income in provinces with lower rural income levels, 1989 provincial rural income distribution data collected by the NBSC indicated that most of China's remaining rural poverty was concentrated in the north-western, south-western, north-eastern and northern regions of the country. The provincial incidence of rural poverty was estimated by applying the national poverty line to the NBSC's 1989 data. The data indicate that in 1989, the rate of absolute poverty among rural households ranged between 17 per cent and 34 per cent in the north-western provinces of Inner Mongolia, Shanxi, Shaanxi, Ningxia, Gansu, Qinghai and Xinjiang, between 11 per cent and 19 per cent in the south-western provinces of Guangxi, Sichuan, Guizhou and Yunnan, and between 12 per cent and 18 per cent in the northern provinces of Hebei and Henan and north-eastern provinces of Jilin and Heilongjiang. These 15 provinces, with less than 50 per cent of China's rural population, accounted for nearly 80 per cent of rural poverty. The NBSC's data concerning provincial incomes also indicated China's worst absolute poverty: 4.6 per cent of all rural households nationwide whose average annual income level was less than 200 yuan per capita. Note that because the populations of these provinces are different,[1] the actual numbers of rural households in absolute poverty vary considerably between even these poorer provinces. It should also be noted that poverty in China is measured by counties rather than provinces.

With the deepening of the rural reform and the constant strengthening of development-oriented poverty relief, the number of people in absolute poverty had dropped to 80 million in 1994. The features of poverty and the distribution of the poverty-stricken population showed obvious geographical characteristics: that is, most poverty-stricken people live in central or western China. The main factors behind poverty are adverse natural conditions, weak infrastructure and backward social development. In 1994, the central government set up a Seven-Year Poverty Alleviation Programme aiming to lift 80 million people out of absolute poverty by 2000. China has so far focused its poverty reduction effects on the western and inland regions. As well as the 11 provinces Inner Mongolia, Shaanxi, Ningxia, Gansu, Qinghai, Xinjiang, Guangxi, Sichuan, Guizhou, Yunnan and Tibet, the 12 target regions also included Chongqing City. Thus, 11 out of 15 of what were the poorer provinces in 1989 are still poor today.

In October 2000, the Chinese government issued a White Paper entitled 'The development of rural China'. It announced that the number of people in rural areas with problems obtaining sufficient food and clothing had decreased from 250 million in 1978 to 30 million in 2000; and that the absolute poverty rate there had decreased from 30.7 per cent to about 3 per cent.

In the present 10th Five-Year Plan period (2001–5), China is giving priority to the rural areas inhabited by ethnic groups and poverty-stricken regions in the middle and western regions of the country.

The rural sector has been dominated by agriculture. The market-oriented economic reform endowed peasants with autonomy of operation. Most of them exploited the chances given by raised prices for farm products, structural adjustment, and development of non-agricultural industries, and allocated their resources in a more efficient way. As a result, their household income grew by leaps and bounds in a short span of several years. In comparison, those inhabiting either areas where there was a lack of both resources and infrastructure or areas which enjoyed resource potential but had poor infrastructure have not been able to keep up with this progress. This has led to the concentration of poverty in poor western and inland areas. In the course of introducing market mechanisms, the gap between these areas and the national average in social and economic development is generally widening.

Rural–urban inequality

As mentioned above, poverty in China is mainly manifested as regional poverty in the rural sector. Owing to rigorous policies that prohibited rural people from freely migrating while China was industrialising, a barrier between urban and rural societies has existed since the 1950s. Furthermore, because of the urban bias involved in the industrialisation strategies, the urban sector has enjoyed more benefit than the rural sector did from the rapid growth of the national economy, partially at the cost of the rural population in a relatively slow socio-economic development before 1978 and after 1985. Even at present, with reforms ongoing, many urban inhabitants still enjoy stable social welfare services to fulfil their basic requirements such as medical treatment, housing and transportation – benefits that have never been available in rural areas.

A more detailed analysis of historic reasons for the rural–urban differences is given in a later section.

The poverty line (basic survival line)

The minimum annual income per capita needed for subsistence in rural areas is calculated by multiplying the annual consumption of staple foods per capita needed to produce the minimum number of calories required for daily subsistence by the average price of the various types of food in the same year.

Experts from the Chinese Nutrition Society have calculated that the average individual daily food intake is equivalent to 2,400 kcal, and the minimum is 2,000 kcal (NBSC, 1992b).[2] In rural areas in China, the staple diet consists of grain and vegetables, which have a relatively low consumption structure and level, so that a slightly larger number of calories are required to compensate for the lack of other nutrients. In view of this, the Chinese government has taken 2,100 kcal as the minimum daily calorific intake required for subsistence.

According to a nation-wide survey of rural households in 1992, the primary foods consumed per capita per annum by those in the 200–250 yuan income group were as follows: grain, 192.7 kg; vegetables, 73.12 kg; edible oil, 5.48 kg; meat, 5.02 kg; and eggs 1.1 kg (NBSC, 1992b). These foods are equivalent to a daily calorific intake of 2,099 kcal, and have therefore been taken as the minimum average food consumption per annum for rural inhabitants. Based on the average prices of these foods in the same year, the minimum amount required to purchase these foods is 220 yuan. If additional expenditure on items such as salt, sauces, vinegar and fuel are taken into consideration, the abject poverty line has for convenience been set at an income of 250 yuan per annum (World Bank, 1992).

The above is the basic method used to determine the poverty line in China. The earliest standard was calculated by the relevant government departments in 1985, on the basis of investigations of the consumption expenditures of 67,000 rural households; that is, the standard of 206 yuan (US$24) in net income per capita in rural areas. In 1978, the poverty line was equivalent to 98 yuan (Tang and Lin, 1995). In practice, the poverty line needs to be adjusted according to the actual conditions in different regions, owing to the differences in living costs and general price indices. In Table 2.1, the differences between several provinces and autonomous regions are shown. By using the basic figure of 250 yuan in 1992 and by taking inflation into account, a poverty line for a given year can be calculated. For example, the poverty line in 1997 was estimated to be 560 yuan in Shanxi.

Table 2.1 Poverty line in different provinces and autonomous regions in 1991

Province or autonomous region	Abject poverty line (yuan)	Poverty line (yuan)	Development line (yuan)
Guangdong	380	530	910
Shangong, Hubei	250	350	590
Jiangxi	240	340	580
Shanxi	200	280	490
Guizhou, Gansu	180	250	420

Source: NBSC (1992b)

The poverty line now set by the Chinese government is 625 yuan (US$75) in terms of net annual income per capita (Gao, 2001). This poverty line, though relatively low, is enough to obtain sufficient food and clothing and have a place to live (Gao, 2001). Using a standard international poverty line of US$1 per day would result in a substantially greater number of absolute poor, but the trend in reduction of poverty is still confirmed.

Another method commonly adopted in China for determining the poverty line is based on the Engels coefficient:

Poverty line = minimum food expenditure / Engels coefficient for poor households

To use this equation, it is necessary to determine the average Engels coefficient for poor households. In 1989, the coefficient was 63.6 per cent (NBSC, 1989), which was determined on the basis of a survey of 11,830 poor households in 23 poor counties.[3] In 1995 and 2000, the Engels coefficient for rural areas in China was 59 per cent and 50 per cent respectively.

In the period 1985–95, more than 40 million rural poor extricated themselves from food insecurity[4] (State Council, 1995). This number was 65 million by the end of 1995 (Jiang, 1997), 47 million in 1998 (State Council, 1998), about 42 million in 2000 (*Beijing Youth Daily*, 21 April 1999) and 30 million at the end of the Seven-Year Poverty Alleviation Programme (Gao, 2001) This means that 30 million rural people still remain in a predicament, and they can be classified as 'hard-core' poor inhabiting seriously deteriorated environments which can also be called hard-core poor areas.

Government aims and basic anti-poverty policies

During the thirty years prior to the reforms, when incomes were low, China provided relief to people in poor areas through government interventions. The long-term commitment to alleviate and eliminate regional poverty in the rural sector since the mid-1980s can be considered an extension of a tradition of public support. First, the anti-poverty actions have been undertaken via intensive public investment. Since 1996, the poverty alleviation funds provided by the central government amounted to 10 billion yuan (US$12 million) each year (Chen H., 1996).[5] In addition, the poverty relief fund has been increased by 1 billion yuan (US$120 million) in 2000 to meet its goal of alleviating rural poverty. This extra money has raised the central government's anti-poverty account to a total of 24.8 billion yuan (US$2.98 billion) in 2000, 30 times as much as in 1980, according to a 2001 White Paper. The additional money has been used to relocate poor farmers and augment other poverty relief efforts in remote areas and ethnic minority regions. Second, there has been extensive social mobilisation, so that poverty issues are becoming a matter of increasing public concern. Besides implementing the development assistance schemes designed by the central government for all poor areas, every functional ministry also allocated additional resources to conduct specific programmes in a few hard-core poor counties. In response to initiatives from the central government, local governments at provincial, prefecture and county levels took similar actions. Statistics indicate that in 1999, local governments spent 1.78 billion yuan (US$214.4 million) on poverty relief, 20 per cent more than in 1998 (Liu F., 2000).

The national Seven-Year Poverty Alleviation Programme for the years 1994–2000 to solve the problem of food and clothing shortages of the present rural poor was included as an important component in the Ninth National Five-Year Social Economic Development Plan. Since the Chinese government set a poverty line in 1985, alongside the attempts to bring progress in infrastructure construction in poor regions, measures were also taken to stimulate local governments and peasants, through the reforms in poverty alleviation policies, to tap their own potential for economic development and extrication from poverty.

The national Seven-Year Poverty Alleviation Programme, an important step towards achieving national common wealth, is of great political, economic and social significance. In 1996, the Party Central Committee and the State Council jointly held a working conference on poverty alleviation. The conference adopted a resolution to get rid of absolute poverty in rural areas. As well as the launching of some political slogans, like 'strengthening the leadership on poverty alleviation' and 'increasing the input on poverty alleviation', some concrete new measures have been taken such as the following:

1   Some large-scale development projects in infrastructure construction and natural resource development in poor regions have been approved. In order to support poverty alleviation in central and western regions, the State Council is making efforts to apply the Ninth Five-Year Plan and the national Seven-Year Poverty Alleviation Programme simultaneously. Examples of these large-scale projects include the Yanghuang project in Ningxia and the Yindaruqin project in Gansu. These large projects are accelerating local economic development.

2   The management and operation systems of poverty alleviation funds have been reformed by enhancing the provincial government's power. Provincial governments can now make overall arrangements for the local use of poverty alleviation funds according to their own situation.

3   Favourable policies have been adopted in poor areas; for example:

    • Poor households living below mere subsistence level are exempt from handing over grain to the state.

- The maturity period of poverty alleviation loans haa been extended and the conditions demanded for mortgages and as collateral have been relaxed to suit those on the lowest incomes.
- Poor households with feeding and clothing difficulties are exempt from agricultural taxes and special agricultural product taxes.
- Subsidies to poor areas have been increased.
- Newly established enterprises in poor areas are exempt from income taxes for three years, and enterprises are being set up in poor areas with assistance from the developed areas.
- As of 1996, the level of funding for reservoir construction and maintenance has been raised and, in accordance with the policy that the displaced must be paid, these funds are now used to help the relocation of the rural poor in the reservoir areas.
- The developed provinces and cities in coastal areas are now being called on to help the poor western areas.

A principal tenet of the Seven-Year Poverty Alleviation Programme was that by the end of 2000, every household in poor areas should have one family member working in a rural enterprise, in a sideline industry, or as a migrant in a developed region (Chen H., 1996). The official slogan was 'The migration of one person frees the entire household from poverty' (Wang Y., 1994).

Although the Seven-Year Poverty Alleviation Programme has ended and the programmes can be credited with much success, the development-oriented poverty alleviation drive in rural China early in the twenty-first century still faces serious challenges and problems. Alleviating and eliminating poverty remains a long-term historical task. The Chinese government has officially issued the Outline for Poverty Alleviation and Development of China's Rural Areas (2001–10), setting out the objectives, tasks, guiding ideology, policies and principles for work in this regard in the 10 years that it covers. The outline is another programmatic document following the Seven-Year Poverty Alleviation Programme for guiding poverty alleviation work in the rural areas.

The outline pointed out that the main difficulties and problems for China in the early part of the twenty-first century in the field of poverty alleviation are as follows. First, though the income of poverty-stricken people obviously has been improved, the current standard of poverty relief in China is very low. Second, restricted by unfavourable natural conditions, a weak social insurance system and their own lack of all-round ability, the people who now have enough to eat and wear may easily sink back into poverty. Third, although the development-oriented poverty reduction drive has greatly alleviated the poverty and backwardness of the vast impoverished rural areas, there has been no qualitative change either in the basic production and living conditions of the poverty-stricken peasant households, or in the social, economic and cultural backwardness in those areas. Fourth, because of its large population, China will face employment pressure for a long period to come. Last, people who still do not have enough to eat and wear generally live in areas with adverse natural environments, a low level of social development and underdeveloped social services, where the contrast between input and result is very sharp.

China's overall poverty alleviation goal from 2001 to 2010 is to help the small number of needy people without enough to eat and wear attain that minimum standard of living as soon as possible, and further improve the basic production and living conditions of the poor areas and consolidate the results gained in this regard. However, China is a developing country, and it will still take a long period of hard work to enable the people in the poor areas to live first a comfortable and then a well-off life.

Alleviation by bank credit

Poverty alleviation programmes in China rely overwhelmingly on domestic resources, in particular on central government's public spending. Besides preferential financial policies, such as reduction of taxation and increasing financial assistance, the central government has mainly promoted two types of programme. In addition to the public works carried out in poor areas to improve regions with poor infrastructure, it is also very important to mention the provision of subsidised credit to poor areas to stimulate local investment activity.

In China, poverty alleviation by bank credit has played an important part in government poverty alleviation and development programmes. From 1994, poverty alleviation credit was transferred to the ADBC (Agricultural Development Bank of China), and some reform of policy measures and the operation of poverty alleviation by credit has been conducted. The basic policy is to stick to the idea of helping poverty-stricken populations to have enough to eat and wear. Poverty alleviation funds are limited strictly to state-designated poverty-stricken counties, especially in extremely poor villages. The credit is aimed at all those poverty-stricken populations who have not had enough to eat or wear. Efforts have been made to ensure that credit was delivered directly to poor peasants. The issue of loans takes two forms. One is to disburse loans directly to peasants: that is, to issue loans to poor peasants with production capability, and help them to develop individual ventures within the private economy. In 1997, outstanding loans of this kind accounted for 23 per cent of all poverty alleviation loans. The other is to issue loans indirectly to households; for instance, for those peasants who do not possess production ability or who can engage in only small-scale family production, loans are issued through intermediaries or entities. These amount to about 77 per cent of all poverty alleviation loans. The indirect loans to peasants normally take one of the following forms: 'company + peasant', 'enterprises

+ peasant', 'rural socialised service system + peasant', 'functional department + peasant', 'intellectual + peasant', 'GB (Grameen Bank) model +
peasant',[6] or 'other intermediaries + peasant' (Zhu L., 1996).

However, there are factors limiting the effects of these. The poor who
live in the mountain areas with an adverse environment and poor
resources are generally not able to make use of the relatively favourable
economic conditions of the areas near county towns, roads and factories,
where the credit projects are often implemented. It is, then, questionable
whether the patterns of credit distribution could enable this group of the
poor to overcome food shortages.

Along with the government's western development plan, some banks
have moved their focus to regions of western China, such as the Huaxia
Bank's 25-million-yuan (US$3.01 million) poverty relief programme. This
programme plans to support 25,000 rural families in starting their small
businesses in south-west China. Instead of distributing money and goods
among the rural poor, the bank offers small credit loans for the farmers to
initiate projects. Training programmes in relevant technologies and
project management will also be offered (Wang Y., 2000).

Anti-poverty work: activities and experiences

Since the reform and opening to the outside world, China has experienced
its fastest economic growth and also seen the fastest decrease in the proportion of its population defined as poverty-stricken. It can be seen that
the Chinese government's key strategies on poverty alleviation have been
changed in different stages according to social economic situation. The
following are the key strategies implemented before 1997 (Jiang, 1997):

1 Give top priority to eliminating absolute poverty.
2 Stick to the principle of development. It is a fundamental change to
   shift from the previous approach of granting relief funds in emergencies to the development-focused poverty alleviation approach after
   learning the lessons over the decades.
3 Focus on grain and livestock production, and on improving agricultural processing industries, which contribute directly to removing
   absolute poverty.
4 To make effective use of the funds, the state has selected 592 counties
   as the key poor counties.
5 Economic development and intellectual enhancement are given equal
   importance. Educational and scientific means are used to raise the
   quality of labour in the poor regions.
6 Make full use of the political influence of party and government agencies and mobilise all the resources of society to support poor regions.
7 Help to build the spirit of self-reliance and hard work and make
   arduous efforts to make a better quality of life a reality for the poor.

8 Strengthen grassroots organisations in poor regions and support the development of the collective economy.
9 Combine poverty alleviation with the birth control programme.
10 Promote exchange and co-operation with international organisations and create a new pattern in the combination of domestic poverty alleviation institutions with international organisations, e.g. domestic poverty alleviation funds with international aid.

One question which must be raised for the decision makers at the top level to consider at this stage is whether they should differentiate regional development projects from anti-poverty programmes. The concepts of 'poor areas' and 'poor people' are mixed up in the policy design for poverty alleviation programmes in China, as it is thought that the richer the areas are, the better the people will do. It might be true in the regions where no absolute poverty exists, but it is not the case for the poor areas, where regional development does not necessarily benefit all the residents.

It seems that the focus should be on the alleviation of long-standing poverty aimed at groups of people rather than a short-term approach to individual cases of poverty. To be specific, in accordance with the definition given by developing countries, 'the poor' refers to those groups of people in absolute poverty. Long-standing poverty can be classified into two categories according to the origins of the poverty (Zhu L., 1994):

1 class-based poverty owing to great disparity in the distribution of property ownership; and
2 regional poverty resulting from an adverse living environment, such as lack of resources and underdeveloped infrastructure.

Of course, in some cases poverty can be attributable to the simultaneous effect of both these factors.

Although the Chinese government has to its credit considerable achievements in poverty alleviation, the task of solving the problem of poverty remains tough. Some economists suggested that raising incomes for large sections of the population in poor regions may be an expensive way for the national economy to reduce poverty.

The following strategies have been put forward in a White Paper, 'The Development for Rural China', to conclude the Chinese government's poverty alleviation programme between 1997 and 2000 (State Council, 2001).

1 adhering to the policy of development-oriented poverty alleviation;
2 bringing poverty alleviation within the reach of individual villages and households;
3 helping the poor with technology and education;
4 mobilising and organising all social sectors to participate in the poverty alleviation programme;

5   co-operation of the eastern and western regions in the poverty allevi-
    ation work;
6   helping the poor by encouraging migration;
7   transferring labour from poor areas to increase the chances of employ-
    ment and the income of workers in poor areas;
8   combining poverty reduction with eco-environmental protection and
    family planning; and
9   promoting international exchange and co-operation in aid for poverty
    alleviation work.

It can be seen that at the last stage of the national Seven-Year Poverty
Alleviation Programme, the Chinese government added three new key
strategies: rural–urban migration, development of the west of the country,
and protection of the natural environment.

Reducing rural poverty in China by rural–urban migration has proved
to be a relatively cheap or even cost-free strategy for the government.
According to Galbraith (1979), it has only rarely required the active inter-
vention of government. More often, it has needed only the government's
acquiescence and, more often still, in recent times, mere non-vigilance. It
has placed no strain on capacity.

Rural–urban migration in China

Migration is caused by a series of forces which encourage an individual to
leave one place (push) and attract him or her to another (pull) (Herberle,
1938). In China, the situation is rather complicated. It seems that the most
fundamental reason for rural–urban migration is the beneficial difference
between rural and urban areas, and the intention of increasing one's
income. In this section, reasons for internal migration in China, the
characteristics of migrants, and their activities in both the sending areas
and the destinations are analysed.

From statics to flow

The movement of China's rural population has undergone a great revolution over the past two decades: from little movement to a considerable flow.

An overview

The impact upon migration of rural–urban income differentials has
become the central focus of many migration studies, stimulated by the
availability of a testable hypothesis developed by Todaro that rural–urban
migration is determined by the income disparity between two regions, and
is conditioned by the probability of securing urban employment (see
Chapter 1).

It seems that the situation in China corresponds to Todaro's model. As in other societies, contemporary rural–urban migration in China is essentially a function of higher income and more job opportunities in the cities. On the one hand, there is the large income gap which became evident from 1949, narrowed after 1978 and has been widening since 1985. On the other hand, economic restructuring has created numerous job opportunities in the cities. For example, almost all cities are undergoing a construction boom as large amounts of foreign and domestic funding are invested in a wide variety of business activities and housing. Very often, rural peasants are organised into construction teams or companies by rural township or village governments. With the increasing liberalisation of the economy, the number of jobs in individual and small-scale enterprises in the urban manufacturing and service sectors has also grown rapidly, which is clearly an important force attracting numerous peasants to the cities (Sabin, 1994).

Rural–urban differences

The unequal exchange between agriculture and industry has existed for a long time in China, and consequently this has been an important reason for the rural–urban differences.[7] The term 'scissors differential' (*jiandaocha*) is closely related to the issue of unequal exchange. There are two types of 'scissors differential'. One is termed the 'price scissors differential', which measures the changes in terms of trade between agriculture and industry. The other is termed the 'value scissors differential', which measures the deviation of prices (of agricultural and industrial commodities) from their values (in terms of labour embodied) (Sheng, 1993). Economists generally agree that the 'price scissors differential' has narrowed by a big margin as prices for agricultural products have been readjusted several times. Using the conventional interpretation of the Marxist labour theory of value, many economists argue that the 'value scissors differential' has widened since 1949 (Chen K., 1982; Xu *et al.*, 1982). They suggest that the unequal exchange between agriculture and industry has not only existed but also grown, in the sense that agricultural commodities have been increasingly underpriced and industrial commodities increasingly overpriced relative to their respective 'labour value'. While prices for certain crops are fixed by planning mechanisms, chemical fertiliser, chemical pesticide and other agricultural materials are sold at market prices. For example, in 1993, 50 kilograms of rice was worth only a bottle of pesticide (Wang G., 1996). It was reported that from 1955 to 1985, the total absolute price scissors was more than 7,000 billion yuan. This is the same as the total investment in fixed assets in this period (Yan, 1988).

As a result, there is a considerable difference between rural and urban income, as shown in Table 2.2. It can be seen that from 1978 to 2001, the average income in urban areas was generally more than twice that in rural areas. Farmers' income per capita increased by 4.6 per cent in 1997, 4.3 per

Table 2.2 The difference in income (yuan/person/year) between urban and rural areas in China (Li, S. 1994; Song, 1995; Zhu, Q. 2000; NBSC, 2001)

Year	Urban/Rural
1978	2.37:1
1984	1.71:1
1992	2.33:1
1993	2.54:1
1994	2.63:1
1995	2.71:1
2000	2.79:1

cent in 1998 respectively. In 2001, farmers' income increased by 4.2 per cent, only half the growth of city residents' 8.5 per cent, the lowest growth rate of farmers' income in twenty years since China began its reform and opening up to the outside world. Slow growth of farmers' incomes has become a major problem. Lack of sales and low prices for farm produce have shown no sign of improvement, and in some grain production regions, farmers' incomes are declining.

Table 2.2 clearly shows the unfavourable position of farmers and agri-culture. The difficult life of some farmers can be partially attributed to the heavy tax burdens and illegal financial levies they bear. According to a 1997 State Administration of Taxation Survey of 5,000 rural households in 12 provinces, each farmer had to pay 149 yuan (US$18.90) in various fees per year, out of a total tax burden per capita of 195 yuan (US$23.50). The income gap between urban and rural residents is continuing to widen. Although some economists have put forward a wide range of arguments to demonstrate that the rural–urban gap in real income was not so great,[8] no attempt has been made to deny that a gap did indeed exist. Moreover, they agreed that average living standards among staff and workers[9] were indeed higher than among peasants (Nolan, 1979). In China, every rural household is entitled to land, and consequently there are very few landless households. Those without land probably have relinquished it voluntarily in order to specialise in non-agricultural rural activities. It is noteworthy that in China, wages rather than assets are the source of high incomes, whereas in other developing countries, agricultural wage workers are the poorest of the poor (Keith and Zhao, 1993). Peasants in China always say that 'without industry it is not possible to become rich (*wu gong bu fu*)'.

The consumption level for the rural population is relatively decreasing compared with urban people's (NBSC, 1997). For example, the consump-tion levels of urban and rural people were 148 yuan and 62 yuan in 1952, 754 yuan and 324 yuan in 1985, and 2,337 yuan and 921 yuan in 1993, respectively (Song, 1995). The differences in consumption levels between urban and rural areas (2.70:1 and 2.99:1 in 1995 and 2000 respectively (NBSC, 2002a)) are even greater than the difference in income.

Besides, urban people enjoy many special privileges. For instance, local government is responsible for job assignment for all those of working age in each locality's registered urban area. All employees receive salaries and bonuses, and retirement pensions, cooking oil and grain rations, foodstuffs subsidies, traffic and bathing allowances, and so on.[10] Experts agree that the urban–rural income difference is more than fivefold if urban residents' privileges and certain unspecified income are considered (Zhu Q., 2000). The government ensures that urban citizens' economic position remains stable even if there is drought or excessive rain. This social insurance alone is enough to attract people.

Rural surplus labour

It is difficult to give an exact definition and universally agreed measurement method for rural surplus labour. A highly rigorous analysis of China's surplus farm labour conducted by scholars at the Chinese Academy of Sciences reveals that as early as 1984 there was a surplus of 95 million peasants in agricultural production (Li R., 1996). By 1990 the size had swolled to 170 million (Ji D. and Shao, 1995). In 1994, the number exceeded 200 million, with predictions of 300 million by 2000 (Li R., 1996). Since the demand for rural labourers in agriculture will decline to 168 million by 2005, rural experts have predicted that around 600 million rural labourerrs will available by 2005–10 (Ministry of Agriculture, 2000). Whereas millions of surplus farm labourers have been absorbed by rural industries that have blossomed since the end of the commune system in the early 1980s (Chen J. and Yu, 1993), millions more have sought their fortunes in cities and towns. In 1984, the State Council issued a directive permitting peasants to move to and settle in towns (State Council, 1984).[11] This new policy officially opened the floodgate that had controlled rural–urban migration since 1958, when the Chinese household registration system (*hukou*) was implemented.[12] With the tacit consent of the state, millions of peasants have moved not only to towns but also to cities. An unprecedented era of massive migration (*da qiyi*) began, and since then the momentum of the waves of peasant workers (*min gong chao*) flooding the cities has increased rapidly and shows no sign of abatement.[13]

In rural areas, various factors in social development, such as the rapid increase in the rural population, and the decrease in cultivated land per capita, have impelled larger numbers of people to migrate from rural to urban areas. The most important factor is the large surplus labour force in rural areas caused by higher labour efficiency since the introduction of the production responsibility system in the late 1970s. Table 2.3 compares the numbers engaged in agricultural and non-agricultural labour. It is seen that the ratio of agricultural to non-agricultural labour is about 2 in the eastern region and greater in central and western regions.

Table 2.3 Comparison between agricultural and non-agricultural labour among various regions in China in 1996 (NBSC, 2001)

	Agricultural labourers (millions)	% of whole labourers force	Non-agricultural labourers (millions)	% of whole labour force
East	149.14	66.50	75.12	33.50
Central	155.25	79.88	39.10	29.12
West	120.02	84.38	22.23	15.62

Rural enterprises

Besides moving to cities, an alternative for people in rural areas is to work in rural enterprises. In 1985, China's rural reform entered a new period of de-agriculturalisation, national and regional development of non-agricultural industries, and the transfer of farm labour to non-agricultural sectors. The upsurge of township and village enterprises has changed the industrial structure in rural areas and provided employment opportunities for surplus rural labour. By 1993, the number of people working in these enterprises had risen to 112 million (Meng, 1996). That is, they employed one of every four able-bodied person in the countryside. This sector absorbed new labour at a more rapid rate than did the state sector (Nolan, 1993). However, with the increase in production efficiency, employment capacity in rural enterprises appears to be decreasing. For example, from 1988 to 1992, the output value of rural enterprises doubled, but the increase in the number of workers was only 10.9 per cent (Guo, 1995). Table 2.4 compares the rate of increase of the total output in rural industries and the number of rural labourers in rural industries from 1990 to 1997. It is interesting to note that the number of rural enterprises was increasing continuously, but the number of rural labourers absorbed was decreasing. However, rural enterprises will continue to be major employers of surplus rural labourers, with an estimated annual increase around 2–3.5 million rural labourers during the next five years (Ministry of Agriculture, 2000).

Chinese government policy has encouraged surplus agricultural workers to 'leave the land but not the village', by taking up jobs in rural industry,

Table 2.4 Increase in output and employment in rural industries from 1990 to 1997 (Jia, 1999)

Year	1990–4	1995	1996	1997
Rate of increase in output (%)	42.2	33.6	21	18
Number of new rural labourers employed (millions)	7.19	7.2	6.47	4.0

transport, services, or other sideline occupations. In some villages, this is feasible, mostly because they are not far from a city market. Villages and small towns near cities can produce light industrial products for the city market and easily transport their products into the city. In addition, some rural areas near China's coasts have begun to produce for the export market.

Nevertheless, the non-agricultural development has incurred a high cost for the entire rural sector of China. Most beginners who established non-private enterprises were not well-trained entrepreneurs but government officers. They had very little capital of their own and mainly depended on bank loans to start their business. Where these enterprises have been successful, they have become part of the achievements of the local government leadership and have provided an extra source of finance in addition to local taxation. However, when they fail, the biggest losers have been and will continue to be the banks and the people who have banking deposits. Most local governments of poor areas have a deficit budget and depend on subsidies from central government finance. A large number of township and county governments are not able to pay salaries on time to their employees.

Moreover, many villages are located in remote places, far from transport lines and very far from city markets. Such villages may find it impossible to employ their local surplus agricultural labourers in non-agricultural jobs.

Urban industrialisation

Urban industrialisation is also an important factor attracting the rural population to the cities. The attractiveness of rural–urban migration depends on the growth rate of the urban economy, especially the growth of employment in the state industrial sector. Many state industries are likely to use rural–urban migrants to add 'new blood' to increase their production without incurring the usual extra employers' on-costs such as pensions.[14] For example, in Jiangnan Shipbuilding Factory in Shanghai, one of the biggest manufacturers in China, one-third of the workers come from rural areas. Also, in one of the main cotton mills in Shanghai, most assembly-line workers are rural women (Zhao M., 1995). In urban construction industries, the number of rural–urban migrants is even greater.

Other reasons for migration

There are also some other reasons for rural–urban migration. For example, rising educational levels encourage people to leave the rural areas. Information through mass media and propaganda allows them to know more of the world outside their place of origin. In addition, improvements in transport networks make migration more convenient, although there have been many reports about how crowded the trains are because of the large numbers of migrants (Zhan, 1994).

For all the above reasons, rural–urban migration is growing from a trickle to a torrent. As Davin (1996a) reported,

> Migration has involved the transfer of tens of millions of people from villages where they are employed (or under-employed) in agriculture to cities, to towns or to other rural areas where they hope to find better economic opportunities. There are flows of cash in the form of remittances, of information in letters, and of returning migrants who bring with them not only more cash and more information, but new skills, ideas, aspirations and life styles. Migration thus has the potential to transform or at least very considerably to change life in the sending areas.

Table 2.5 shows the direction of migration in China. It can be seen that the flow of migration is mostly from rural to urban areas and from inland provinces to east coast provinces.

Characteristics of rural–urban migration

Migration is selective (Lee, 1966). If migration is selective of individuals in terms of sex, age and economic or social attributes, their movements will result in changes in the demographic and socio-economic composition of the population of both the sending and the destination areas. Migration is a two-way process: it is a response to economic and social changes and equally it is a catalyst for change in those areas gaining and losing migrants (G. J. Lewis, 1982). In this section, some selective factors for migrants in China are briefly analysed. These factors are sex, age, educational level and income level.

Table 2.5 The direction of floating population and distribution of outmigration/immigration by provinces/cities (NBSC, 2002)

Number of floating population	121.07 million		
Within the same province	65%	To another province	35%
To rural	25.6%	To urban	74.4%
Outmigration by provinces		Immigration by provinces and cities	
Sichuan	16.4%	Guangdong	35.5%
Anhui	10.2%	Zhejing	8.7%
Hunan	10.2%	Shanghai	7.4%
Jiangxi	8.7%	Jiangsu	6.0%
Henan	7.2%	Beijing	5.8%
Hubei	6.6%	Fujian	5.1%
Other provinces	40.7%	Other	31.5%

Sex

There are two opposite opinions regarding the differences between male and female in terms of migration. Beaujeau-Garnier (1966) indicated that the male is a mobile creature, capable of enquiring, susceptible to suggestion, and endowed with imagination and initiative. Similarly, G. Lewis (1982) showed that males tend to be more migratory than females. By contrast, from his observation of large numbers of women in domestic service in Victorian Britain, Ravenstein (1885) claimed that females are more migratory than males. Richmond (1969) indicated that as economies develop, females take a more active part in the labour force and therefore sex selectivity becomes less significant. There is evidence for both opinions. For example, rural–urban migration in Ghana (Caldwell, 1969) is certainly dominated by males, yet in Chile the opposite is true, owing to the availability of female-dominated employment in the urban areas (Shaw, 1975). In West Usambaras, Africa, land is inherited only by sons, and women's access to land is conditioned by their marital status. Consequently, those women who do not have access to land are likely to enter the labour market (Sender and Smith, 1990).

Generally speaking, China has brought more women, both unmarried and married, into gainful employment outside the home (Hawthorn, 1978). According to a survey in 1992 (NBSC, 1992b), in China the proportion of male migrants was slightly over half (54.4 per cent). One possible reason is the traditional attitude that 'males are for outside work and females for inside work (*nan zhu wai nu zhu nei*)'. However, in comparison with many other developing countries, where migration is dominated by one sex, usually but by no means universally males, the sexes are comparatively evenly balanced in China's internal migration. It is interesting to note that the importance of male and female migration is different in various regions. A survey of migrant workers in 149 factories in the Pearl River Delta region showed that 74.7 per cent of interviewees were women and 25.3 per cent were men (Research Group on Peasant Workers, 1994). In northern China, conversely, it appears that migration is dominated by males. A survey in 1994 in the capital of China, Beijing, showed that of the 3.29 million migrants, the percentages of males and females were 63.5 and 36.5 respectively. Besides the regional variations, distance also affects the sex ratio: it seems that women dominate short-distance migration and men dominate long-distance migration. An investigation by Yang Z. and Xiao (1996) showed that in short-distance migration, the ratio of male to female migrants was 3:5, whereas in long-distance migration, the ratio of male to female was 4:1. A similar phenomenon has also been observed in Africa (Adepoju, 1983).

It is noted that the impact of marriage migration is rather different from that of economic migration. Studies on marriage migration in China have been carried out by Goldstein and Goldstein (1990) and by Lavely (1991).

Age

In general, there has been plenty of evidence to support the hypothesis that people in their twenties and early thirties are the most mobile. G. J. Lewis (1982) indicated that young adults are the most mobile segment of the population. The reason often advanced as to why that is the case is that they are best placed to take advantage of new opportunities as they are without the economic and social ties which constrain older groups, holding them to their place of residence. Almost everywhere, migration is concentrated extremely heavily among villagers aged 15–30. Connell *et al.* (1976), in their study in north Indian villages, found that within the adult migration group, 60 per cent of the total adult population were aged 15–24. Similar results have been reported in Africa (Gugler, 1968). Moreover, Lipton (1977) found that most migrants first left their village at the lower end of their 'working age period'. However, the migration of females tends not to show such a marked age selectivity.

The case in China is very similar to the above. Figure 2.1 shows the age distribution of unofficial migrants in 1995 (NBSC, 1996). It can be seen that there is a peak of migrants at age 20–24.

Education

The role of education in determining migration patterns is very important. Many of the studies on migration point to the high degree of educational

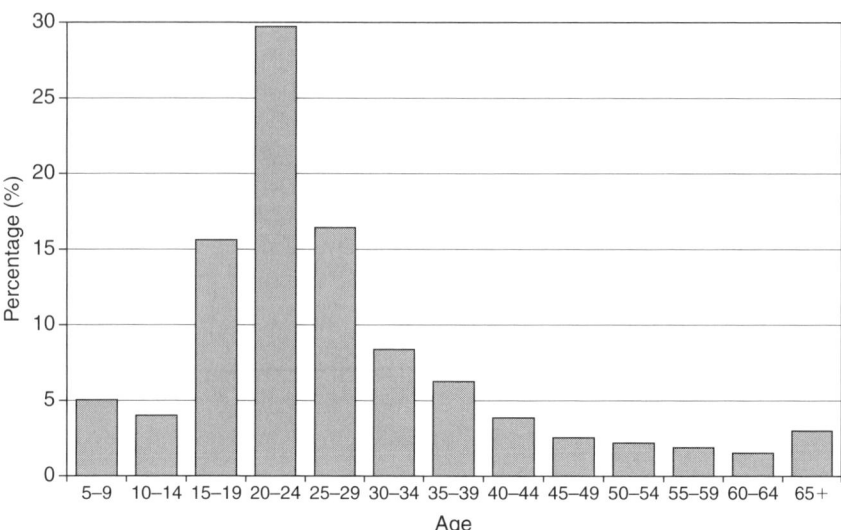

Figure 2.1 Age distribution of unofficial migrants in 1995 (NBSC, 1996). The sampling proportion was 1%.

selectivity in migration patterns. The tendency to migrate increases with the acquisition of educational qualifications, though the educated comprise a minority of total migrants in many developing countries. Even if within the migrant group a large majority are illiterates, they are followed a long way behind by those with secondary or higher education. In between, the proportion with lower educational qualifications is relatively small (Connell *et al.*, 1976).

In China, the vast majority of migrants are not illiterates. According to the Chinese Education Constitution, the five years of primary and four years of secondary school education are free. In post-reform China, there is evidence that the majority of rural migrants have had at least junior middle school education (Mallee, 1996). On average, rural residents have 5.5 years of education (NBSC, 1994).

Income

The evidence on the characteristics of individual migrants suggests that both rich and poor people move out of villages, depending on the resource structure of the village. But the majority of migrants from rural areas come from relatively poor villages (Connell *et al.*, 1976). Moreover, it is by no means the case that migration has typically tended to be of those with the highest income from the poorest regions (Baines, 1991).

The case in China is rather complicated. In Sichuan, a province which has high population density and is often regarded as a poor region, there are enormous numbers of migrants. In recent years, 5.5 million people have moved out from this province annually. This number is 5 per cent of the total population there. By contrast, in another relatively poor province, Shanxi, only 0.12 million people (0.4 per cent of the total population) move out each year.[15] In many poor villages, only five to six people per village work away (Zhan, 1994) – an administrative village typically has 300 households. One reason is that they are too poor to move, and the other reason is that traditional values still dominate (Wang X. and Bai, 1987). They believe that 'staying at home in poverty is better than earning riches far away (*hao chu men bu ru lai zai jia*)' and 'our own poor home is better than someone else's plush apartment (*jin ou yin wo bu ru zi ji de gou wo*)'. In Zhejiang and Hunan, two provinces which are generally regarded as having a middle to high income level, the number of migrants each year is 2 and 4 million (4.7 per cent and 6.3 per cent of the total population respectively).[16] The main reason is that these provinces are near economically developed areas on the coast.

Activities of migrants in their destination areas

It is useful to give a brief account of the employment structure and income distribution among labour in urban areas before analysing the activities of migrants in the cities.

The proportions of employees in state-owned and collectively owned enterprises have shrunk drastically, but those in the private sector have snowballed. Personal income is related to education level, age and gender. Personal income increases with education level. People with college or higher degrees, who account for 12 per cent of the total employees, are at the top of the income tower with 980 yuan (US$118.4), while high school graduates made only 664 yuan (US$80.2) and illiterate persons are at the bottom with 481 yuan (US$58.1). The people with higher education degrees are among the youngest workers; this group is paid the most. People who are under 30 earn more money than other age groups. Earnings decrease with age and reach their lowest level for people aged 41–45, who earn 30 per cent less on average than those under 30. This is in contrast to what is found in most developed countries, where middle-aged people tend to have the highest income levels. Furthermore, there is a widening income gap between the two genders. The ratio of incomes between male and female in August 1999 was 1:0.77, compared with 1:0.83 in 1990. In addition, in August 1999, 6 per cent of urban families' incomes were less than 100 yuan per capita per month (US$12). Most of them were laid-off workers from state-owned enterprises.

Wages and salaries

Attempts have been made to regulate wage levels for migrant workers in many parts of the country. In places such as some of the special economic zones in southern China, a minimum wage system has been introduced based on local price indices. However, so far it seems that the system has not been at all effective. A general check on labour conditions in 1993 demonstrated that salaries in some enterprises were far below the stipulated minimum level. For example, in the Longhua handbag factory in Hangzhou City, more than 90 per cent of the peasant workers received less than 200 yuan per month, including their overtime pay.

According to a bi-variant analysis in the Pearl River Delta (Research Group on Peasant Workers, 1994), salary levels depend on gender, education and type of enterprise. Generally speaking, the percentage of women receiving a salary of less than 300 yuan is much higher than the percentage of men, while the percentage of men receiving between 500 and 800 yuan and more than 800 yuan is much higher than the percentage of women.

There is a strong positive correlation between education and salary. Most of those who receive a monthly salary of more than 500 yuan have graduated from senior high school or above.

Salary also depends on the type of enterprise. There are five types: enterprises run by towns or townships; those run by villages; private enterprises; joint ventures; and foreign enterprises. Generally speaking, the salaries of workers in enterprises run by towns or townships are lower than in most other enterprises, but salaries in private enterprises are the lowest.

Similar differences in salary have also been reported in India. On the basis of a survey, Breman (1996) showed that the lowest paid received five to six times less than the highest paid. These figures are for adult males. Children up to the age of 15 or 16 who work as unskilled labourers are paid no more than half the adult wage, and the rate for women is at least 20 per cent lower than that for men doing the same work.

Knight and Song (1998) studied migration from the census, and their case study of households and migration in the Handan area of Hebei Province showed that poor people may have escaped from rural poverty, but in some cases they have entered urban poverty instead.

Working conditions

Many, but not all, of the jobs that peasants take are indeed low-paid, dirty or tedious jobs that are avoided by local residents even when they are unemployed. Some of the jobs are offered by state-owned units with a short-term contract. Such units are willing to hire peasants, as they do not have to provide them with regular staff housing or benefits, such as retirement and health care for family dependants. At the same time, the state's decision to allow the non-state sectors of the economy to grow has also created numerous jobs in the tertiary sector available to rural peasants.

Rural–urban migrants' rights have become an important issue in local government policies. Some local governments have promulgated their own labour laws and regulations, specifying limits to working hours, especially overtime. For example, the Labour Regulations of Guangdong Special Economic Zones and the Regulations Concerning Contract Labour in Shenzhen Special Economic Zone, both issued in 1993, stipulated that 'Workers shall not work more than 40 hours a week or more than 8 hours a day, and overtime shall not be used routinely to increase regular working hours.' However, it appears that those laws and regulations exist only on paper. An investigation into the working conditions of peasant workers (Research Group on Peasant Workers, 1994) found that those with a poorer educational background work more overtime.

It was also found that there are many complaints about physical conditions in the workplaces, such as the temperature being too high or too low, there being too much dust or noise, and too much exposure to poisonous or otherwise dangerous chemicals. Compared with private enterprises, the employees' general welfare is better in enterprises run by towns, townships and foreign companies.

Means of employment and occupation distribution

There is only a weak recruitment system in China to transfer rural labourers to urban areas directly. Most migration in China is an individual or household arrangement made without outside help, except sometimes from local governments.

Generally speaking, there are four means by which a migrant can find a job:

1   with the help of co-villagers who are already temporary workers in a destination area;
2   by him- or herself;
3   with the help of local labour services in the sending or destination areas; and
4   through other channels.

According to a survey by the Research Group on Peasant Workers (1994), these four means of finding employment were used by 42.7 per cent, 45.3 per cent, 4 per cent and 8 per cent of migrants, respectively. Recent research by the State Council Development and Research Centre (2001) showed that 76 per cent of migrants found their first job through their friends or relatives. It is clear that independent job seeking is becoming the norm.

Because there are many surplus labourers in urban areas and the competition for jobs is stiff, the most common occupations for rural–urban migrants are those which are regarded as heavy work with low social status and bad working conditions. Migrants normally work in coal mining, the textile industry, civil engineering, transport, commerce, food and other service-sector jobs, environmental sanitation and domestic work. It is very difficult for rural migrants to find jobs in government departments or in the finance sector since they would be expected to hold the relevant qualifications, such as a university degree. In 2000, the Ministry of Labour and Social Security issued an emergency document instructing provincial labour departments to control the number of transient rural labourers seeking jobs in urban areas, especially big cities. In Beijing, non-Beijing residents will be banned from 103 kinds of jobs, such as working as an accountant. The new rule has been issued as an important way to ease employment pressure, which many Beijingers believe is cranked up by the influx of migrant labourers. Most enterprises, except for high-tech ones, are heavily restricted from hiring migrants.

The distribution of rural–urban migrants by branch of industry in 1990 is shown in Table 2.6.

According to a survey (NBSC, 1996b), Beijing's construction industry employed more than half a million peasant workers in 1994. These migrants accounted for 90 per cent of the total number of the city's construction workers. Many were recruited directly by various organisations, production units and businesses through some 'labour service bases' (*laowu jidi*) that were established throughout China for this purpose. In an attempt to better control and manage peasant workers, in 1992 Beijing's

Table 2.6 Distribution of rural-urban migrants by branch of industry as a percentage of total rural-urban migrants working in industrial enterprises (NBSC, 1990)

Industrial sectors	Percentage
Coal mining and processing	20.7
Cotton textile industry	11.4
Wool textile industry	10.3
Fibre products	4.4
Garments products	15.2
Other sewing products	4.3
Leather products	7.1
Furniture manufacturing	12.4
Civil engineering, construction	7.5
Glass and glass products	6.6
Sum of the above	100

Bureau of Labour required that hiring units must sign a labour contract with the bureau of the labour-exporting county. Meanwhile, the city also permitted various provinces and counties to establish liaison offices in Beijing (*zhujing banshichu*) to assist labour recruitment.

Having a common place of origin affects migrants' employment in another way. In Beijing and other cities, most construction workers are recruited by the leaders of individual construction teams (*baogongdui*) from their fellow villagers (*laoxiang*).[17] A team leader must find work for his team, often through the city's liaison office that represents the government of his home county or province. After a job is secured, he must provide a service fee to the office that may amount to 16 per cent of contract income (Zhou, 1996). Such teams tend to be small and work on small projects, often providing labour only. Larger construction projects are frequently contracted to teams organised by township and town enterprises, which invariably also employ *laoxiang*. Aside from construction, about 35 per cent of Beijing's peasant workers are employed in various businesses and services (Zhou, 1996).

Although numerous peasant workers make their living as small street traders – for instance, selling vegetables and small household goods or providing repair services to urban residents – a significant number should be seen as rural entrepreneurs who have brought their capital or skills to the cities. They have come to Beijing not because they are unable to make a living in the countryside, but because they wish to make more money quickly or perhaps also because their local culture puts a high value on going out to the outside world to get rich. Collective or group behaviour is essentially shaped by public opinion on migration at the village of origin. In the village setting, with limited exposure to the mass media and information spread by word of mouth through intimate personal contact, the success stories of earlier migrants can inspire all who wish to earn more. Such stories can thus provide the impetus that prompts under-employed villagers to leave for a certain city.

Women's migration

When rural women migrate, their first destination tends to be a nearby village or township, where the majority of them are absorbed by locally run enterprises. Particularly common is assembly-line work in one of the special economic zones. The second most common destination for women migrants is larger towns and cities, where rural women take up dirty, tiring and less rewarding jobs rejected by urban residents.

According to a survey report issued by the Institute of Rural Development under the Chinese Academy of Social Sciences, about 130 million rural labourers migrated from rural areas during the period 1978–88. Of these, about 33 million, or 25 per cent, were women (Liu C., 1995). A survey conducted by the Ministry of Labour and Social Security of labour markets in 62 cities across the country found that the demand for women labourers was slightly higher than that for men. However, there are many more male migrant workers than female ones (Ministry of Labour and Social Security, 2001).

Migrants' social and economic status

Although the employment and income patterns of migrant groups differ markedly, they tend to be seen as a single urban lower social class. It is still difficult for them to be integrated into urban culture. However, there are major exceptions to the perception that all migrants are poor, socially and economically marginalised and trapped by the *hukou* system in the lower stratum of a supposedly dualistic urban society, capable of leading only a life of hardship by selling cheap labour. Conversely, in many cities some of the poorest people are local citizens who have urban *hukou*, whereas many of the rural migrants are comparatively rich. According to a recent survey in 20 cities, the percentage of low-income households has increased from 16.8 per cent in 1998 to 19.5 per cent in 1999. This is mainly caused by the 'job suspension' in many state-owned industries[18] (Zhao Y., 2000).

Summary

It can be seen from the above that rural–urban migration plays an important role in the development of urban areas. Migrants play a vital part in many job sectors such as the construction industry. They also provide an indispensable part of the social facilities of the cities. Without them, most cities could not move. Generally speaking, the more migrants there are in an area, the faster the economic development is in the area. Urbanisation in China is increasing to a certain extent as a result of rural–urban migration. However, migrants are normally working in the lowest-level jobs on low pay. They are not entitled to any state welfare. Many social problems caused by rural–urban migration have emerged in urban areas. Nevertheless, according to a survey in 1994 of 149 factories in nine cities in the Pearl River Delta region, peasant workers' awareness of their rights is growing, and the number and quality of migrating peasants are enough to influence the structure of society as a whole (Research Group on Peasant Workers, 1994). Overall, it appears that the effect of rural–urban migration on the destination areas is more positive than negative.

Activities of migrants in sending areas

In many agricultural provinces and poor areas, rural–urban migration has become an important path leading the rural poor to *xiao-kang*, which means 'to get a better life' or 'rise to beyond subsistence level'.[19] The remittances from migrants can significantly improve standards of living. Peasants have a saying about migration: 'Enough to eat after one year, wear new clothing after two years, and build a new house after three years (*yi nian chi bao fan, liang nian chuan xin yi, san nian gai xin fang*)'. Moreover, many returned migrants invest in rural enterprises or set up private enterprises which increase employment. Furthermore, migrants play an important role in socio-economic activities in their sending areas. They bring back not only money but also new ideas.

Remittances

A major consequence of migration is the transfer of cash or other resources between migrants and the family members remaining in the village. This is different from what happens in some other countries, such as India, since poverty in China is not associated with landlessness because of land-use rights. Consequently, China has created a relatively secure present and a relatively predictable future for a majority of rural people, whereas India has not (Hawthorn, 1978).

In China, all rural–urban migrants have a piece of land in their home village even if it may be very small. They have to maintain links with it. It has been reported by Pei (1994) that Chinese migrants keep close ties with their home villages. In Sichuan Province, about 70–90 per cent of the migrants return home at least once a year, usually at Spring Festival. Also, the 'spread effect' (Myrdal, 1957) brings chain migration, and this helps to maintain frequent communication. However, such a 'spread effect' may be affected by backwash effects leading to divergence rather than convergence.

Although the term 'remittances' usually refers to money transmitted to villages by migrants while they are away, the meaning has been extended here to include savings brought back by returning migrants, and any reverse flow of either remittances or savings in cash or kind (Connell *et al.*, 1976).

The role of remittances appears to be very important in rural development in China. Remittance money is used not only for improving standards of living for migrants' families but also for rural investment. Statistics indicate that China's farm workers send home about 100 billion yuan (US\$12.1 billion) each year (NBSC, 2002a). Migrant labourers are essential for development of the rural economy. Close investigation found that in 1994, the rural–urban migrants in China earned a total of 1,500 billion yuan, an average of 3,649 yuan per person. After allowing for living and travelling expenses, at least 832 billion yuan returned to rural areas in the form of remittances (Song, 1995).

The scale of remittances has had a significant impact on economic development in several provinces of southern China. In Sichuan Province, for example, about 8 million migrants brought back 30–50 billion yuan in 1995. In the same year, in Zhejiang Province 2 million migrants earned 4 billion yuan, and the income of 4 million migrants in Hunan Province was 40 billion (Li S. Z., 1996). In Anhui Province, remittances in 1993 amounted to 75 billion yuan, which was more than the total budget of the local government in that year, 55 billion yuan (Yang X., 1995). However, in western and central areas of China, the income from migration is much less. For example, in Shanxi Province there were 0.12 million migrants in 1995 and they brought back only 3.6 billion yuan in remittances, although there were 3 million surplus labourers and this number is increasing at a rate of 0.15 million per year (Zhan, 1994).

There is no doubt that the nature of remittance flows, whether regular or intermittent, large or small, depends on the nature of the links between the migrants and their families. If migrants' families also move to cities, which might be the case for permanent or long-term rural–urban migrants, the total flow of remittances would be reduced.

Attitudes and values

At a societal scale, it has been suggested that migration acts as an agent for the transformation of a society from a traditional one into a modern one. Away-from-home work experiences not only help farmers understand the market economy, but also bring urban influences to less developed rural areas. In addition, returning migrants act as a means by which more advanced forms of human activity are received from different parts of the country, and therefore form an essential part of the modernisation process.

Clearly, labour migration in China has changed the economic and material life of the sending areas. More importantly, this change may also result in substantial improvements in their standard of living, although this still needs to be further investigated. It appears that attitudes towards farming are being changed, from the pursuit of subsistence to commercial ideas. Mallee's survey of 2,835 households in seven provinces found that of the 28.8 per cent villagers who engaged in agriculture as their sole pursuit, 56 per cent were women (Mallee, 1997, 1998; Pieke and Mallee, 1999). This survey, indicating that women now make up a majority among full-time cultivators, but that men still play a substantial role in agriculture, is probably a better indication of the situation in China as a whole. In the meantime, many women have given up agriculture in order to engage in local and regional trading. Also, migration strengthens the economic infrastructure through the need to develop both rural industry and the rural public infrastructure such as roads and transportation facilities. As mentioned previously, in many areas the money sent back home by migrants has been used not only to improve the immediate quality of life, but also to invest in further economic development.

Other issues relating to rural–urban migration

The following sub-sections introduce a number of issues related to rural–urban migration in China that may improve understanding of the phenomenon.

Blind flows (mangliu)

'Blind flows' (*mangliu*) is a term implying random and disorganised movement. It refers to situations where migrants have no prior knowledge of job opportunities in their destinations. This is often the case when there are no identifiable forces that channel the rural migrants to a specific place or particular type of employment. Doubtless there are 'floaters' in small towns and cities, but discussion of the floating population is almost exclusively concentrated on the big cities such as Beijing, Shanghai, Guangzhou and Wuhan, where this population is estimated to form between one-fifth and one-third of the total (Solinger, 1997).

However, any view that peasant migrations are 'blind flows' is contradicted by the fact that peasant workers are actively recruited by urban industries, government units and state enterprises. Various work units have directly recruited peasant workers, and the working term is often relatively long, say more than one year.

Two types of population movement

It is important to indicate that there are two types of spatial shift of population in China. The first is permanent or formal migration (*qianyi*), which is approved and often planned by the state, and allows a migrant to move to a predetermined place and re-register their *hukou* there. This mainly involves people with urban *hukou* who move between urban places.

The second type of population movement (*renkou liudong*) is unofficial, mainly involving spontaneous movement of peasants, although also including travellers in transit and individuals on official business in a different place. Such people are called the floating population (*liudong renkou*), or temporary migrants, non-*hukou* migrants, peasant workers (*nong min gong*), or simply people coming from elsewhere (*wailai renkou*) (Ma and Xiang, 1998). Those wishing to stay in a city for more than three days are required to register as temporary population (*zhanzhu renkou*) and are not entitled to the privileges provided by the state for regular urban residents (Cheng and Selden, 1994). From the early 1980s on, two sub-types of floating population can be clearly recognised: those who have registered as temporary residents and those who have not. The size of the latter group has been expanding since then.

Cleared and returned

When the authorities deemed that there were too many outsiders flowing into the cities, action would be taken to drive them out. This occurred between 1961 and 1963, when 26 million peasant workers were 'cleared and returned' (*qingtui*) from the cities, most of whom (19 million) had been recruited to support the frenzied industrialisation programme of the Great Leap Forward in the cities. The major reason for their removal was to alleviate the burden on the state of supplying grain to the cities (Ma and Xiang, 1998). During the past ten years, many migrants have still been sent back, although the reason may not be the food supply in cities.[20]

Government policies

A major influence on migratory movement is public policy. Although a government is rarely concerned with migration *per se*, it seeks to influence it as a means of effecting policy goals. Usually such a policy is developed for the benefit of society as a whole rather than the personal objectives of its members (Houston, 1979).

During the two decades of rural economic transformation, the Chinese government recognised this dilemma and loosened its formerly tight control on internal migration. The central government and local government played a role in organising long-distance migration in poor areas. In poor areas, it was often the township government in particular which helped to organise migrants, giving them training courses and information about job opportunities, in the belief that their migration would benefit the local community (Nolan, 1993). Moreover, in some very poor areas, local governments are planning to move people to places which are more suitable for agriculture or where jobs may be found in rural enterprises.

Kang (1996) argued that the government should help people to move to the areas where labour is needed rather than simply attempt to alleviate poverty by giving them relief. For example, the Shanxi provincial government is planning initially to relocate 50,000 people from poor mountain areas. Some other provinces, such as Shaanxi and Fujian, have also carried out such projects (*zao fu gong sheng*). Shandong's government has relocated 1.6 million people (304 villages) from areas regularly flooded by the Yellow River (*People's Daily*, 13 February 2000).[21]

However, it must be stressed that the majority of migrants move through private channels. Surplus labourers from villages, especially economically depressed villages, have been allowed to migrate seasonally for work elsewhere, to adopt mobile occupations such as transport and trading, or even to settle permanently in small towns or cities. As a consequence of the reforms which relaxed state control of food to free market trading, it became possible for migrants to get food supplies in cities. Thus, internal migration in China in the past two decades has helped ameliorate the problem of rural underemployment, has enabled migrants to become more productive than before, and has contributed to the impressive economic growth that took place.

The policy which has allowed peasants to move into small market towns since 1984 is subject to many preconditions. For example, they are not qualified for state food supply, financial subsidy and job allocation.

In these past twenty years, many local governments have allowed the issue of special residence permits to encourage farmers to reside in small cities and towns. Some big and medium-sized cities have also loosened their restrictions. Shanghai, Shenzhen and Zhuhai have regulations that allow anyone who buys local commercial property to apply to become a permanent resident. Beijing allows technical workers with senior professional titles to move there without complications.

The hukou *system: effects on agricultural and non-agricultural populations*

By the *hukou* system, most Chinese people are assigned a registration status, as either 'agricultural' or 'non-agricultural' population. For a newborn baby, *hukou* status is passed along the maternal line; in other words, the baby must register with the mother's household registration unit, where her permanent address is.[22] Any transfer of *hukou* registration status from agricultural to non-agricultural has to go through official channels, as either a regular or a special transfer. Under the Chinese political economy, the most regular channels of transfer are recruitment by an 'urban' enterprise (*zhao gong*), enrolment in an institute of higher education (*zhao sheng*), or promotion to a senior administrative job (*zhao gan*).

The *hukou* system serves as another boundary by which the state can regulate the size of the urban population to suit its own interests. Through the regular channels, the granting of non-agricultural *hukou* depends on the proprietary nature (state owned or collective owned) of the work unit (*danwei*) to which one is going to be assigned, not exactly on the geographical location of the *danwei*. In other words, if one gets a job in a collective-owned *danwei*, one might not be able to transfer one's registration, but if it was a state-owned *danwei* then one would.

The basic function and features of the *hukou* system remained intact after 1980. Since *hukou* status is politically delineated and is an important way of maintaining social control, there is no incentive for the state to change it fundamentally. The classification of citizens as agricultural or non-agricultural based on the *hukou* regististration still exists. Persons holding different *hukou* still have different political and economic rights and obligations. Transfer of *hukuo* status from agricultural to non-agricultural is still subject to policy and quota controls. Change of permanent residence to anywhere outside the jurisdiction of one's original place of residence still requires a certificate of transfer. The *hukou* system *per se* is not as relaxed as is conventionally perceived.

Hukou status does not necessarily reflect a person's occupation. In fact, many urban residents who are classified as agricultural by the *hukou* registration system actually engage in non-agricultural jobs. Also, since rural–urban migrants who are classified as agricultural workers are not statistically counted into the urban population, the increase in urban population does not officially reflect a labour shift from agricultural to non-agricultural sectors.

Statistically, since 1986 the official concept of non-agricultural population has been linked to actual occupation, not simply to registration status. This new official concept of non-agricultural population, which is mainly based on occupation, appears to be more realistic than the concept which defines population by *hukou* status. Although in practice the actual statistics might still exclude some portion of agricultural-*hukou* holders who are engaged in non-agricultural jobs, owing to the failure to capture all such people, its appropriateness has become more apparent than the aggregate totals classified by the *hukou* system.

Considering the needs of China's economic development and the process of urbanisation, the barrier that restricts people's freedom to migrate and divides the country into distinctive urban and rural worlds is expected to be broken very soon. A reform of the existing residence system has been introduced into all the country's county-level cities and administrative towns starting 1 October 2001. According to the government's plan, non-natives with a legal and static dwelling place and a stable occupation and source of income can apply for permanent residence in the cities and towns where they work and live.

Some small cities and towns in the country have already conducted trial reforms, For example, Ningbo, a city in the economically developed east China province of Zhejiang, has totally revamped its registration system, allowing people to register as permanent residents in cities and towns where they work and live. The city's new system allows all non-urban residents and non-natives to have a legal and fixed address, and a stable job and income. Their family members can also apply for permanent residency in urban areas.

Experts hailed Ningbo's reform as a big breakthrough in China's existing 43-year-old household registration system.

Official documents relating to population movement

There were different types of migration in China before the reform period of the 1980s. For example, over 20 million urban people, Red Guards, intellectuals and politically disgraced officials were sent to the countryside to settle. Some of the rusticated urbanites retained their urban registration while living in the villages and many peasant migrants to the cities continued to be registered as agricultural population (Scharping, 1987).

In 1985, the Ministry of Public Security issued another *hukou* regulation, which stipulated the compulsory registration of temporary residents in all urban areas. This was not previously required.

In 1985, with the relaxation of migration control, 'resident identification cards' (*jumin shenfen zheng*) were issued to all citizens over 16 years of age. The resident ID card has contributed to greater spatial mobility. The card can be used to seek employment, register at a hotel, apply for business licences, and to register as a temporary urban resident in cities.

On 29 October 1988, the General Office of the State Council issued a circular on stopping the overt 'sale' of urban *hukou* in certain cities and counties. When necessary, the government enforces the *hukou* registration and takes action to send back any 'illegal' migrants.

Meanwhile, in some cities, such as Shanghai, there is a special type of urban *hukou* for rural migrants, called the 'blue seal *hukou*'. Those who hold this kind of *hukou* can stay permanently in the city but their privileges are limited in comparison with those who have normal urban *hukou*. To obtain a 'blue seal *hukou*', considerable amounts must be paid to the local government as official fees, and in addition, many other strict requirements have to be met.

In 1991, the State Council issued a directive concerning the hiring of peasant workers by state-owned enterprises (State Council, 1991).[23] Labour contracts may be signed with recruited peasants who agree to work for more than one year. Such workers are supposed to be treated in the same way as contract workers from urban areas, but unfortunately this is usually not the case.

In 2001, the State Development Planning Commission planned to end the decades-old residence permit system and scrap restrictive migration policies. China said it would scrap policies limiting the movement of labour in the next five years as the government tries to find jobs for tens of millions of rural workers. The intention was that the restrictions would first be lifted in the richer coastal provinces, and then throughout the nation. The commission announced that China would abolish the policy during the next five years to increase employment and establish a unified labour market for both urban and rural areas of the coastal provinces. The new system is meant to alleviate the situation by allowing people to go where the jobs are. Under the new system, each person will be given his or her own social security number, similar to the system in Western countries, which will be used to keep track of their wages and tax them for social security.

In 2003, one year after China's accession to the WTO, the State Council issued a directive concerning equal opportunities for hiring peasant workers in cities. It seems that the barriers that prevent migrant workers remaining in urban areas are still in existence. Moreover, the unemployment rate in cities remains high, and some 2.12 million college graduates will pour into China's labour market in 2003. Thus the 2001 plan which promised to end the old residence permit system has not been fully implemented.

Urbanisation level

Compared with most developing countries, particularly Asian countries, China has a relatively low level of urbanisation despite the fact that it has experienced rapid industrialisation in the past five decades under socialism. According to the census publications (NBSC, 1985–2000), China's urbanisation level was 20.1 per cent in 1985, 26.2 per cent in 1990, 28.9 per cent in 1995, and 30.5 per cent in 1999.

By considering designated towns' population as urban population, some research has shown that China's urbanisation level on the whole is higher than the official estimates. Zhang L. and Zhao (1998) indicated that China's urbanisation level has grown substantially and consistently since 1980 – from 19 per cent in 1980 to 33 per cent in 1995, an increase of almost 1 per cent per year. This confirms that rapid economic growth in the past years of economic reforms has truly speeded up Chinese urbanisation.

It is noted that there are substantial differences between various regions. In 1995, the eastern region had the highest level, reaching 40 per cent, almost double the western region's figure, which ranked the lowest, only 22 per cent. In the central region, the urbanisation level was 30 per cent (NBSC, 1996).

Another important issue is the quality of the urban environment, which has become a very serious social problem along with the heavy flow of rural–urban migration and with increasing urbanisation levels (Jahiel, 1997, 1998; Lo and Laung, 2000; Tang, 1997). The problem is mainly caused by increasing pressures on daily living with the increasing population in urban areas. Many cities, especially some southern cities such as Guangzhou and Shanghai, have paid great attention to the issue of urban environment and development.

Overall, China has made great progress in urbanising. Currently there are more than 55,000 small cities and towns, and more than 100 million farmers have become permanent urbanites in the past decade, according to official statistics. Zhejiang Province, for example, has chosen 105 small cities and towns in which to try out its reforms since 1998. Those cities have absorbed more than 1.24 million new residents, of whom 80 per cent are from rural areas.

China still has 800 million rural people. With the country's plan to change from an agricultural giant to an industrial power, the promotion of urbanisation is urgent. Experts predicted that as many as 8 million of these people will become residents of small cities and towns each year as China's urbanisation starts to roll. More than 46 million people will enter the urban labour force in the next five years (*Xinhua News*, 2001).

Summary

It can be concluded from this chapter's discussion of poverty and migration in China that although considerable progress has been made, the task of solving the poverty problem remains tough. From a socio-economic viewpoint, rural–urban migration has played a positive role both in helping to solve the problem of poverty, and also in the overall social and economic development of China. Existing research on rural–urban migration has contributed significantly to the field, but much work, especially relating to the central region of China, is still required. The following chapters describe one such study.

3 Case study region and methodology

Patterns of migration and poverty in the central provinces of China were largely unknown prior to this study. This chapter introduces Shanxi Province, a poor region of inland China, and the areas selected for the field study. In addition, this chapter also describes the research methodology in detail.

General information on the region

Geography

Shanxi Province lies to the south-west of Beijing (see Figure 3.1). The name means 'west of the mountains', as it is separated from the Huabei plains by the Taihang mountains. It is often referred to as the 'coal sea' because of its rich coal resources. A population of 32,710,000 (NBSC, 2001)[1] lives in an area of 156,266 square kilometres. Ranges of hills cover most of the province. The western regions border the Loess Plateau of Shaanxi and Inner Mongolia, and exhibit the characteristic rolling hills of yellow earth, heavily eroded by rain and flash floods. The Fen River starts in the north, collecting what little rain runs off the parched earth, and meanders down the central valley to meet the Yellow River in the south-western tip of the province. The south of the province, nestling in the bend of the Yellow River, is known to be one of the ancient cultural centres of China. About 200 palaeolithic and 500 neolithic sites have been unearthed in the region, as well as 500 tombs and other ancient ruins (Bao, 1995).

A significant geographical feature of Shanxi is that it is located on the Loess Plateau. Its soil and special climate strongly affect the lifestyle of the inhabitants. The Loess Plateau is an ancient land form which extends over some 624,000 square kilometres of north-western China, covering much of Shanxi, Gansu, Ningxia and Shaanxi. The soils, formed from accumulated wind-borne deposits, are of uncommon depth. Large tracts are 50–100 m deep. Mean annual rainfall varies from less than 200 mm to more than 800 mm, with most areas receiving about 400 mm. About 75 per cent of the

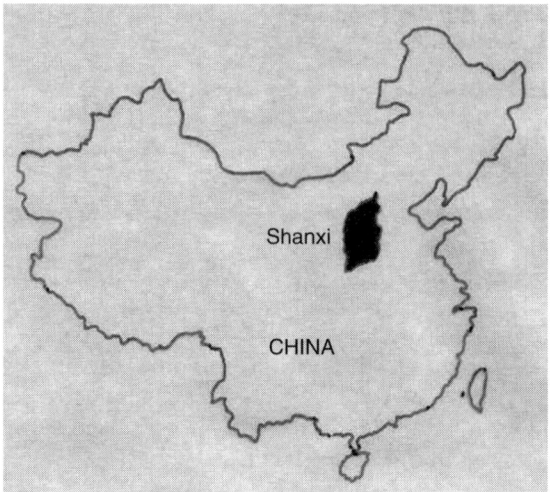

Figure 3.1 A map of China showing the location of Shanxi.

annual rainfall occurs in the four-month period June to September, and frequently comes as sporadic heavy falls. The brief season of effective rainfall fortunately coincides with the period of highest mean air temperature, and provides the most favourable period for plant growth. The efficiency of rainfall use is reduced, however, by limited infiltration on steep slopes and surface crusting (Zheng P., 1999).

Shanxi is China's most important energy base. The Loess Plateau abounds in coal. In Shanxi Province, almost every county has coal deposits. Shanxi coal was formed mainly in the Palaeozoic Era and the early period of the Mesozoic Era 100–200 million years ago. Coal deposits have been found under one-third of the total area of the province, or 60,000 square kilometres. They are concentrated in six coalfields: Datong, Ningwu, Xishan, Huoxian, Qinshui and Hedong, where combined proven coal deposits exceed 200 billion tonnes, one-third of the national total. Coal from these areas is of good quality and of a whole range of varieties. Shanxi coal has old ash, sulphur and phosphorus content, and a high calorific capacity. Furthermore, coal deposits in Shanxi are easy to mine thanks to the simple geological structures and shallow coal seams. After years of construction, Shanxi has become China's biggest coal supply base with an annual output of more than 200 million tonnes, about one-fifth of the national total (Zhou X., 1999). Datong in northern Shanxi is the country's biggest coal mine. It is also one of the biggest coal mines in the world. Datong produces mainly power-generating coal known in China and abroad for its superior quality. The Yangquan coalmine is the country's biggest producer of anthracite. Shanxi coal is exported as well as supplied to other parts of the country.

Land degradation and rural poverty

Expanding and exploitative agriculture, in combination with geological erosion of the naturally fragile soil, has progressively removed the Loess Plateau's vegetative cover (Chen Y. *et al.*, 1989). Since unprotected loess is easily eroded, the removal of the vegetative cover has by now resulted in the advanced environmental destruction of most of the plateau. Streams, which in many areas have cut through to the underlying sandstone, have heavily dissected the plateau, leaving a landscape of steeply sloped hills of relatively uniform height. It is estimated that of the 530,000 square kilometres of the Loess Plateau situated along the middle reaches of the Yellow River, more than 450,000 square kilometres (85 per cent) is severely eroded 'badlands'. Erosion products are transported out of the area by the silt-laden Yellow River, leading to heavy silting of dams and irrigation systems downstream and dangerous increases in the height of the riverbed itself.

Extensive environmental degradation is both an important cause and a result of low productivity and severe poverty in the rainfall agricultural areas of the Loess Plateau. Agricultural productivity and income were diminished during the 1960s and 1970s when, as part of the national policy of achieving local self-sufficiency in grain production, upland farmers were encouraged to switch from pastoralism to extensive cultivation of grain. Unfortunately, extending grain cultivation to steeply sloped land exacerbated land degradation and ultimately led to a reduction in carrying capacity. Many of the 81 million rural inhabitants of the Loess Plateau continue to suffer from extreme poverty, and the effort to improve their well-being receives attention and support from both central government and provincial government.

The rural household net income per capita in Shanxi was 1,557 yuan in 1997 (NBSC, 1997).[2] This figure, although slightly higher than that for some of the poorest provinces in China, such as Shaanxi (1,165 yuan), Yunnan (1,229 yuan) and Guizhou (1,277 yuan), was considerably lower than the national average, 1,926 yuan. The household net income per capita in Shanxi was also lower than for Anhui (1,608 yuan) and Henan (1,579 yuan), which in China are often regarded as poor provinces.

In terms of the rural household living expenditure per capita, Shanxi ranks even lower. In 1997, this figure (NBSC, 1997) was 1,174 yuan,[3] which was much lower than the national level, 1,572 yuan, and also lower than that for Anhui (1,309 yuan), Sichuan (1,350 yuan) and Henan (1,206 yuan).

It was reported by the Shanxi government that in 1996, there were 3.8 million people living in poverty, defined as those whose income was lower than 500 yuan per year (Zheng S., 1996). In other words, about 14 per cent of the population in Shanxi were below the 'poverty line'. These people were living in 50 counties and 492 towns, classed as the poorest or poverty areas, mostly in the Taihang mountains, Lulang mountains and the Datong–Yanbei area. 'Poverty alleviation' has been one of the three most important tasks for the local governments. In 1996, the poverty alleviation funds allocated by the local governments totalled 100 million yuan (Zheng S., 1996), and this amount is increasing every year (*People's Daily*, 2 February 2000).

The workforce and rural–urban migration

It is well known that China's population is increasing relatively fast compared with that of many other developed and developing countries. The population growth rate in Shanxi was 1.034 per cent in 1996, which was similar to the national average, 1.042 per cent (NBSC, 1997).[4]

In China, the workforce increased 1.66 times in the past forty years in comparison with a 1-fold increase in some developed countries in ninety years (Gu and Li, 1995). Currently the natural growth rate of the workforce is 2.5 per cent in average per year.

From national census data, the gross domestic product (GDP) indices,[5] and other relevant indices from 1990 to 1999 (NBSC, 1985–2000), the workforce supply and requirement between 2000 and 2015 in Shanxi has been predicted by the author using the method of curve extension.[6] The data from 1995 to 2015 are shown in Table 3.1.

As shown in the table, there are, and will be, plentiful human resources in Shanxi. The total workforce is increasing considerably each year. There will be about 440,000–690,000 new workers of working age each year in spite of the annual retirement of 210,000–440,000. However, the workforce requirement is also increasing, and thus the ratio of workforce require-

Table 3.1 Workforce supply and requirement between 1995 and 2015 in Shanxi. 1, Total workforce; 2, workers of working age;[7] 3, new workers of working age per year;[8] 4, retired workers of working age per year;[9] 5, workforce requirement;[10] 6, ratio of workforce requirement and supply (%), i.e. ration between item 5 to 1. The unit in the table is million.

Year	1	Population (in million) 2	3	4	5	Ratio (%) 6
1995	18.7	18.5	0.44	0.21	14.0	74.79
1998	19.6	19.3	0.48	0.24	14.5	74.18
2000	20.2	19.9	0.54	0.22	16.5	81.6
2005	21.6	21.2	0.63	0.25	16.6	76.88
2010	22.6	22.4	0.66	0.37	17.6	77.94
2015	24.0	23.6	0.69	0.44	18.6	77.54

ment to workforce supply is approximately constant from 1995 to 2015. In other words, both state industries and rural enterprises will be able to absorb 75–80 per cent of the labourers. Nevertheless, in terms of absolute number, the high rate of increase of rural surplus labour[7] will continue because of the rate of increase of the population as a whole. Hence, leaving the village to find work is almost the only choice for the surplus labourers.

It should be noted, however, that in Shanxi fewer people are migrating outside the province than in some provinces in southern China. Possible reasons include the following:

1   Some people are too poor to move out.
2   As Shanxi is an inland province, people's way of thinking is relatively traditional. They would rather stay at home, and do not want to take a risk.
3   The development of local industry is not as fast as in some southern Chinese provinces, and this has limited people's positive view of migration.

As mentioned previously, a particular feature of the migration in Shanxi is that it is greatly affected by the province's special position as 'China's energy base'. The migration of coal mine workers has been an important phenomenon for over seventy years as the coal industry has developed, and migrant coal miners continue to be an important factor in Shanxi's development.

The case study area

The survey that forms the basis of this dissertation was carried out in three counties: Daixian, Jingle and Wutai. The selection of the three counties was based on their economic level and migration situation. In 1996, by using a multi-index evaluation system, the Statistical Bureau of Shanxi defined 50 of the province's 150 counties as 'poverty counties'. The evaluation system was based on geographical and economic conditions, as well as social and human factors. The 50 counties were divided into three categories: counties with a traditional agricultural structure (including Daixan), counties with rich but unexploited natural resources (including Jingle), and counties with other resources such as tourist attractions (including Wutai). The three counties were chosen at random from their respective category.

Jingle and Wutai were also among the 563 national 'poverty counties'. In other words, Daixian is more developed than Jingle or Wutai. In terms of migration, Daixian and Jingle were about average for Shanxi, whereas Wutai had well above the average migration rate for the province. In each county, three villages were randomly sampled, and the one which was

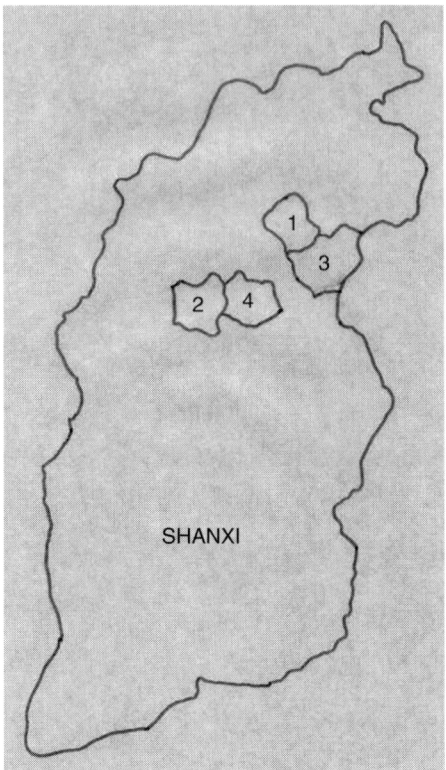

Figure 3.2 A map of Shanxi showing the locations of the studied counties (1, Daixian; 2, Jingle; 3, Wutai) and the county used for the pilot study (4, Xinxian).

typical of the general case of the county was chosen for case study.[8] The locations of the three counties in the province are shown in Figure 3.2.

Daixian County is located in the Taihang mountain area. There are 253 villages in the county. Jingle is in north-western Shanxi. Its underground resources, mainly coal, are rich. There are 22 townships (*xiang*),[9] of which 17 have coal deposits with workable reserves totalling 6 billion tons. Wutai is well known because Wutaishan, one of the sacred mountains of Buddhism, is located in this county. Tourism to this famous scenic spot brings in 100 million yuan extra income for the county every year.

Population and income

Table 3.2 shows the population of the three counties between 1978 and 1997. It can be seen that there was a dramatic population increase in the

Table 3.2 Population (in thousands) of the three counties in this case study. Data compiled from the NBSC and the county governments' reports.

		1978	1980	1985	1990	1993	1996	1997
Daixian	Total	175.4	174.2	182.0	188.8	199.2	200.3	200.4
	Rural	160.0	159.2	163.0	163.2	167.6	163.1	162.5
Jingle	Total	127.5	129.1	136.4	144.4	151.3	153.5	154.1
	Rural	122.1	122.6	128.5	130.2	133.6	135.7	135.6
Wutai	Total	292.5	293.6	296.8	305.5	310.5	310.8	309.7
	Rural	277.4	276.5	278.9	282.4	284.7	278.7	277.0

three counties during this period except for a slight decrease in Daixian and Wutai around 1980. The main reason for this decrease was that many young people who had come from big cities for 're-education'[10] in the countryside went back to cities. In 1997, the total population of all three countries was 665,000 of which the rural population (577,000) accounted for 86 per cent of the total.

It is noteworthy that in contrast with the conventional picture, the rural population in these three counties fell slightly in recent years. An important reason is that some of the rural residents bought township *hukou* and moved into towns.[11] Also, many young women and even men 'escaped' from these three counties through marriage. The population is decreasing every year in some of the poorest villages, such as Tongqiangou *xiang* in Wutai.[12]

Since 1978, the net income per capita[13] of rural residents in the three countries has increased dramatically. Table 3.3 shows the change in net income from 1978 to 1997. However, the economic development level in the three counties is still much lower than the national average, and so is the standard of living. In 1997, the net income per capita of rural residents in Daixian, Jingle and Wutai was 1,175, 859 and 986 yuan respectively, considerably lower than the average for the province, 1,557 yuan, or the nation as a whole, 1,926 yuan. The average grain production per capita in the three counties was 305 kg, which was 82 kg lower than the national level (NBSC, 1996).

Table 3.3 Comparison of net income per capita (in yuan) among the three counties studied, the national level and the provincial level. Data from the NBSC and the field study database.

	1978	1980	1985	1990	1993	1996	1997
China	133.6	191.3	397.6	686.3	921.6	1,577.7	1,926.1
Shanxi	101.6	155.8	358.3	603.5	778.3	1,208.3	1,557.2
Daixian	86.5	88.0	261.4	353.3	556.1	1,018.5	1,175.3
Jingle	60.8	68.3	162.1	291.1	381.5	663.7	858.9
Wutai	96.7	89.5	320.4	343.0	461.3	913.9	986.1

Natural resources and basic social and economic conditions

The three counties are located in mountainous areas and have always suffered from natural disasters. Water resources are insufficient and survival is difficult for both people and livestock. Communication infrastructure is quite backward. Local government reports[14] provide the following background data on the three counties in the field study:

1   *Roads*. About 82 per cent of the villages in the three counties are on the township-level road network,[15] although the road quality is normally very poor – some are very narrow and some are in need of modernisation and upgrading.
2   *Electricity*. Only 79 per cent of the villages in the three counties have electricity. In those villages with electricity, power shortages and electricity blackouts are quite common, especially in spring and autumn, when agricultural activities are in full flow.
3   *Telecommunications*. The development of telecommunications is way behind the times in these three counties. Automatic switchboards for programmed telephone have been installed only in some of the main townships and villages with coal mines. Some village officers are still using old-style cranking bar telephones. About 83 per cent of the villages do not have any telecommunications link and half of the townships have no switchboard – partly because they cannot afford the bill and partly owing to the lack of technical support.
4   *Education*. The education facilities in the three counties are very poor. Over 95 per cent of the villages have no middle school, and 17 per cent of them do not have a primary school. Many children have to walk a long distance to school. About half the school buildings are in very bad condition. In 1997, one-third of the schools had to bring their summer holiday forward because of the potential danger that leaking roofs might flood the classrooms. Only 50 per cent of the teachers are qualified. Each year, only 70–80 students in each county are able to go to universities and colleges because of their reasonably good marks, a proportion much lower than in the cities.[16]
5   *Medical treatment and health care*. In recent years, the healthcare situation has improved – 32 per cent of the villages have clinics or village doctors. It is reasonably convenient to see a doctor, but many rural peasants have to walk more than 20 km to get medicine.
6   *Water supply*. Generally speaking, Shanxi is short of water resources. Exploiting coal is very water-consuming.[17] As a result of the huge exploitation of coal, the remaining available water resources fell from about 14.2 billion cubic metres in 1956–79 (average) to 9.0 billion cubic metres in the 1990s. The decrease in the shallow groundwater level in the three counties has caused serious problems for the supply of clean drinking water, and water for irrigation.

Jingle is one of the 563 poorest counties in China. Of the 305 villages, 262 are not on the township-level road network. Drinking water is in short supply in 80 villages. The central government has sent two groups of volunteers to this county as part of its Anti-poverty Project. The county has also been visited by officials from the United Nations (UN).

Land and agricultural productivity

In Daixian, Jingle and Wutai, the cultivated land areas per capita are 2.5 *mu*,[22] 3.6 *mu* and 1.7 *mu*, respectively.[18] Compared with the provincial level, 2.6 *mu*, and the national level, 1.66 *mu*, the amount of cultivated land per capita in the three counties is not low. However, 97 per cent of the cultivated land is dry land and one-third is classed as impoverished soil.

Table 3.4 shows the variation in the land area under cultivation and the gross agricultural output value in each of the three counties. It can be seen that the total cultivated land has decreased from 1978 to 1997, but the agricultural productivity is increasing. An important reason for the decrease in cultivated land is that more houses have been built. The reason for the increase in the yield of agricultural products is that the effects of the rural economic reforms are becoming more widespread, and also the conditions for agricultural production are being improved. New agricultural technologies such as thin plastic ground cover and deep ploughing have been widely used and local governments also encourage peasants to develop forestry, animal husbandry, fisheries and commodity industries run by rural households. As a result of the above changes, there has been an increase in rural surplus labour[19] in the three counties studied.

Development of rural enterprise and industry

The coal industry and other heavy industries in Shanxi have been developed over a period of many years. The structure of the three types of industry – primary, secondary and tertiary industry – is reasonably in balance. In 1997, the three types of industry made up 15.2 per cent, 51.3 per cent and 33.5 per

Table 3.4 Land area (10,000 *mu*) under cultivation and agricultural output (million yuan) in the three counties studied (Local government reports).

	County	1978	1980	1985	1990	1993	1996	1997
Area (*10,000mu*)	Daixian	48.12	48.04	44.75	43.87	43.49	43.47	43.46
	Jingle	53.10	52.80	49.90	49.50	49.31	49.30	49.00
	Wutai	57.34	57.11	52.31	51.03	50.82	49.78	48.56
Agricultural output (*million yuan*)[24]	Daixian	5.58	5.38	6.56	7.94	7.77	17.62	18.06
	Jingle	3.32	3.17	3.48	4.49	4.73	9.97	11.33
	Wutai	6.75	7.24	8.99	9.08	9.48	20.20	17.21

cent of GDP respectively, compared with the national level: 21.0 per cent, 47.8 per cent and 31.8 per cent (NBSC, 1998). The percentages of employees working in each of the three types of industry in Shanxi were 43.3 per cent, 29.4 per cent and 27.2 per cent, compared with the national levels 50.5 per cent, 23.5 per cent and 26.1 per cent respectively.

The industrial level in Shanxi is relatively high in many cities. However, the surrounding countryside remains backward. The three counties studied are dominated by a typical traditional agricultural economy. The level of industrial development is significantly lower than the national and provincial level. Table 3.5 shows the GDP and the breakdown of employee by industry type in the three counties, compared with the provincial and national levels. In the three counties, the percentages of employees in primary industry are higher than the national level (the differences in the percentages being 8.9 per cent, 13.4 per cent, and 8.5 per cent for Daixan, Jingle and Wutai respectively), and also higher than the provincial level (16.1 per cent, 20.6 per cent and 15.7 per cent respectively). Conversely, the percentages of employees in secondary industry are lower than the national level (3.7 per cent, 1.4 per cent and 4.4 per cent) in the three counties. Similarly, the percentages of employee in tertiary industry are 5.9 per cent, 12.0 per cent and 4.2 per cent lower in these three counties compared with the national level.

Figure 3.3 shows the number of rural enterprises, the number of employees, and the total output of the enterprises in the three counties in the period 1995–7. It can be seen that the number of rural enterprises in the three counties decreased dramatically: in 1995, the numbers were 9,851, 1,757 and 2,175 in Daixian, Jingle and Wutai, and in 1997 the numbers were 582, 172 and 485. Corresponding to the decreasing number of rural enterprises, the employees of rural enterprises in these three counties also fell dramatically. In 1996, the peak period, the numbers were 26,448 in Daixian, 15,217 in Jingle and 39,025 in Wutai. In 1997, the figures were reduced to 16,657 in Daixian, 4,449 in Jingle and 20,602 in Wutai. It

Table 3.5 The GDP and compositions of employee by industry type in the three counties in the field study, compared with the provincial and national levels (NBSC, 1997; Local government reports)

	National	*Shanxi*	*Daixian*	*Jingle*	*Wutai*
GDP (%)					
Primary Industry	21.0	15.2	40.0	45.0	45.4
Secondary Industry	47.3	51.3	36.9	29.5	27.5
Tertiary Industry	31.8	33.5	22.2	25.5	27.1
Employee (%)					
Primary Industry	50.5	43.3	59.4	63.9	59.0
Secondary Industry	23.5	29.4	19.8	22.1	19.1
Tertiary Industry	26.1	27.2	20.2	14.1	21.9

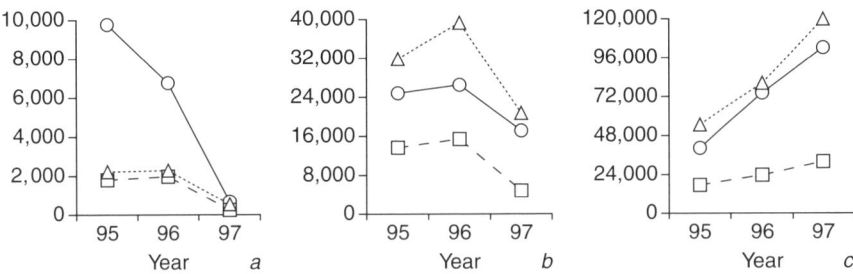

Figure 3.3 The number of rural enterprises (a), number of employees (b), and the total output of the enterprises (c, unit in the figure 10 thousand yuan) in the three counties in the period of 1995–7 (Local government reports). ○, Daixian; □, Jingle; △, Wutai.

is interesting, but not surprising, to see that the total output from the rural enterprises actually increased from 1995 to 1997.[20] This suggests that the rural enterprises which survived are those that were, and continue to be, successful.[21] In general, the tendency shown in Figure 3.3 is in line with the overall situation in China (see Chapter 2).

Figure 3.4 shows the number of non-rural industries[22] in the three counties

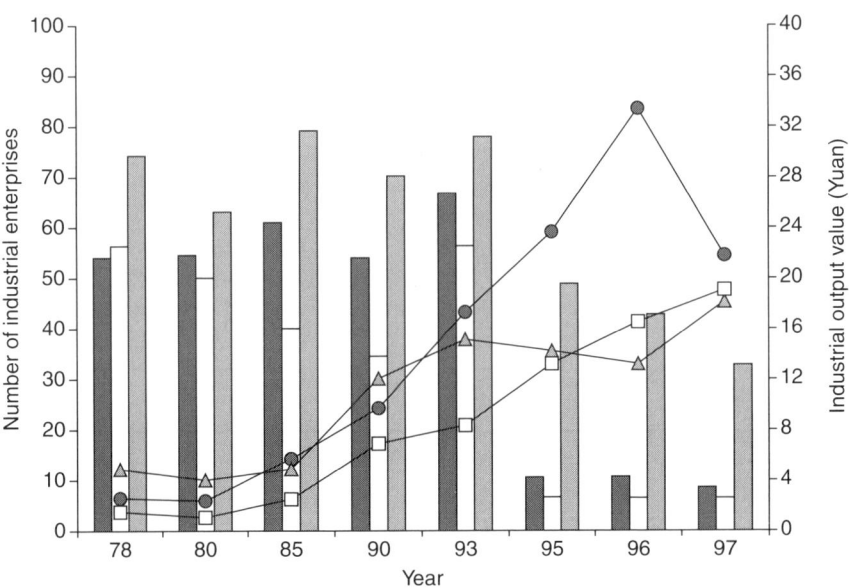

Figure 3.4 Number of the non-rural industries (bars, ■, Daixian; □, Jingle; ▨, Wutai) and their total output (lines, ■, Daixian; □, Jingle; ▨, Wutai. unit: 10 million yuan).

and their output in the period 1978–97. It can be seen that, as in Figure 3.3, the number of employees has decreased, especially since 1993, but output has increased.

Case study methodology

The case study was carried out from October 1997 to July 1998. First, a typical township was selected as a pilot study site to pre-test the case study methodology. Then, in-depth semi-structured interviews were conducted in four sampled villages in the three counties. Two hundred households, 100 with migrants and 100 without, were interviewed. For the households with migrants, a two-ended approach was made, namely, interviewing the migrants in their destinations as well as their families in their villages of origin. In addition to the above interviews, some informal discussions were held, and a number of special interviews were conducted.

Apart from a first-hand database which resulted from the above inductive field survey approach and site observation, statistical data and relevant information were compiled from published documents as well as internal circulated official reports, from village level to provincial level. With all these data,[23] it has been possible to carry out an in-depth analysis, both qualitative and quantitative, of the changing nature of rural–urban migration and its socio-economic effects in Shanxi since the economic reforms of 1978.

Questionnaire design

A set of preliminary questionnaires, including questionnaires for migrants, for households, and for local officers and village cadres, were designed. An outline for informal discussions was also formulated. The final versions[24] of these are all included in the Appendix.

The design of the questionnaires was based on an intensive study of relevant theories and case studies on migration and poverty, as reviewed in Chapters 1 and 2. Apart from gathering factual information about the migrants, such as demographic data – age, gender, marital status, and so on – the questionnaires were focused on the causes and effects of rural–urban migration in Shanxi. Three major aspects were considered in the design of the questionnaires, and each aspect contained ten major items:

1 Sending area:

- socio-economic characteristics of migrants and their villages;
- main factors affecting migration-decision making;
- reasons for not migrating out.

2   Destination:

- migrants' occupation distribution;
- urban adjustment system;
- migrants' social and economic situation;
- the role of migrants in industry and other sectors;
- future plans of current migrants.

3   The socio-economic effects of rural–urban migration:

- would rural–urban migration be helpful in solving rural poverty?
- would rural–urban migration benefit the overall economy?

Each questionnaire was divided into two main parts which dealt with tutored and untutored questions, respectively. In the tutored part, questions were asked in order to investigate the interviewees' attitude to migration. Most questions were designed in a form of multiple choices, so that it was easier for the interviewees to answer. For some questions, the interviewees could tick more than one choice. In this case, the total percentage may be greater than 100 per cent, which can be seen in the results in Chapters 4 and 5. In the untutored part, the interviewees' opinions about government policies were asked. The main questions in the questionnaires were in the following areas:

1   The *demographic selection* of rural–urban migrants: Which members of the family migrate? What are their social and economic character-istics? Is there a link between the sort of village and sort of migration?
2   *Reasons for migration*: Is there a link between rural poverty and migration, and between rural surplus labour and migration?
3   *The role of women and children*: Are more women than previously involved in rural–urban migration? What occupations do they take up? Has rural–urban migration had any effect on other tasks tradition-ally undertaken by women, such as their agricultural work and house-work? Has migration from rural areas had any effect on the role of children, especially on their share of the workload?
4   The *change of relationship*: How is the relationship changing between migrants and their families (spouse, parents and children)?
5   The *organisation of family and village development* in terms of inter-household co-operation and inter-village co-operation. How do the employment activities of migrants affect their home villages: are there any changes in the way the village is organised (for instance, the divi-sion of labour and new styles of co-operation between villagers)?
6   *Influence on agriculture*: Has there been any change in the land-usage rights? Is there a new style of collective farming corresponding to the reduction in agricultural labour? What has happened to migrants' lands (formal and informal policies)?
7   *Remittances*: How do the remittances affect social and economic activ-

ities in sending villages? How do remittances affect the standard of living in the sending villages? In what kinds of rural enterprises do the migrants prefer to invest?

8 *Changes in values and ideas*: Does rural–urban migration affect values and ideas in the sending villages? Are there any differences between households with and without migrants?

9 *Returned migrants*: Why do they return and what are they doing in the village? Do most migrants return because of failure or success? How do the other villagers regard the returned migrants?

10 *Social change*: What is the relationship between the economic activities of migrants and socio-economic innovation in the villages? How do the economic activities of migrants affect the development of the sending villages?

11 *Local policies*: Does rural–urban migration affect the anti-poverty policies of local governments? Do local governments take some responsibility for arranging migration or providing information for those who want to move?

12 *Migrants' occupations and socio-economic activities* in their destinations: Is there a correlation between age, sex, education level and income? How about their well-being and working environment?

13 *Different views about city and village life* between migrants themselves and other members of their families and between them and households without migrant members.

14 *Different views about a sense of poverty* between migrants themselves, their families and other households without migrant members.

The pilot study

To test the effectiveness of the above questionnaires and to modify them accordingly, a pilot study was carried out in a typical township. After consultation with the Anti-poverty Office of Shanxi Province, it was considered that Yangjiape Township in Xinxian County would be suitable for such a pilot study.

Some basic data concerning this township are as follows: elevation, 920 m; total area, 103.5 km²; cultivated land, 38 km²; population, 9,729; population of working age, 3,315; population density, 89/km². The land is very barren, although the cultivated land per person is considerably higher than the national level. Also, natural calamities are often a problem. The township is classified as a semi-drought region, and the water conservancy facilities are very inadequate. The township consists of 36 villages. Only 14 of them are on the network of township-level roads. In 1995, the average income per person was only 286 yuan. The percentages of 'poor' households and 'poor' people, according to the government-defined standard, were 69 per cent and 68 per cent, respectively. Consequently, quite a number of people are working outside the township.

The pilot study to test the questionnaires was carried out by sampling 35 households. The sampling was based on income. Some special cases were interviewed as well, such as households which had become rich owing to migration, or the owners of rural enterprises. Interviews were also carried out with village cadres, anti-poverty officers, and so on. In addition, one informal discussion group meeting was organised.

As a result of statistical analyses of the above information, the preliminary questionnaires and outlines for informal discussions were modified. Some questions that most people agreed or disagreed with were deleted or changed. Also, at household level, the way of asking about loans was modified. In the village discussion group meeting, village cadres did not want to mention the question of the ways the poverty-alleviation fund could be used, so this item was deleted from the discussion outline. Some modifications were also made after consulting experts in China.[25]

Sample survey in the three counties

Three administrative villages, one in Daixian, one in Jingle and two in Wutai, were sampled. The reason for sampling two villages in Wutai was that the population of this county is greater than that of the other two. The selection of villages was based on factors such as the distance to cities, the transport system, the number of rural enterprises, the migration situation and so on. The basic situations of the four villages studied are shown in Table 3.6.

In each village, the households were divided into two groups, one with one or more migrants, and the other without. In each group, 25 households were randomly selected. In other words, in each village, 50 households were sampled. In addition, in the three villages, 41 returned migrants were sampled and interviewed.

The survey was performed through questionnaires circulated at three levels: one at individual migrant level, one at rural household level, and the other at village community level. The household questionnaires were filled in on the basis of in-depth interviews with household head couples. General questions were also put to other household members about their social and economic situation. For the village community questionnaires, the interviewees were the leading members of the village committees. Some local government officers and people from relevant Chinese media were also interviewed.

Two informal discussion meetings were held, one in Daixian and the other in Wutai. Village cadres, schoolteachers, people in rural enterprises, families and relatives of migrants, and other ordinary peasants were invited to attend. The discussions were chaired by a well-respected member of the village and by the author.

I conducted all the interviews with households and migrants. In each county, at my request an officer from the county's Anti-poverty Office

Table 3.6 Some background information on the four villages studied

County	Daixian	Jingle	Wutai	Wutai
Village	Dongrucun	Tongmengcun	Shicun	Dashicun
Population	2,735	2,988	2,800	2,878
No. of household	705	884	801	813
No. of migrants	About 500	560	About 500	Over 500
Drinking water	1 deep well, spent 70,000 yuan in 1997	1 well, no water,[31] getting from 7.5 km away	No problem	No problem
Electricity	Supplied	Occasionally supplied	No supply for lighting, OK for machines	Occasionally supplied
Doctor	one	none	none	none
Medicine	convenient	5–6 km	5 km	4 km
No. of pupils	300	200	400	
Class/Teacher	6 class/3 teachers	4 class/1 teachers	8 class[32]/5 teachers	The only teacher just left
Shops	4	2	5	1
Year of first migrant	1973 (coal mine)	1987 (iron mine)	1978 (coal mine)	1979 (coal mine)
Village enterprise	Mill, 3 workers, closed 1996	Pig farm, 4 workers, closed 1996	None	None
Income/person/year	880 yuan (US$108)	701 yuan (US$86)	801 yuan (US$98)	797 yuan (US$98)

helped with organising interviews and informal discussions.[26] The local cadres were also very helpful in organising interviews and discussions.

Some special cases warranted interviews being arranged elsewhere. For example, during the peak period of tourism, namely August to October, many peasants are working in Wutai, opening restaurants and operating transportation. Interviews were carried out during this period there. Also, some women migrants who were making their living by prostitution in the restaurants were interviewed personally.

In addition to the above, a number of interviews also investigated some other, more exceptional forms of migration, such as going to university or joining the army.

To facilitate the flexibility of conversation in a friendly environment, interviews with sampled households, returned migrants, local officers and other people were conducted by the author in a semi-structured and informal manner. Except for a number of essential questions, conversations during the interviews, especially with local officers, were guided by interviewees as the situation allowed. The advantage of this approach is that more information can be collected than might be expected from a formal question-and-answer interview.

To better understand the reality of rural poverty and rural–urban migration in Shanxi, I worked in an anti-poverty team in Wutai for a month. This valuable experience not only allowed me to understand how the local anti-poverty work is operating, but also provided numerous opportunities for me to talk with different people informally, including village cadres, small-business owners, and some of the poorest villagers. Moreover, the experience enabled me to observe rural poverty from another viewpoint.

Two-ended approach

The two-ended approach to rural–urban migration has been employed by a number of researchers such as Connell *et al.* (1976) and Du and Bai (1997). It has been proved that such an approach is invaluable for a better understanding of rural–urban migration.

Corresponding to the interviews in villages, a two-ended approach was also made in this study. Eighty-four migrants from the four villages were interviewed personally in their destinations. Twenty-one migrants were interviewed when they were back to their own villages on vacation. The total number of interviewed migrants is 105, which is greater than the number of households.[27] This is because in some households there are more than one migrant. All the interviews in the destinations were conducted by the author.

Most firms where the sampled migrants were working were located in Shanxi and Beijing. Coal-related industries and the construction industry were the dominant sector of employment – over 50 per cent of the migrants were working in these sectors.

To assess the socio-economic impact of rural–urban migration, I travelled to many cities and towns in Shanxi. In addition to the migrants in the sample, I also talked to many city residents, local government officers in cities, and migrants from other provinces (such as Anhui and Jiangsu). Such first-hand information has been valuable for this study.

Summary

Examination of the general situation in Shanxi indicates that there is indeed a need for an in-depth study of rural–urban migration and poverty in this region. The basic characteristics of rural–urban migration and poverty in the three field study counties are described, all being essential for analysing and understanding the data from the field survey. Careful attention was paid to the case study methodology, and a pilot study of the methodology proved to be very useful. In the next two chapters, the results from the field study are presented and analysed.

4 Case study analysis
Sending areas

This chapter is mainly an analysis of the questionnaires A.1 and A.2 (see the Appendix), which were used to interview two samples of households in the villages: those whose family members did or did not include a migrant. The main objectives of the analysis are:

1   to compare these two groups of households in various aspects such as the basic objective data, their subjective opinions, their general views on city and village life, and general attitudes to life; and
2   to gain an understanding of the current extent and characteristics of migration in the region studied and the social and economic effects this migration is having on these sending areas.

Attention is also paid to the differences and similarities between this case study region and the general situation in the rest of China.

Comparison of socio-economic characteristics of households with and without migrant members

This section attempts to identify the social and economic characteristics of households associated with migration. Why do socio-economic conditions result in migration in some sorts of household but not in others? What is 'the set of unique circumstances which induces a particular migrant to leave his rural area' (Clyde-Mitchell, 1959)? Is it because a village has a large proportion of poor people because it enjoys few economic resources per person, or because its resources are very unequally distributed? Based on the results of the questionnaires, this section compares households with and without migrant members in terms of objective reasons, including demographic factors, geographic factors, economic conditions, and so on.

Demographic analysis

This sub-section compares demographic differences between households with and without migrant members. The factors compared are household size, age distribution, labour capability and education level.

Household size

Figure 4.1 compares households with and without migrant members in terms of household size. It can be seen that in comparison with households which include a migrant, the size of households without any migrant is generally smaller. The average number of people in a household with a migrant member is 3.84, whereas for a household without, this number is only 3.19. A Student t-test shows that this difference in household size between the two groups is significant ($p = 0.009$, one tail, different variance). This suggests that an important reason for migration is that for those households with more members, it is possible to send someone out and at the same time still retain sufficient of a labour force to carry out the farming work in the home village.

Age distribution

The age distribution and family structure are also important for migration. Generally speaking, the suitable age range for working away from the village is about 15–45, especially 20–35. In this age range, a migrant is young, strong and brave, and finds it relatively easy to get a job. Also, normally the parents of the migrant are still not old, so they can do the farming work at home and look after the grandchildren if there are any. Figure 4.2 shows a comparison of age distribution in households with and without migrant members, where seven age groups are used, namely, under 15, 16–25, 26–35, 36–45, 46–55, 56–65 and above 65. It is seen that for the households with migrant members, the proportion of family members in the age range of 16–35 is 43 per cent, which is significantly greater than for households without any migrants, 32 per cent. Conversely,

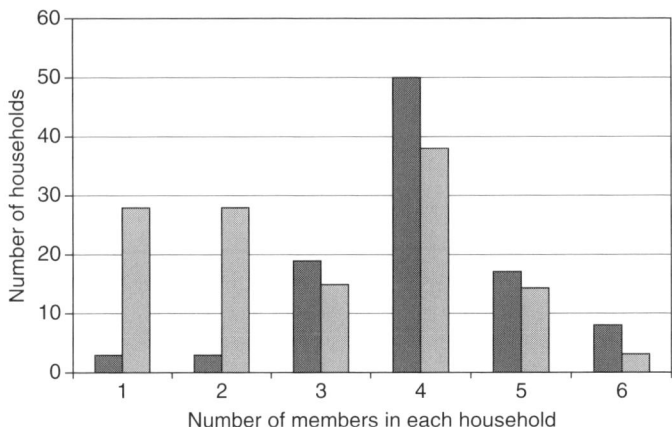

Figure 4.1 Number of people in a household. ■, Households with migrant; ▨, households without migrant.

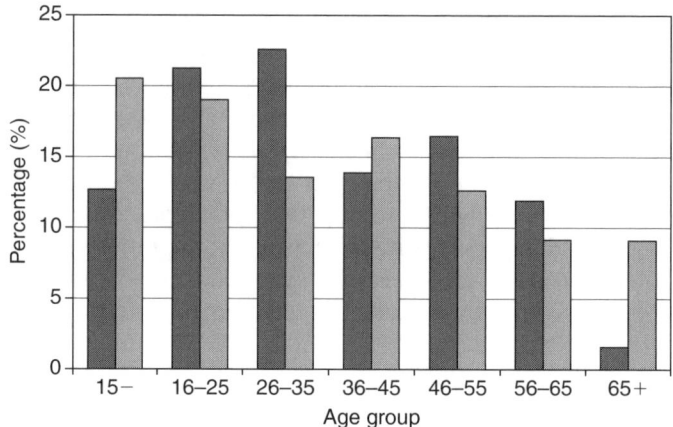

Figure 4.2 Age distribution. ■, Households with migrant; ▨, households without migrant.

in the households without any migrants, the percentage of children (under 15) and elderly (above 65) is considerably higher. Further analysing the age distribution shows that many households with migrant members are in a two-generation structure: the parents are 46–55, and have the labour ability to maintain the agricultural work in village, and the children are 26–35, and are suitable for working away from home. The Wu family in the village of Tongmengcun is a typical example of this type: father, 52; mother, 49; son (working away), 25; daughter, 22. Conversely, the households without any migrants tend to be in a three-generation structure, namely, the grandparents are over 65, and therefore less able to carry out the agricultural work, and the third generation are under 15, and need to be looked after. A typical example is the Liu family in the village of Shicun: grandfather, 66; grandmother, 61; son, 35; son's wife, 34; granddaughter, 10; grandson, 6. Two daughters of the family are married and living in other villages.

Physical labour capability

Further to the family structure and age distribution, it is useful to investigate the effect of labour ability. A comparison of the labour ability between two groups of people – those in households with migrant members and those in households without – has been made. Ability to perform physical labour is graded into three categories, namely, strong, weak, and unable to work.

It appears that in the group with migrant members, the percentage rated as having strong labour ability is significantly higher (at about 22 per cent) than that in the non-migrant group. By contrast, the percentage rated as unable to work or with only weak labour ability in the group with migrant members is considerably less. This result suggests that physical labour capability is an important factor that affects migration.

Education level

Education level has also been found to be an important factor affecting migration, as indicated in Chapters 1 and 2. Figure 4.3 compares the education level between two groups of people: those in the households with migrant members and those in the households without a migrant. According to the current situation in China, eight levels of education are used in the questionnaires, namely, illiteracy/near-illiteracy, junior primary school, senior primary school, junior middle school, senior middle school, special secondary school, high school and higher education. From the figure, it is interesting to note that the education level of the migrant group is generally higher than that of the non-migrant group.

By carrying out a weighting average, a single-index comparison between the two groups can be made. Simply assume that the weighting factor is 0.1 for illiteracy/near-illiteracy, 0.2 for junior primary school, 0.3 for senior primary school, 0.4 for junior middle school, 0.5 for senior middle school, 0.6 for special secondary school, 0.7 for high school and 0.8 for higher education. Then the average education level can be calculated, which is 3.95 for the migrant group and 3.29 for the non-migrant group.

From Figure 4.3, it is also seen that for the people whose households

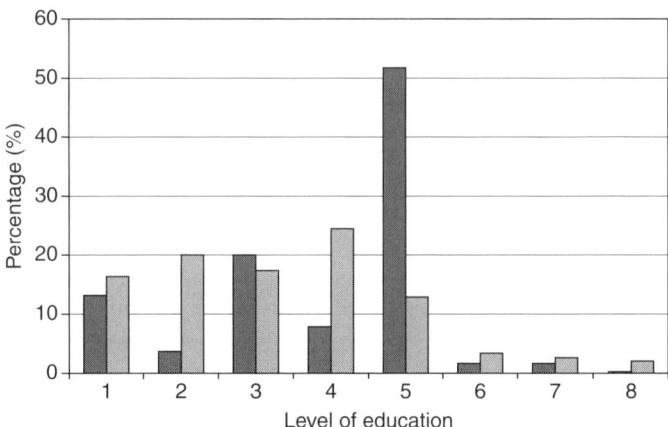

Figure 4.3 Education level of the studied household members. ■, Households with migrant; ▨, households without migrant. 1, illiteracy/almost illiteracy; 2, junior primary school; 3, senior primary school; 4, junior middle school; 5, senior middle school; 6, special secondary school; 7, high school; 8, higher education.

include migrants, there is a strong peak at education level 5, namely senior middle school level. A detailed analysis shows that most migrants themselves are at this level (see also Chapter 5).

Land

In an economy where most people earn their living off the land, its availability must be relevant in determining villages' rates of emigration (Connell *et al.*, 1976). A number of studies have shown a positive relationship between high population:land ratios and propensity to migrate. Walsh and Trlin (1973), from a study of 13 villages near Auckland, indicated that there was a significant correlation between migration and population:land ratios. The Ministry of Village Affairs (1965–8) in Turkey found a slight positive correlation between the number of seasonal migrants and the village man:arable land ratio. In a group of Pakistani villages, Rochin (1972) found an inverse relationship between cropped land per capita and the number of off-farm migrants. In China, the overall situation is similar. For example, studies by Huang P. (1997) and Du and Bai (1997) in south China have all shown the above relationship. However, the relationship works badly where the arable land is relatively plentiful but of poor quality, as appears to be the case in the present case study region.

For the households with migrant members, the land availability is 7.21 *mu* per household or 1.91 *mu* per person, which is slightly more than for the households without a migrant, 6.62 *mu* per household or 1.89 *mu* per person. This seems to suggest that the population:land ratio is not a main reason for migration in the studied villages.

In the context of the economics of migrating villages, the significance of land availability lies in its income-generating potential. Poor-quality land often results in a low level of agriculture – either because low demand for cash crops reduces income, or because poverty compels peasants to play safe. Observations in Shanxi suggest that migration is generally in proportion to the lack of opportunities for agriculture, especially seasonal work in autumn, because there is little quality land suitable for cropping.

Agricultural poverty resulting from the lack of cash crops often stimulates emigration, but emigration can sometimes help relieve financial pressure on the household. In Shanxi, circular migration is common. Such a migration pattern is dependent on the availability of short-term cash-earning opportunities, either in towns or on plantations.

It is also interesting to look at the soil quality. For the household group with migrant members, the average score of soil quality is 2.85, which is somewhat higher than that for the household group without, 2.67, although the difference is not significant. In the questionnaire, the classification of soil score is: 1, very good; 2, good; 3, not good; and 4, bad. The scores are based on relative comparison with other land in the village and region, rather than on an absolute level. This seems to suggest that in the cases studied, the effect of land quality on migration is negligible. It is possible that such an effect might show itself only if a great number of villages in a bigger region were considered, or if there were a wide disparity in soil quality.

In some cases, the availability of opportunities for fish farming, forestry land and uncultivated land also affects migration. But this is not common in the villages studied. Within the sampled household group without any migrant members, one household has uncultivated land and two households are engaged in fish farming. Their income is relatively high and they do not have any plans to work away from home.

Geographic location

There is some evidence that the proportion of migrants to towns is greatest in the nearby villages in the early stages of urbanisation, but this effect is seen in more distant villages at a later stage (Kolars, 1963). Ideas on urban opportunities eventually diffuse to the more distant villages, but those closer to the town have by then contributed their most suitable migrants (Connell *et al.*, 1976). These theories are plausible in the case of Shanxi, especially for coal mine workers. In the past fifty years, villages which are near Taiyuan and Datong,[1] two coal-based cities in the region, have produced huge numbers of coal mine workers. These workers went to the cities but left their families in the villages. In the past ten years, the situation has changed. Most of the early coal mine workers have retired and their replacements of a younger generation are from isolated areas in Shanxi or south China. The new generation in the villages near big cities like Taiyuan and Datong enjoy many of the advantages of urban life without having to migrate. As the head of a county near Taiyuan said to his villagers, 'Keep your eyes on the city near us – we are in an excellent position to get cash by supplying the city's needs without moving into it.'[2]

The villages studied are all in relatively remote regions, and the situation is different from that in the county just mentioned. In Table 4.1, the distances from the villages to the county capital and from the county capitals to the provincial and national capital are shown.

As indicated by Skinner (1977), a market town forms an economic system with essential characteristics. Transport, trade and the sharing of information are all structured within it, spatially according to the principle of centrality, and temporally by the periodicity of its market day. The standard market town, which typically services a hinterland of 15–30 villages (even more today), meets the week-to-week marketing needs of peasant households.

It appears that the distance to towns and markets is still a factor affecting migration. Table 4.2 compares the households with and without migrant members in terms of the minimum, maximum and average distance from the household house[3] to the nearest and farthest towns and to

Table 4.1 Distance (km) from the villages to the county capital and from the county capitals to the province and state capital

To state capital (Beijing)	
Daixian, Jinle, Wutai	About 500 km
To province capital (Taiyuan)[3]	
Daixian	175 km
Jinle	50 km
Wutai	135 km
From village to county capital	
Dongrucun	15 km
Tongmencun	20 km
Shicun	20 km
Dashicun	30 km

the markets to which they often go. It can be seen that on average, the households with migrant members are farther from towns and markets than the households without. This may suggest that those who are in relatively remote areas tend to migrate.

Corresponding to the distance to towns and markets, the households with migrant members are also farther from train or bus stations, although the difference is not great. A comparison between households with and without migrant members is shown in Table 4.2.

It is also interesting to note that in comparison with households without migrant members, households with migrants tend to go to more markets. According to the survey results, 70 per cent people in the migrant group often go to five markets, 10 per cent of them to four markets and 25 per cent to three markets whereas this number is normally two or three for the

Table 4.2 Comparisons between households with and without migrant members on distance (km) to the farthest towns where they often go, distance (km) to the nearest markets where they often go and distance (km) to the nearest railway or bus stations

Questions\levels	Minimum	Maximum	Average
Distance (km) to the farthest towns			
Households with migrant	30	65	38
Households without migrant	27	55	34
Distance (km) to the nearest markets			
Households with migrant	14	27	23
Households without migrant	10	16	18
Distance (km) to the nearest railway or bus stations			
Households with migrant	6	13	12
Households without migrant	5	12	11

households without migrant members, with 10 per cent of them going to four markets, 56 per cent to three markets and 33 per cent to two or fewer markets. One possible reason for the difference is that for those who are farther from markets, there is no great difference between going to different markets. Another possible reason is that there is a correlation between those who would like to compare different markets and those who migrate. Also, it might be because the households without migrant members tend to be those with more dependants (children and old people), which might make it more difficult to make the trips to market so often.

In addition to the distance, the transport system is also an important factor affecting migration. Very often, better transport systems result in commuting rather than migration. Though commuting can be time-consuming and expensive, the higher cost of living in urban areas often results in a preference for continuing to live in the village. In general, well-developed integration into the urban nexus may also enable villagers to enjoy many benefits of urban life without engaging in migration. In 1997, a new highway in north Shanxi was built from Taiyuan to Yuanping.[4] Since then, there have been more commuters and fewer migrants in this area. Also, many people have moved from remote mountain areas to the towns near the highway junctions to enjoy getting money from their doorstep.

Rich and poor

Do richer or poorer villages produce more migrants? Do richer or poorer villagers from the same village tend to migrate more?

Villages

Generally speaking, the majority of rural migrants come from poor villages. However, if a village is very poor and remote, the psychological and financial costs of working away from home may prove prohibitive. This tends to be the case in the region studied. For people in the poorest villages, the cost of staying in a provincial city for one month is equivalent to the agricultural income per labourer per year. Very often they do not want to take such a risk. It seems that there is a positive correlation between migration and the amount of income from non-farming sources. For example, peasants in villages near Wutai Mountain[5] can get extra income every summer by selling their agricultural products or handicrafts to tourists, and consequently, they can afford to look for opportunities in cities. A similar phenomenon has also been observed in south China: migration is more common in villages with a higher income per capita from the sale of agricultural goods.

On the other hand, if the lack of prospects in a village induces emigration, then improvement of prospects, often due to migrants' remittances or promotion changes, can cut future migration or induce existing migrants to return. This is supported, for example, by Murphy's (1999) study in south China.

Villagers

It is difficult to compare quantitatively the financial situation before migration between households with and without migrant members because the year of migration varies significantly among different households. Nevertheless, it seems that in the cases studied, both rich and poor people in a village migrate, except for the very poorest villagers. In other words, within the same village may be found migrants from relatively prosperous households, and from poorer sections of the population. The better-off households in a village where resources are unequally distributed finance the migration of their sons and daughters. In rather poor households, the poverty forces them to migrate in search of work. For the poorest households in the village, the expectation of increased income in cities turns out to be less important than the cost of moving.

Decision-making in connection with migration

Lea (1964) summarised the factors affecting the decision to migrate and the process of migration under four headings: factors associated with the area of origin; factors associated with the destination area; intervening obstacles; and personal factors. This section discusses some aspects relating to these. As indicated by Connell *et al.* (1976), both objective factors and perceptions of them are important. Contributory factors often include imperfect information, a high element of risk, and the general tendency to assume that one's chosen undertakings will be successful, so the decision to migrate is never completely 'rational'.

Migration type and decision maker

There are two types of migration, individual and linked. Individual migration refers individuals leaving largely for their own good. They are single and have no family in the village, and thus their action does not need to be likely to benefit their village or family. Linked migration is intended to be necessary for or useful to relatives remaining in the village. In the former case, it is certainly the individual who determines everything, and in the latter case the process of migration is less likely to be determined solely by the individual who leaves.

The study revealed the situations in which the migrants interviewed left their villages. The vast majority would be described as taking part in linked migration. Of these, seven migrants left the village with their spouses and one with his family (i.e. with children), but most (74 per cent) left the village alone while their families, including parents and/or spouses and children, remained in the village. This means that the migrants still have a close relation to their villages and they will bring information and money back, and are likely to influence the attitudes of the villagers.

In the households studied, there are only two cases of individual migration.[6] These two migrants are both single and in late middle age. They have land in the village and are working in coal mines. Also, there are several special cases; for example, the spouse and other family members frequently go to the destination to visit the migrant.

It is difficult to identify who decides on an act of migration or in what social and economic structure the decision is made. Generally speaking, in the cases studied, the head of a household decides which member will continue farming and which member will seek off-farm employment. Household heads plan and finance the migration of young members in order to bring about socio-economic goals. The linked migration acts as a form of risk spreading: a household has one member in the city whose remittance can offset a bad agricultural year. Moreover, through linked migration a household can gain a surplus income to meet their immediate requirements, such as a small rural investment, money for a marriage, and other family needs. Certainly, some young people work away from home just to find out what cities look like, and they may not save money until the second or third time they migrate. Household heads have to take such a risk when sending the migrants out.

In some cases, the decision-making is affected by a unit larger than a household. For example, the World Bank is arranging for a large number of rural people in three provinces in south-west China to work in cities in order to reduce rural poverty (Centre for Human Resources Development of West Region, 1995). Some local governments and villages in the region studied have also arranged or even funded contractors to some cities to establish a bridge or find construction projects for subsequent migration.

Choosing destinations

The diffusion of information to potential rural migrants regarding the opportunities available in cities may encourage new migration. Television, newspaper, radio, returnees and visitors build up a picture of life and prospects in the cities. In particular, the letters and money sent back by early migrants are concrete evidence of success (R. K. Lewis, 1967).

It is interesting to note that in the sampled households, 79 per cent get information from relatives or friends, whereas fewer than 7 per cent get theirs from the media (all sources). In other words, the choice of destination is mainly based on the information from private channels.

Kinship also affects the choice of destination. In the villages studied, relatives in cities not only send information back to the village, but also control recruitment. They tend to recruit people closely related to themselves. Such a way of choosing a destination appears to be more common for the relatively poor members of a village; if such information is not available, their mobility is limited. Better-off villagers tend to use other, more formal channels to get a job.

Rural–urban migration in China is essentially chain migration structured on the basis of the migrant's place of origin. Aside from the common aspiration to increase their income that all migrants share, place, especially native place, plays a powerful role in shaping migrant behaviour at both ends of the migration spectrum. More often than not, migrants from one place tend to move to a city in small groups rather than as individuals. It is rare to find any peasant in the city who is not living or working with a few fellow villagers, or others from the same native place (*laoxiang*). Migrants who are *laoxiang* normally have a shared sense of common experience, and they are emotionally attached to their common place of origin. This strong feeling is best displayed at the place of destination. Living with the dominant 'they' group, *laoxiang* from the same place tend to voluntarily cluster in a 'we' group for mutual support, assistance and friendship.

The formation of such groups should not be seen as a result of any strategy designed deliberately by migrants to better protect themselves against the dominant population or the other 'they' groups. Some local residents may be contemptuous of outsiders, but there is no detectable hostility towards them. However, there have been some reports of confrontation between migrants and local residents. For example, at a brick factory in the Daixing county capital, there was a serious confrontation between migrants and local workers in 1997.

Based on the questionnaires, Table 4.3 shows the reasons for choosing a particular destination. Results from households with and without migrant members are all listed. Note that for households without migrant members, the question was 'If you had relatives or neighbours who were working away from home, in your opinion, what would be their reasons for deciding where their destination would be?'. Only about 70 per cent of the households without migrant members answered this question. Table 4.3 shows the percentages for each choice of the 70 per cent who did respond.

Table 4.3 Reasons for choosing a city to work: comparison between households with and without migrant. 1, More opportunities; 2, with relatives or friends; 3, organised by local government; 4, organised by labour contractor; 5, factory recruitment.

	Reasons (%)				
	1	*2*	*3*	*4*	*5*
Households with migrant	33.8	31.9	0	32.4	1.9
Households without migrant	18.8	36.3	5	35	5

From Table 4.3 it is seen that, corresponding to the above, for both groups 'with relatives and friends' is a major reason. The main difference between the two groups is on 'more opportunities'. This appears to suggest that the households without migrant members tend to be less 'brave'.

Choosing migrants

Sometimes the decision making has a clear objective: either to maximise the household income or to achieve a special cash target. Consequently, 'who is going to go away to work' would be an important part of the decision making. In the questionnaires, households with migrant members were asked what was the most important factor in choosing who should migrate.

The research showed that 33.6 per cent of the households thought that age is the most important factor in choosing a migrant. An important reason is that it is easier for young people to find a job. For young people, the choice of destination and occupation is less limited. According to the traditional view in Shanxi, anyone over 45 years old is considered 'old', and at this age it is thought that one should not work away from the village. Another possible reason for the importance of age is that the longer a migrant's expected remaining working life is, the greater the expected total cash return.

Of the households questioned, 30.8 per cent responded that sex is also an important factor, which means that males tend to dominate the migration. This is mainly because in the region studied, most job opportunities are in coal mines and the construction sectors.[7] In the villages studied, the most common way for young women to migrate is to join their husband. This means that if the males' migration to the cities is long term, then the rate of female migration may well increase. Also, those young wives who migrate with their husbands are less likely to return to the village because they often find city life more attractive than they had expected. Relatively older women whose husbands work away usually stay in the village to do farming work and to look after children.

Of the households studied, 25.2 per cent thought that experience and skill are the third most important factor. Clearly, this is because more experience of working in towns can help reduce the job-hunting period, and the level of skill is usually related to income. In one of the construction teams, the daily payment is 10 yuan (*c.* US$1.2) for an inexperienced worker (*xiaogong*), 20 yuan (*c.* US$2.5) for an experienced worker (*dagong*) and 25–35 yuan (*c.* US$3.1–4.3) for a skilled technical worker (*jishugong*).[8]

Only 0.9 per cent and 9.4 per cent of households studied thought that marital status and education level were important factors.

Which child is important? – a related question

Clearly, sons are more important than daughters in terms of migration, at least in the current situation in Shanxi, given the fact that the majority of migrants are young males. To investigate the households' attitude in this aspect, a question was asked about 'which are more important, sons or daughters?'

Interestingly, it was found that there was a significant difference between the households with and without migrant members: 86 per cent of the households with migrant members thought that sons are more important than daughters, whereas this proportion was only 48 per cent for the households without a migrant. There was also a similarity between the two groups: only about 10 per cent of the households thought that daughters are more important than sons. The difference between households with migrant members and households without is that 40 per cent of households without any migrant members agreed that boys and girls are equally important compared with only 5 per cent of households with migrant members.

A question was also asked about the reasons for the above. Four choices were given, namely, carrying on the family name; capability for physical labour; the possibility of receiving more education and thus a better future; and others. It is noteworthy that in the group with migrant members, the percentage choosing 'capability for physical labour' was 59 per cent, which is much higher than for the group without a migrant, 38 per cent. This suggests that there is a relationship between migration and people's attitude towards gender and work.

For the reason 'carrying on the family name', the percentage was only around 20 per cent in both groups, which appears to be rather different from the Chinese traditional view. This indicates the effects of economic factors.

It is surprising to see that the percentage choosing 'possibility of receiving more education and thus a better future' was only around 10 per cent in both groups. This is quite different from the common view. Usually, further education is regarded as the only formal way for rural people to change their farmer's status. Perhaps the situation of rural education has disappointed the majority of villagers for a long time. As a result, the economic aspects are much more important than other aspects.

Staying in the village

Despite the enormous rural–urban labour flow, most people in the region studied are still staying in the villages rather than leaving them for work in the towns. In addition to the analysis in Chapter 2 on objective differences between households with and without migrant members, questions were put to the households without migrant members about why they are staying in their village.

It is interesting to note that about 39 per cent of the households chose 'no opportunity to work elsewhere'. In other words, for the sending areas, the potential for further migration is rather great. On the other hand, various reasons, including 'too old', 23 per cent, 'no money for going out', 12 per cent, 'busy with farming work', 11 per cent, and 'looking after parents and children', 10 per cent, may prevent about 50 per cent of the households in the non-migrant group from seeking work elsewhere.

It should be indicated that a number of people have no intention of working anywhere else because their social and economic position in the village is relatively high. This group of people includes a village doctor, four village heads and three village shop-owners. They are remaining in the villages, but are not engaged in farming. One of the shop-owners is rather familiar with Marx's theory of extended reproduction,[9] and his management philosophy and operation style fit the cost–benefit theory very well. He gave me a very good explanation of why he did not migrate to a city. By running the shop with his wife, they make a profit of around 10,000 yuan (US$1,225) per year. They can look after their small children even when the shop is open. Their land is looked after by the husband's parents. During the harvest, they close the shop for a couple of days in order to give his parents a hand on the farm. He said that they and their children are greatly attracted by life in the cities. However, if they moved to a city, they would have to pay rent and for food and childcare, as well as the costs when looking for jobs. Meanwhile, they would lose part of their income from their land. After considering all these various factors, they decided to stay in the village, at least for the next few years.

The opportunities for working away from the village are closely related to the information channels to the cities. Table 4.4 compares the two groups of households regarding their information channels. It is seen that the major difference is that the non-migrant group gets more information from local friends and relatives, whereas the migrant group obtains more information from friends and relatives in cities. Some in-depth interviews show that friends and relatives in cities often send back positive information, whereas local friends and relatives tend to spread information about vagaries of urban employment opportunities and some experiences of 'failed' migrants such as 'one has to wait up to six months to get a job'.

Table 4.4 The information channels: comparison between households with and without migrant. 1, Televison, radio and newspaper; 2, local friends and relatives; 3, friends and relatives in cities; 4, from local officers; 5, to get information by oneself.

	1	2	3	4	5
Households with migrant	23	20	29	11	17
Households without migrant	17	37	15	16	15

Another important reason for the lack of opportunities is the lack of contact with contractors and 'bridgehead'[10] migrants. As mentioned previously, contractors and bridgehead migrants are for poor villagers the main means of getting a job. However, both contractors and bridgehead migrants are likely to bring out their relatives or friends because they are relatively easy to control, and will not let the contractors and bridgehead migrants down.

Social differentiation

Attitudes to migration are also an important factor in decision making concerning migration. For any given opportunity, some people may take it but others may not. Some questions were designed to study the differences between households with and without migrant members.

In some small towns where the people in this case study often go, there are a number of migrants from south China. For both households with and without migrant members, questions were asked about their opinions of these people. The comparison is shown in Table 4.5. A major difference between the two groups of households is that households with migrant members tend to regard the migrants from south China as people who can 'bear hardship'. This seems to suggest that this group of households is likely to take up the challenge if opportunities arise, even if this might be quite a hard option.

Another question concerned their reactions if there happened to be a factory nearby, which could be an opportunity for migration. The comparison between the two kinds of household is shown in Table 4.6. It is interesting to note that for households with migrant members, the percentage choosing 'try to work there' is 57.1 per cent, which is much higher than for the non-migrant group, 39.4 per cent. However, it is noteworthy that of the non-migrant group, 13 per cent of the households choose 'do some small business', whereas of the migrant group none made this choice. It seems that the two groups may have different opinions about grasping an opportunity.

Comparison was also made between the two groups about their views on taking 'low-class' jobs in cities. The results are shown in Table 4.7. It is clear that the households with migrants are much more positive about

Table 4.5 Opinions about migrants from south China: comparison between households with and without migrant. 1, Bear hardships; 2, more migration experience; 3, brave; 4, more stratagems; 5, don't know.

	1	2	3	4	5
Households with migrant	44.8	26.7	13.3	15.2	0
Households without migrant	26.7	30.7	16.8	13.9	11.9

Table 4.6 What could you do if there were a factory nearby?: comparison of the opinions of the households with and without migrant. 1, Try to work there; 2, go there to have a shower, see film, or see doctor, if possible; 3, do some small-capital business; 4, try to send son or daughter to work there.

	1	2	3	4
Households with migrant	57.1	18.1	0	24.8
Households without migrant	39.4	27.3	13.1	20.2

Table 4.7 If there were an opportunity for you to go to the cities to be a pedlar, street shoe-repairer, rubbish collector, domestic help worker, what would you think?: comparison of the opinions of households with and without migrant. 1, Wouldn't want to do it; 2, wouldn't dare to go because not familiar with cities; 3, yes if no skill is needed; 4, yes if more income; 5, it may be difficult because there are already too many people.

	1	2	3	4	5
Households with migrant	19	0	38.1	42.9	0
Households without migrant	39.4	20.2	20.2	18.2	2

doing this kind of job – about 80 per cent of them chose 'yes' (choices 3 and 4), whereas this proportion was less than 40 per cent for the non-migrant group.

Overall, from the above analysis it can be seen that those in the migrant group tend to be more active in grasping possible opportunities than those in the non-migrant group. It is likely that such attitudes did affect their decision to seek work in the cities. Of course, there is also the possibility that their attitudes have been affected by the migration experiences of members of their households.

The causes of such social differentiation are rather complicated. From the interviews, it appears that there are three possible reasons. First, some families are strongly influenced by traditional views, both from traditional society and from Mao's time. They firmly believe that only those moves such as going to university,[11] going to a stated-owned enterprise or becoming a schoolteacher can be regarded as positive. Social position is more important than income. In these families, one or more family members, or at least some of their relatives, or the previous generation(s), often have, or had, a good social background and/or a good education level. Second, some families are influenced by the positive migration experiences reported by their family members, including old people. They believe that if they work hard and bear hardships, they will manage to improve their quality of living. Third, households' social attitudes are also affected by their current economic situation. Generally speaking, for many better-off households, they would like to start from a better job even though taking a 'low-class' job could immediately improve their living standards.

Effects of rural–urban migration

This section describes the general situation of migration in the sending villages, and the effects on the villages. It is divided into four main parts: remittances, intra-rural inequality, consequences of absence, and the situation of women and children.

Remittances

It is known that remittances are a major consequence of rural–urban migration. Migrants transfer cash or other resources to their family members remaining in the village. Generally speaking, remittances include either money transmitted to villages by migrants through the post and friends, or savings and goods brought back by migrants themselves.

Considering the Shanxi case, it seems that four aspects should be studied: the sources of remittances, including region and sector; the type and level of remittances; the relationship between household type and remittance; and the use of remittance money. An overall aim is to assess the contribution of remittances to development in rural areas, especially its role in reducing rural poverty.

Sources of remittances

Figure 4.4 classifies the studied migrants in terms of their work sectors and regions. It can be seen that the coal and related sectors are dominant, followed by construction and services. In other words, they are all to be found in some rather traditional work sectors. In terms of region, only seven people are working within their own county. This is mainly because the industrial level is rather low in the three counties studied. The majority of the migrants are working outside the county but within the province. Within the province, the major work is still in coal and related industry, but other sectors, such as construction, also provide opportunities for migrants. Outside the province, the main work sectors are coal,[12] services and catering.

Corresponding to Figure 4.4, Figure 4.5 shows the total remittances from the various sectors. In accordance with the results in Figure 4.4, in terms of region the major remittance source is within the province but outside the county. In terms of sector, the major sources are the coal industry, coal-related industries and construction.

In order to examine remittances on a household scale, it is useful to compare the remittances per migrant between various sectors. Such a

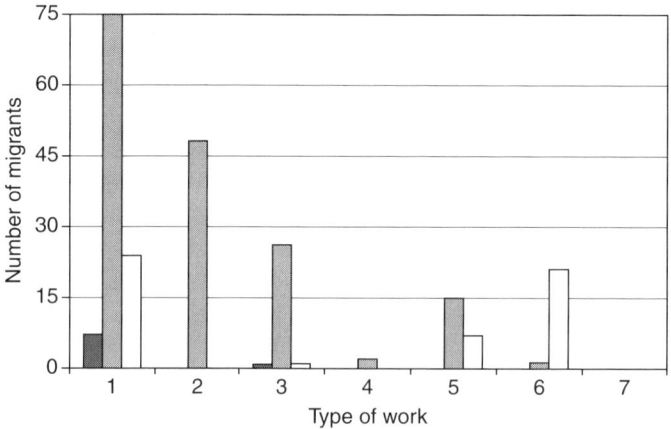

Figure 4.4 Number of migrants in various sectors. 1: Coal industry; 2: coal related industry; 3: construction; 4: transportation; 5: catering; 6: services. ■, Inside county; ▨, within province; □, outside province.

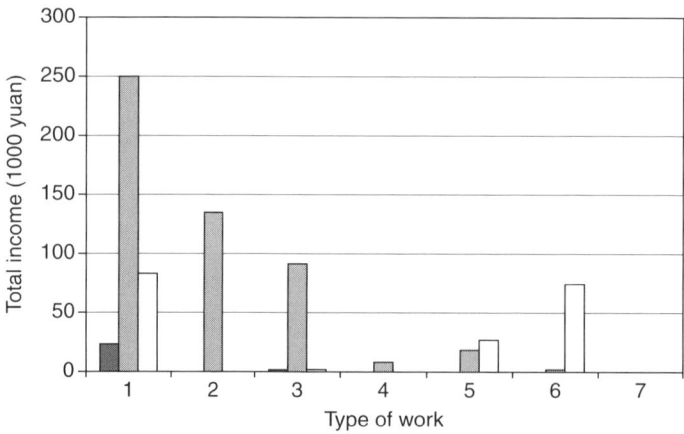

Figure 4.5 Total remittances of households with migrant. 1, Coal industry; 2, coal related industry; 3, construction; 4, transportation; 5, catering; 6, services. ■, Inside county; ▨, inside province; □, outside province.

comparison is shown in Figure 4.6. Generally speaking, there is no significant difference between the various sectors or between the different regions. The main difference worth pointing out is that the remittances from migrants working within the province in catering and the service sectors are much lower than from those outside the province. The highest remittance, 4,000 yuan, is from the transportation sector. It should be

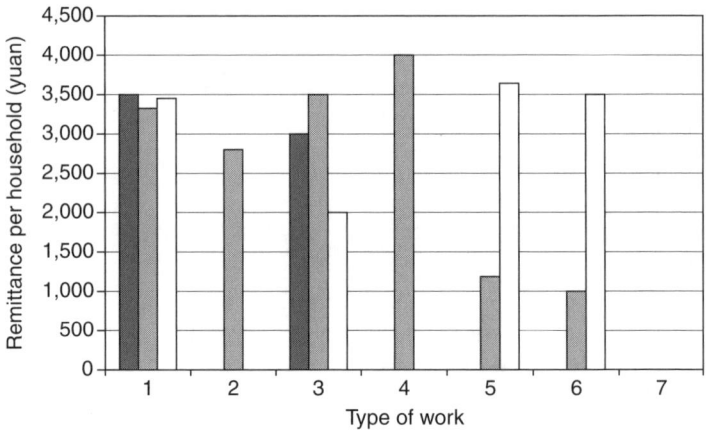

Figure 4.6 Average remittance per household per year in various sectors. 1, Coal industry; 2, coal related industry; 3, construction; 4, transportation; 5, catering; 6, services; 7, other non-farming. ■, income from inside county; ▨, income from within province; □, income from outside province.

noted that because the sample size for those sectors is rather small, it is difficult to draw any general conclusions based on these findings.

Type and level of remittances

> Rural–urban migration may involve a high proportion of migrants in sending back remittances, but the sums involved, absolutely and as a proportion of income, reflect lower earnings and are therefore usually smaller.
>
> (Johnson and Whitelaw, 1972)

Figure 4.7 shows the distribution of the remittance per migrant in 1996. Presents are also included. It can be seen that the amount is generally 2,000–4,000 yuan, which is less than the corresponding figure for south China. Note that 6.7 per cent of the migrants studied sent back less than 500 yuan, and two migrants did not send anything home.

For comparison, an overview of levels of non-agricultural income in Wutai County is shown in Table 4.8. It is seen that the remittance levels shown in Figure 4.7 are higher than the average non-agricultural income in the county. Note that the level of industry in Wutai County is higher than that of the other two counties studied.

It has been shown from the case study that there are two factors affecting levels of remittances: migrants' net income and their purpose of

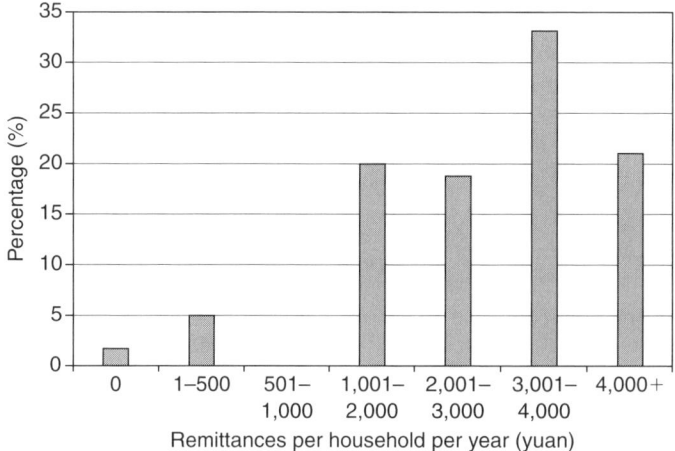

Figure 4.7 Remittance (including presents) received per household in 1996: distribution by level.

migration. Net income determines the general level of remittances. Wage-earners, usually the coal mine workers in state enterprises, send remittances home regularly. Non-wage-earners, such as workers in construction teams, self-employed workers and those who work for private businesses, send back money irregularly, and the remittances are sometimes large and sometimes small. Apart from net income, the level of remittances is also affected by the initial purpose of the migration. Some migrants keep only a small proportion of the net income for themselves, and distribute the rest to the family and relatives. For some migrants, usually the relatively young, remittances are sent only to meet specific needs, such as illness or a wedding in the family.

Whether remittances are regular or intermittent, large or small, depends on the nature of the links between the migrant and his or her family, and on the needs of the village household. If a migrant comes from a nuclear family, and the migrant's parents or wife and children rely on the remittances to achieve a given consumption target, a regular and substantial flow of remittance money seems to occur. If the native villages are exceptionally poor and villagers treat remittances as a big sum of money, a certain level of remittances is likely to be received.

Certainly, if the original act of migration was attempt to relieve rural poverty, as in the case of the World Bank's project in south-western China, migrants have to send back remittances to help pay the debts.

Not all remittances are cash flows. Over 50 per cent of the migrants' remittances comprised goods or presents, although 46.7 per cent of the migrants did not give presents. Among those who did, the presents were

Table 4.8 Non-agricultural income of Wutai county in 1996: sector distribution and corresponding income (Local government report)

Total income (10,000 yuan)	9,055		
Average income of each worker (yuan)	1,896		
Total number of workers	47,758 (25,812 male and 11,946 female)		
Average income per capita (yuan)[14]	325		
Construction			
Total income (10,000 yuan)	6,230		
Average income of each worker (yuan)	2,000		
Total number of workers	31,151		
	State	*County level*	*Private*
Number of construction teams	3	29	48
Number of workers	801	14,680	2,570
Coal industry			
Total income (10,000 yuan)	1,334		
Average income of each worker (yuan)	2,000		
Total number of workers	6,670		
	Township level	*Village level*	
Number of industries	41	438	
Number of workers	2,420	4,250	
Tertiary Industry			
Total income (10,000 yuan)	1,491		
Average income of each worker (yuan)	1,500		
Total number of workers	9,937		

	Small business	*Hotel*	*Domestic helper*	*Others*
Number of businesses	2,945	302		1,517
Number of workers	5,318	2,200	500	1,919

evenly distributed between food, 14 per cent; clothes, 13 per cent; goods for everyday use, 15 per cent; and others, 11 per cent. Valuable presents like jewellery and electrical appliances are rare. Generally speaking, migrants who have been away for a longer period bring more expensive goods back. Usually migrants are expected to bring back money and goods on every trip, and as Riddell (1970) also indicated, the pressure to meet this expectation has stopped some migrants from making regular return trips.

In the villages studied, 80 per cent of the remittances are taken back by migrants personally and 20 per cent sent back through the post.

Household type and remittances

Since poorer villages usually feature higher migration rates, remittances tend to make up a higher proportion of income in villages with low income per capita. In some villages, a very high proportion of households receive remittances, mainly the poorer households. Extreme poverty in a village requires heavy remittances to support village households. In Wutai County, all the migrant households studied receive cash remittances. This is mainly because the villages are rather poor and there is a lack of alternative ways of earning cash.

Remittances are beginning to introduce much wider differentiation in the village social structure: some households with one or more working migrants may depend heavily on remittances. The case study suggests a positive and significant relationship between the level of remittances, the proportion of adult labour absent from the villages, and the proportion of women, elderly people and children in the villages.

Not all households in receipt of remittances are the poorest in the village. Some remittances from wage-earning coal mine workers contribute greatly to the prosperity of better-off households in the villages. As was also found by Hart (1971), many households in receipt of remittances are relatively prosperous compared with their neighbours. Some migrant households continue to receive a substantial sum in remittances, but they depend much less on this income source than do poorer households. Some migrant households are becoming another 'social class' because they gain their main income from the migrants working in cities and have little economic contact with non-migrant households in the village.

Use of remittances

The evidence in Shanxi suggests that the use of remittances reflects the poverty, the traditional values and the lack of investment opportunities in the sending villages. The majority of remittances are consumed in normal household needs, such as building and refurbishing houses, and in conspicuous consumption, such as weddings.

Main uses of the remittances from migrants[13] include building or refurbishing house, 43 per cent; buying production materials such as chemical fertiliser, 14 per cent; everyday expenses, 31 per cent; investment for factory or business, 1 per cent; children's education, 15 per cent; and others, 15 per cent. It is seen that nearly half of the households used the remittances for house-building and refurbishing. This is actually a very common phenomenon in China as well as in other developing countries (Caldwell, 1969). Housing is one of the village developments that may be strongly stimulated by remittances. A possible explanation is that the social demands upon a migrant and his or her family require that he or she displays the correctness of the decision to migrate and it means that the migrant's family will acquire enhanced standing and prestige in the village.

Everyday expenses are another important use of the remittances. Given the fact that the agricultural income may normally be sufficient for just the very basic requirements of everyday life in this region, this addition from remittances can be used to improve rural households' living standards.

Relatively less of the money is spent on farming and agricultural invest-ment. The low level of investment potential in poor-quality land leads to the failure to use more remittances for this purpose. Detailed interviews show that the remittances are sometimes used to meet some basic agricul-tural requirements, such as buying agricultural materials, paying taxes and other fees. Some of the households use the remittance to hire labour in order to replace the missing labour power or to counteract the overbur-dening of women with agricultural work.

It is important to note that investment in industry or business is even lower than on agricultural development. In the cases studied, only one household used the remittance to invest in business. It appears that this is different from the situation in some regions in south China (Murphy, 1999). There are four possible reasons for this. First, in comparison with some regions in south China, migration in Shanxi is still in its initial stage, and thus some basic requirements, such as housing and everyday expenses, are still rather urgent. Second, the region studied is less developed than many other parts of China, and a suitable investment environment has not been formed yet. As a result, it is difficult for the migrants to find a suit-able place to invest their remittance. Third, most migrants in Shanxi are in job sectors like coal and the construction industry, and thus the technical skills they learn are less suitable for setting up small-scale rural enterprises or small businesses. Finally, the amount of remittance is generally small, and it is often insufficient for setting up a new business. However, it is expected that with the further development of migration, as well as of the overall economic environment in Shanxi, more remittances will go towards investment.

Instead of putting their remittances into poor-quality land, some house-holds tend to use the remittances to invest in their children's education. However, the investment in education is still low. One important reason is that for many rural households, putting money into education is not for stimulating further migration but involves sending their children out of the village to get further education. Given that the quality of education is rather poor in the villages, and children can hardly pass exams for high schools, let alone for higher education, it is difficult to achieve the objec-tive of investing in education. It is noted that some migrant households have financed their children to go to school in a town, but this is much more expensive.

Remittances are not just an economic phenomenon, but involve compli-cated social perspectives as well. When basic requirements have been met, remittances may flow into conspicuous consumption, including weddings, buying or repairing graves, and so on. In Shanxi, some migrants spend a huge amount of money on their marriages. A young worker in a construc-tion team spent 50,000 yuan on his wedding, and his daily wage is only 15 yuan. A young couple spent 10,000 yuan on repairing their ancestral grave. Thus, remittances are essentially conservative, reinforcing a traditional set of values (Ahiauyo-Akakpo, 1974). These migrants try to demonstrate their economic and social prestige through such traditional values. As Caldwell (1969) indicated, much of the money that flows to the villages is undoubtedly spent on mundane necessities. The Indian evidence suggests that while remittances can be substantial, both in terms of migrants' income and as a proportion of village income, such money transfers stimulate village-based development only in rather special circumstances, and even then the benefits rarely reach the poorest section of the community (Connell *et al.*, 1976).

Intra-rural inequality

Although at the regional level, the net benefit produced through migration could be seriously questioned, at the individual household or village level certain groups definitely benefit from migration. As a result, rural–urban migration increases intra-rural inequality and leads to different opinions about income, different attitudes to money and different levels of family expenditure between migrant households and non-migrant households.

Opinions about income

From the fieldwork, it was found that on the one hand, remittances are useful for reducing rural economic differentiation since some relatively poor households tend to send out migrants and the remittances can thus support other family members. On the other hand, the poorest non-migrant households have no choice but to stay in poverty, owing to their lack of sufficient resources to cover the initial costs for migration.

Table 4.9 shows a comparison between the two kinds of households' opinions regarding whether migrants' income is higher than that of other villagers. It is seen that 68 per cent of the households without migrant members believe that the income of normal villagers is lower than that of the migrants, whereas 78 per cent of the migrants' households think that there is no such difference. This result indicates that the households without migrant members are strongly attracted by the remittances from migration.

Similarly, questions were put to the households with and without migrant members about whether their income is different. The households with no migrant members think that they are poorer, whereas most households with migrant members think that they are slightly better off than, or the same as, non-migrant households.

Table 4.9 also shows the opinions regarding whether the rural households' income is higher than that of city residents, again from both households with and those without migrant members. It is seen that the households with migrant members are fairly confident about their economic position. Only 2 per cent of them think that their income is lower

Table 4.9 Opinions of households with and without migrant members on income of migrants in comparison with normal villagers; income of households with migrant members in comparison with households without migrant; and own household's income in comparison with city residents, %

Questions/Levels	Higher	Same	Lower	Don't know
Income of migrants in comparison with normal villagers				
Households with migrant members	8	78	10	4
Households without migrant members	68	23	3	6
Income of households with migrant members in comparison with households without migrant				
Households with migrant members	11	77	12	0
Households without migrant members	81	15	2	2
Own household's income in comparison with city residents				
Households with migrant members	31	68	2	0
Households without migrant members	0	42	40	18

than that of city residents, whereas the households without any migrants tend to think that city residents' income levels are higher.

A question was also asked about other incomes, such as subsidies from relief funds and support from relatives. The answers are all 'none' except that in the group without migrant members, three households received 1,000–2,000 yuan from relatives.

Attitudes to money

Usually migration brings major net remittances only to those households that can afford the forgone income and initial costs involved in sending out migrants. This may merely result in new and more extreme social differentiation in the village. Commonly, the highest returns to migration accrue to those households that can afford the high initial costs of sending migrants out. This certainly raises questions about how non-migrant households use their surplus money.

The way households use their money is indeed a relevant factor relating to migration. One question was asked about how they use their surplus money, and a comparison between the two kinds of household is shown in Table 4.10. It is seen that those in the migrant group tend to use the money to build or refurbish their houses, and those in the non-migrant group tend to save. This might suggest that those in the migrant group are more 'show-off' or want to be more comfortable, and those in the non-migrant group are more 'reserved' – they feel less secure financially and would like to save money for emergencies. There is no noticeable difference between the two groups in other ways to use their money. The percentage spent on 'doing business' is zero in both groups, which indicates that they are still not at this level.

Table 4.10 The ways of using surplus money: comparison between households with and without migrants. 1, Save in bank; 2, build and refurbish house; 3, children's education; 4, marriage; 5, business; 6, others.

	Saving	House	Education	Marriage	Business	Others
Households with migrant	13.4	54.6	21	10.1	0	0.8
Households without migrant	29.2	33.3	25.2	9.3	1.3	1.3

Questions were also put to both kinds of household about whether they would be willing to borrow money to extend the family economy or to spend money on learning a skill, and if so, how much they would be prepared to borrow. Overall, the majority of households without migrant members were not willing to do either. However, surprisingly, none of the households with migrants would borrow at all for either purpose. A quarter of non-migrant families responded more positively to these suggestions, though most of these would borrow only between 500 and 1,000 yuan. This again suggests that these non-migrant households do have some intention to migrate.

Further to the above, questions were asked of the households without migrant members about whether they would be willing to borrow money to work away from the village. Only about 6 per cent of the households were willing to do so, and the amount they wanted to borrow is rather limited: from 500 to 2,000 yuan.

Following on from the above, all the households were asked whether they currently had any loans, whether from a bank, collective, private lender or any other debt. Among household groups with migrant, none had any loan. In the group without migrant family members, none had any loan from a bank or collective, but three households had loans from private sources, and one from other sources. Overall, it seems that currently, migrants in the region studied are less involved in credit markets. However, given that in some other regions in China, bank credit has played a useful role in poverty alleviation (Chapter 2), it is to be expected that it will also become more important in the region studied.

Expenditure

The questionnaire also asked about family expenditure. Most households keep careful accounts of their agricultural input, so that it was possible to obtain this figure.[14] Conversely, exact figures for other items are hard to get, especially for living expenditure, since peasant families use their own products.

According to the household interviews and discussions with village cadres, there is a great discrepancy between peasants' income and the cost of inputs required to cultivate the 'responsibility' land.[15] It was pointed out that many items for agriculture are rather expensive and are thus the major family expenditure. These items include irrigation water, electricity, agricultural machinery like tractor ploughs, roads for agriculture, payments for special agricultural teams, and the costs of furnishing grain quotas to the state. In addition to the above, rural households have to invest more than 100 yuan per year in fertiliser and pesticide per *mu*. With the costs for seeds and labour, the total expenses for agriculture are about 300 yuan per *mu*. However, the profit is only 100–200 yuan per *mu* in a normal year and 300 yuan in a year with more favourable natural conditions. In the cases studied, there are no substantial differences between households. This means that they have to rely on sideline production. Rural peasants also pointed out that agricultural costs are governed by market forces while the prices paid for grain quotas have been set by the state regulations or plan and have not been adjusted to cover the rising costs of inputs. For example, in 1996 the price of corn rose by 40 per cent and the price of fertiliser rose by 50 per cent. Agricultural production is also affected by migration (see pp. 98–102).

A question was also asked about whether the households have surplus money, including savings and money for buying luxuries. It is seen that 96 per cent of the households with migrant members have surplus money, whereas the corresponding figure is only 66 per cent for the households without.

Impact of absence

In the region studied, most migrants are young males. The absence of many young men from the villages increases the relative proportion of women, children and the old. This affects agricultural production and changes the socio-economic structure of the villages. This section mainly deals with these two aspects.

Land-use rights

Chinese peasants are different from those in many other developing countries since they all have land-use rights. This study shows that rural–urban migration does not affect migrant households' land-use rights.

Land reforms in China since the late 1970s have resulted in important changes to the rural land system.[16] There are five basic provisions concerning the use of farmland.[17] Essentially, peasants have only use rights, not ownership of the land they contract, and the land cannot legally be rented or sold. Their land-use rights are long term, normally for 30 years starting from 1999. Whenever the collective needs to readjust the land, the collective (i.e. administrative village) must consult peasants who contract the land and get their approval. However, peasants are allowed to transfer the land-use rights to other private parties.

In the villages studied, the households with migrant members were asked whether their land-use rights had been changed because of migration. Ninety-seven per cent of them said 'no change', and 3 per cent said 'changed'. Further study shows that one village readjusted the land according to soil quality and increased population, and a single migrant did not want to keep his land, with its poor soil, and wanted the village to readjust it. These, however, do not mean a change in land-use right.

A question was asked about the duration of the land-use rights. It is interesting to note that the answers ranged from three to ten years and most people reported five years. It seems that this is not an important issue for them. Perhaps this is because households all expect to be able to extend the term of their land-use rights for another period.[18]

Impact on agricultural production

The impact of migration on agricultural production is related to many factors. Generally, it can be divided into two parts: crop farming and side-line production. The sidelines include animal husbandry, forestry and fish farming.

Farming is mainly based on the cultivation of wheat, corn, legumes, sorghum, rice and potatoes. Many studies have shown that farming production is less affected if the previous contribution of migrants to farming was small.[19] Other remaining male labourers as well as women, children and the old can replace migrants. Migrants' work can also be taken over by using new technologies. The effects are even less significant if migration is seasonal according to the cycle of farming production. Studies in south China show that there is no evidence that migration affects the yield of major farm crops or the total sown areas of farm crops (Bai, 1998). On the contrary, peasants in south China believe that migration is supporting farming because remittances are helpful for meeting the rising costs of farming production together with the payments required for village services, taxes and fees. Overall, it seems that the negative effects of labour shortages caused by migration are less significant than the positive effects of remittances on farming input, especially in some poor regions. In other words, migration may have a positive effect in farming. In addition, migration may stimulate differentiation between peasants in terms of farming income.

This case study in Shanxi does not show a significant difference in farming income between migrant households and non-migrant households. In 1996, incomes from farming, sideline production and wage labour[20] were 563 yuan, 702 yuan and 4.8 yuan per person for households with migrant members and 603 yuan, 995 yuan and 34.4 yuan per person for households without migrant members. The figures refer to the net income after deduction of taxes and fees. It is seen that for the households without migrant members, their farming income is only about 7 per cent more than that of households with migrants. In-depth interviews show that although natural conditions and soil quality are relatively poor in these villages and farming income may not constitute the mainstay of migrant households,[21] they still continue to put great effort into their contract (responsibility) land. In addition, it is rare to see changes in cropping patterns – for example, from more labour-intensive to labour-extensive cropping which involves few male-specific jobs.

Generally speaking, after a working migrant has gone, their household must seek a less labour-intensive form of sideline production. For example, in animal husbandry, they tend more to keep sheep or cattle and are less likely to pursue chicken farming or fish culture. Conversely, households without migrant members, especially those who have no plans to migrate,[22] tend to develop a variety of sidelines to obtain more cash. From the above figures, it can be seen that for the households without migrant members, their income from husbandry and forestry is about 40 per cent more than that of the households with migrants. In the villages studied, the overall level of animal husbandry is increasing each year. The scale of livestock farming is becoming greater, with herds increasingly being raised on a collective rather than household basis.

Labour structure and land transfer

Both households with and those without migrant members were asked about changes that may have arisen in the way agricultural labour has been structured since villagers began to leave in larger numbers generally. The results are shown in Table 4.11. It can be seen that for both groups, 70–80 per cent of the households chose 'hiring labour' and 'transferring land'. According to Friendland (1971), this may reflect a more long-term response by households receiving regular migrant remittances who are able to use remittances for changing the nature of the household's agricultural production and transferring land. It is interesting to note that the pattern of the production team[23] has almost disappeared.

A question was asked about whether there is some work that cannot be done because of the shortage of labour. Of households with migrant members, 46.5 per cent answered 'yes', whereas for the non-migrant group, the corresponding figure was only 19.2 per cent. This indicates that migration does cause a shortage of labour. Corresponding to this, 75.2 per cent of the households where someone has migrated think that their work is heavier than it was before that person migrated.

Clearly, from both the financial and security viewpoints, it is more acceptable to use labour exchange and kinship group help as a labour reserve for a household where labour absence is critical to production. Where labour exchange and kinship group help are not available, rural households may hire labour. Typically, during harvest some peasants help out other villagers who have more land. In Shaanxi, a province bordering

Table 4.11 Changes relating to agricultural labour structure after migration, opinion from both households with and without migrant members. 1, Similar to the cooperation in the production team; 2, cooperation between friends and relatives; 3, hiring labour; 4, transfering land; 5, others. (%)

	1	2	3	4	5
Households with migrant members	0	16.2	29.5	47.6	6.7
Households without migrant members	3.9	30.8	44.2	18.3	2.9

Shanxi, this is a very common phenomenon. However, this pattern is not common in the villages in this case study. In the non-migrant group studied, only one person was receiving this kind of income, which is about 1,000 yuan per year.

All kinds of co-operation reflect new patterns of capital accumulation. Increased remittances and increased shortage of labour are often offset by increased expenditure on hiring labour or other ways of replacing labour and transferring land. In south China, such as Jiangsu, migration households are likely to transfer their land to those households that do not have members able to migrate for work. As a result, the remaining households in the villages can get more income from agriculture to cover their living expenditure. Some of them even earn more than those who migrate for work. This is because those who remain do not need to pay for expensive accommodation in the cities, and also do not need to take the risk of waiting for job opportunities.

Households without migrant members were asked about whether they have received transferred land from other households. It was found that 7 per cent of the households have received transferred land, ranging in area from 1 to 4 *mu*.[24] Among them, four households received 2 *mu*; two households got 3 *mu* and only one household received 5 *mu*. Further interviewing showed that in the region studied, the transferred land comes mainly from households with migrant members, but in a small number of special cases households without migrant members also transferred their land to others. Overall, the results suggest that although land transfer is allowed, it remains at a very low level. An important reason is that the land quality in this region is rather poor,[25] and thus the profit involved in transferring land is insignificant, especially for the households receiving the transferred land. For this reason, normally the household that is losing the land pays the tax and other fees for the land. Migrant households tend to ease their labour shortage through exchanging labour and kin group assistance.

The above is similar to the situation in Anhui, where the proportion of households that are involved in land transfer is 6 per cent (Bai, 1998). Bai (1998) indicated that although at present the scale of land transfer and labour hiring is small, it has been predicted that this will increase in line with the increasing migration stream.

Connell *et al.* (1976) indicated that where the absence of men is critical to agricultural production, in that the production forgone cannot be substituted by purchased food, new forms of organisation must be employed or old forms adapted. In the villages studied, the round of village-based activities seems to adjust quite successfully to high rates of absenteeism.[26]

Women, children and the old

Women, children and the aged in rural areas have been affected in the wave of rural–urban migration. If it is young males who are the predominant migrants, other groups who remain in the villages – women, children and the old – have been involved either directly or indirectly in agricultural activity, to take up farming and domestic tasks. Women and children especially play important roles in village life. Many of them tend to become independent labourers in the field.

Such cases have also been reported in some other developing countries. Cohen (1972) provided a good account of the extra work taken on by women and the resultant impact on their prestige and by children in Israel. Connell *et al.* (1976) suggested from an Indian study that with the migration of adult males, the economic importance of other groups is enhanced.

Women

'Men migrating and women on the land' is becoming an important labour pattern for a considerable number of households in the region studied.[27] In Shanxi, since the majority of migration opportunities are in coal and its related industries and the construction sectors, it is not surprising that this pattern is emerging, whereby men migrate in search of jobs and women are bound to the village. This new division of labour along sex lines is in contrast to the traditional pattern of 'men tilling while women weave cotton cloth' – or in other words, women just carry out traditional tasks like cooking, childcare and forms of sideline production that can be done in the home. In the villages studied, sex discrimination in work roles is not strong,[28] at least not between husband and wife, and thus, this new division of labour is an accepted pattern. Such a pattern is likely to take hold among households in which both husband and wife are strong and healthy. As a result, migration can mean merely an extension of female responsibilities without any dramatic social consequences (Anderson, 1972).

In the questionnaire, one question was addressed particularly to women, to investigate the extra work for women caused by migration. For the group with migrants in the household, 91 per cent of women thought that they had extra work. Of the extra work, 44 per cent was farming work, 45 per cent was domestic work, and 2 per cent was looking after children and elderly people. Nine per cent of the households answered 'no extra work for women'. For those households, a further question was asked about who was doing the migrants' share of the work. Seven per cent said that the extra work was being carried out by the older family members. The other 2 per cent answered 'relatives or friends'. Overall, the results seem to suggest that everyone was working harder than before.[29]

It is interesting to note that for the households without migrant members, 52 per cent of the women thought that they have had extra work since migration became more common in the villages: 29 per cent farming work, 20 per cent domestic work and 3 per cent childcare. This is rather typical in China, at least in this region. Households in a village are related to each other in many ways, hence the effect is not on each household separately, but on the whole society.

A question was also asked of the women about where they get help when there are difficulties. The results show that parents on the husband's side are the most helpful: 43 per cent of migrant families and 35 per cent of non-migrant families get help from them. An important reason is that in the region studied, a young couple usually lives in the same village, or sometimes the same house, as the husband's parents. Thirty-four per cent of migrant families and 23 per cent of non-migrant families call for help from relatives and friends. In addition, the women's own parents are rather helpful for 16 per cent of migrant families and 24 per cent of non-migrant families. It seems that the level of governmental help is considerably lower than before. The major reason might be privatisation, and peasants feel that they are more independent. However, the percentage is still 16 per cent from migrant families and 9 per cent from non-migrant families.

Connell's (1973) Indian study suggests that women are called in to replace the men who have migrated, but that in general women have less strength, or have acquired a lower level of farming skills than men, and in consequence more women must join the workforce than the number of males who migrate. It seems that there is a somewhat different picture in rural Shanxi. Many rural women have developed skills, either directly or indirectly, as a result of their involvement in the process of rural–urban migration. The efficiency of their participation in economic development has been greatly improved. An important reason for such a consequence might be the concept insisted on in Mao's time: whatever men can do, women can do the same.

Under the new division of labour, many rural women must undertake farming work alone. They have to take many decisions, such as those relating to farming work, field management, the buying of agricultural materials in short supply, the buying of the means of production and articles for daily use, the education of their children, and they have more contact with their relatives and the rest of the community. In many instances, women assume these roles, and where this represents significant new responsibilities, as in the case study villages, women change from being dependent to being independent labourers, and create a new image for themselves in the society.

Agricultural work is a combination of human labour and biological processes. Since the biological processes change constantly, timely decision making is demanded to meet the concrete conditions at each link of the production chain, such as sowing, irrigation, the use of insecticides, weeding, fertilising and harvesting. There is much room here for women to bring into play their subjective initiative. When males are engaged in urban occupations and females work on the land, rural women have no alternative but to be independent. Overall, this should be regarded as another 'liberating' result for women.[30]

Local anti-poverty offices have also paid attention to rural women by training them in useful farming skills and improving these women's general knowledge about animal husbandry and the operation of household businesses. The development of rural women is becoming one of the strategies to reduce rural poverty. Sender and Smith (1990) suggested that there is an association between female education and the emergence of more progressive farmers. In the long run, women's access to education, and therefore to higher-status waged and salaried employment, enables them to question and resist the prevailing bases of intra-household distributions of power and resources.

In summary, profound changes have taken place in the following three respects:

1   In subjective consciousness, rural women have changed from labourers-in-themselves to labourers-for-themselves.[31] As a new type of rural women, they have rapidly developed their subjective consciousness, which manifests itself in the following ways in the work process (Meng, 1996). First, they have a strong desire to become rich through their own labour. Second, they are self-reliant. Third, they have a clear understanding of the whole process of production, the general objectives and the aims of various stages, and they can work independently in most links of the production chain. Finally, they are hard-working and do their best to learn to use agricultural technology.
2   In terms of authority within the household, they have ceased to be dependent on their husband and become the 'number one' in both production and household affairs.
3   In the past they had no say in the allocation of income; now they have taken economic rights into their own hands.

The 'men migrating and women on the land' pattern may also have some negative effects. Agricultural activities often require physical strength, but women generally may have a lower level of strength for some physical work, and thus such work could be detrimental to their health. Also, normally the education level of rural women is lower than that of men and consequently the introduction of new technologies in agriculture may be impeded. Overall, it seems that in rural areas like the region in this case study, the use of mechanised technologies and the hire of male wage labourers should be strongly encouraged, especially on a low cost-basis. In this aspect, the government's involvement would be very useful.

Children

As to children of primary school age, a question was asked about their activities after school. For the households with migrant members, a comparison is made before and after migration, and the results are shown in Table 4.12. It is seen that children's activity has changed dramatically. After migration they play less and work more. In-depth interviews[32] show that although no child has been deprived of education as a result of migration,[33] their education quality has indeed been affected because many of them have to work after school rather than study and play.

Table 4.12 also compares households with and without migrant members. It is seen that for the households without migrants, only 3 per cent of children need to work after school, whereas this ratio is 47 per cent for the households with a migrant or migrants. It is also important to note that for the non-migrant group, the percentage of 'study' time is considerably higher than that of the migrant group, both before and after migration. This may suggest that they are more concerned with their children's education.

The migrants' households were asked about whether they would be prepared to pay money for childcare. Only one household said yes, and the amount is only 100 yuan per year.

Children were asked about whether they wanted to go to the cities, and if so, why. The vast majority of the children did want to go. Two major reasons were 'better food' for 44 per cent of children in migrant families and 39 per cent of children in non-migrant families, and 'better education level' for 29 per cent of children in migrant families and 48 per cent of children in non-migrant families. None in either group chose 'fear to go' or 'cities are not good'.

General changes

As a summary of this section, Table 4.13 shows some of the general changes that have emerged since migration began in the villages studied.

Table 4.12 Major activities of children after school: comparison before and after migration, and between households with and without migrant members.

	Play	Study	Work
Households with migrant, before migration	61	32	7
Households with migrant, after migration	27	26	47
Households without migrant	37	60	3

Table 4.13 General changes after migration: comparison of the opinions between households with and without migrant. 1, Higher living standard; 2, more information; 3, better education for children; 4, everybody has work to do; 5, more work for women and the old; 6, lack of people to look after children.

	Changes					
	1	*2*	*3*	*4*	*5*	*6*
Households with migrant	50	27	7	33	13	0
Households without migrant	38	19	16	12	14	1

About 40–50 per cent of the households believe that living standards are higher than before, which means that the effect of migration is generally positive in the sending villages. About 20–25 per cent of the households think that they have access to more information. This is also rather positive. Households with migrants tend to think that everybody has work to do, but the opinion of households without migrant appears to be different. It is interesting to note that the negative effects, such as 'more work for women and the old' and 'lack of people to look after children', are relatively less important among the main changes.

Overall, from the above results it is clear that the positive effects of migration outweigh the negative ones. The level of remittance is considerably higher than the income from agriculture and sidelines. This further supports the positive side of migration.

Returned migrants

It is also important to investigate those migrants who returned to their native villages. Who are they? Why do they return? What impact do they have on the village economy and social structure? What is their socio-economic role in the life of the village?

Circular migration and temporary return

A special feature of migration in China is that every rural resident has his or her roots in the village. The land system is such that every household has its own land which it is not allowed to sell.[34] This system has significantly affected the migration pattern in China.

There are different forms of migration – migrants have different intentions at the time of leaving the village and their subsequent actions are also different. There are two major types of return, which can be viewed as temporary return and permanent return.

In the cases studied, an important migration pattern is circular migration. Most of the people involved believe that they will return home someday, and this belief determines their relations with those remaining in the village. Most of the migrants in cities are working in construction teams, coal mines or coal-related industries, and it is possible for them to return occasionally to meet special and short-term agricultural demand. This kind of migration can be regarded as a risk-minimising strategy – the households are committed both to agricultural income and to waged employment. Another advantage of this pattern is that the migrants do not need to move the whole family to the city where they are working, and this can significantly reduce the cost of living.

There are a number of typical examples of temporary migration in the village of Shicun in Wutai. In September, a seasonally busy time for agriculture, among the 25 sampled households with migrant members, 8 migrants had been away for over one year and did not return during the summer; 12 migrants had returned for several days every six months, both in summer and in winter; and 12 migrants were returning on an irregular basis. This means that two-thirds of the migrants were in the village during the peak agricultural seasons.

Analysis of reasons given for returning home in the questionnaires by households with migrant members showed that over 28 per cent of them came back because agricultural work was busy; 43 per cent of them came back because there was something to deal with at home, such as a wedding or funeral, or the illness of a family member; 19 per cent of them returned because of a slack period for work in the city; and 10 per cent of them took a holiday.[35] In-depth interviews show that 'something to deal with at home' is mostly agriculturally related. Overall, it seems that the pattern of return and duration in Shanxi tends to follow the agricultural cycle. This is different from many cases in south China, where the migration pattern tends to be long term and long distance, and migrants are not able to go home very often. For example, 78 per cent of the migrants from Sichuan are working outside the province, and this proportion is 91 per cent in Anhui Province (Du and Bai, 1997).

Permanent return

Apart from temporary return, the villages studied also have a number of migrants who have returned permanently. Permanent return can be divided into two types, successful and unsuccessful return.

Connell *et al.* (1976) reported that there are four types of successful migrants who return and three types of unsuccessful migrants:

SUCCESSFUL RETURN

1   Some migrants achieve their target, which can be a larger amount of capital, or sufficient capital to build a house, or for a marriage or small investment.

2   Some return after retirement from work outside the village.
3   The decision to return may be related to the level of economic or social opportunity available in the native village or to the migrant's ability to create economic opportunities.
4   Some student migrants return after completing their higher education elsewhere.

UNSUCCESSFUL RETURN

1   Some return after being unsuccessful in finding employment elsewhere.
2   Some migrants whose work outside the village ends after a limited period find that nothing else is forthcoming in that area.
3   There are migrants who return because they are unable to adapt to social and cultural life outside the village.

Thirty permanently returned migrants were interviewed in the villages studied, and were asked their reasons for return: 1, end of contract; 2, not enough income for family; 3, health reasons or getting old; 4, cannot find a job; 5, lack of necessary expenses in the cities; 6, earned enough money; 7, others.

Their answers indicated that about 42 per cent of them returned because of health reasons or because they were getting old.[36] Migration to coal mines has been a fairly common phenomenon in Shanxi since the 1950s, and currently many of these migrants have retired and returned to their villages of origin. This should be generally regarded as successful return.

The results show that over 50 per cent of the returned migrants can be classed as cases of 'unsuccessful return', for reasons including 'income is not enough to support family', 29 per cent; 'cannot find a job', 7 per cent; and 'contract ended', 22 per cent. It should be indicated that only 7 per cent of the interviewees chose 'cannot find a job', which means that in cities there are still considerable possibilities. It is interesting to note that none chose 'lack of necessary expenses in the cities', and none returned because they had 'earned enough money'. This appears to be different from the cases in some other developing countries and regions (Elkan, 1973), and also different from the situation in some regions in south China – where some migrants return after reaching a certain savings target or when they have learnt skills which would benefit them in their home villages.

Current situation of returned migrants

Some migrants learn skills such as making furniture and motor-repairing in the cities and then return to the village to use these skills. This will benefit the migrants as well as contribute to the development of the village economy. Such examples have been reported in Murphy's (1999) study in Jiangxi. In Shanxi, however, it seems that the situation is somewhat different. Most returned migrants have worked in construction teams, coal mines or coal-related sectors, and thus their skills are unlikely to be useful in the home village. In the villages studied, there is little evidence to suggest that returned migrants are a particularly important source of non-agricultural skills in the villages. Most of the returned migrants have no choice but to take up cultivation of the land. As mentioned previously, the land quality is normally very poor in the region studied.

The current situation of the returned migrants in the villages studied is: farming, 88 per cent; business or establishing a rural enterprise, 5 per cent; and others, 7 per cent. It is seen that most of them are farming. Only a few people are doing business or establishing rural enterprises, which is one of the expected activities for those returnees. None of them is working in a rural enterprise.

There are, however, some very successful returned migrants, though not in the villages studied. It was reported[37] that in 1997, two migrant brothers went back to their home village and took over[38] all the land in the village.[39] The two brothers worked in the eastern coastal region for seven years in a foreign enterprise. The experience has given them great ability for such local and regional development. They became village leaders. All the villagers have been rearranged according to their work ability: some farm by using large agricultural machines, some work in rural enterprises which were set up with investments by the two brothers, and the relatively old women look after the children. Currently this village is one of the richest villages in Shanxi. Unfortunately, in most cases the remittance flow into the villages from migrants is small. This means that the benefits of remittances would mainly be reaped by the migrants' households rather than at a village level.

As to income, 43.9 per cent of the returned migrants think that their current income in the village is lower than their income when they were migrants. The rest think that there is no significant difference between their current and previous income, or that it is difficult to compare them. Overall, it seems that working away from the village is better from the viewpoint of income.

Returned migrants were also asked about the way they used remittances, and the results show that 82.5 per cent of them use their money for housing. Caldwell (1969) found a similar phenomenon in Africa in the 1960s.[40] Other uses include investment, 3 per cent; education, 8 per cent; saving, 5 per cent; and so on.

Considering the rural–urban differences in income and living standards, a question was asked of both successful and unsuccessful returned migrants about how the other villagers regard them. It was found that 44 per cent of the returned migrants did feel that other villagers thought that they could not find a job in the city, whereas none of them believed that other villagers thought that they had got enough money. It seems that migrants felt their return was more likely to signify failure than success, although the determinants of success or failure were not always within their own control. Thirty-five per cent of the returned migrants, mostly those retired, chose 'return is normal'. The remaining 21 per cent of the returned migrants had no comment.

Future plans

What of the future plans of the returned migrants? It is interesting to note that the percentages planning to 'migrate again', 'stay in agriculture' and 'don't know' were rather low: only 7 per cent, 12 per cent and 22 per cent, respectively. In comparison, 59 per cent of the returned migrants thought that they were going to do something else. Further interviews showed that the things they wanted to do included moving to a town nearby,[41] setting up a small business, and developing animal husbandry such as rabbit warrens, pig farms and fisheries. This appears to indicate the effect of the migration experience.

The sampled households with migrant members were also asked, 'In what circumstances should a migrant not move out again?' Reasons of an economic nature, namely, 'earned enough money', or 'need labour at home', made up about 55 per cent of the total, and reasons on the social side, namely 'having difficulties away from home' and 'missing each other', made up about 34 per cent. This is somewhat different from the traditional view, like 'it is a good life if someone has 2 *mu* of land, a cow, wife and children, and a warm bed' (*liang mu di, yi tou niu, laopo haizi rekangtou*). The change can also be regarded as one effect of migration.

City and village

Rural households' attitudes to city and village life, as well as their general attitude to life, are also related to migration. It would be useful to investigate the differences and similarities between households with and without migrant members. In the questionnaire, a section was designed for such an investigation.[42]

General comparisons between city and village

A multi-item comparison was made between city and village life for both groups of households. The results from the households with migrant members are shown in Table 4.14. For each item, there are three options: good, normal and bad. Accordingly, a single index is calculated by weighting 'good' as 2, 'normal'[43] as 1, and 'bad' as 0. In other words, if the index is higher than 1, it tends to be good, and if the index is lower than 1, it

Table 4.14 Comparison between city and village life, opinion of the households
with migrant members

	City				Village			
	Good	Normal	Bad		Good	Normal	Bad	
Score of satisfaction	2	1	0	Overall	2	1	0	Overall
Living standards	48.6	50.5	1.0	1.48	2.9	30.5	66.7	0.36
Housing standards	32.4	43.8	23.8	1.09	33.3	17.1	49.5	0.84
Adequate food and dress	39.0	61.0	0.0	1.39	1.0	28.6	70.5	0.30
Medical services	42.9	57.1	0.0	1.43	0.0	8.6	91.4	0.09
Transport	55.2	42.9	1.9	1.53	7.6	22.9	69.5	0.38
Shopping	34.3	65.7	0.0	1.34	0.0	41.0	59.0	0.41
Environmental pollution	14.3	11.4	74.3	0.40	59.0	41.0	0.0	1.59
Family relationships	10.5	71.4	18.1	0.92	17.1	70.5	12.4	1.05
Neighbours	1.9	89.5	8.6	0.93	24.8	74.3	1.0	1.24
Education level	79.0	21.0	0.0	1.79	0.0	1.0	99.0	0.01
Social security	0.0	30.5	69.5	0.30	61.0	39.0	0.0	1.61
Opportunity	33.3	66.7	0.0	1.33	0.0	51.4	48.6	0.51
Social welfare	10.5	81.9	7.6	1.03	0.0	20.0	80.0	0.20
Power using	0.0	41.9	58.1	0.42	7.6	32.4	60.0	0.48
Income	20.0	71.4	8.6	1.11	0.0	45.7	54.3	0.46
Labour intensity	10.5	89.5	0.0	1.10	10.5	60.0	29.5	0.81
Farmer status	0.0	8.6	91.4	0.09	54.3	44.8	1.0	1.53
Power of office	14.3	12.4	73.3	0.41	18.1	41.0	41.0	0.77
Personal motivation	15.2	82.9	1.9	1.13	2.9	44.8	52.4	0.50
Overall	24.3	52.6	23.1	1.01	15.8	37.6	46.6	0.69

tends to be bad. Using an even weighting system for all items, an average
score is calculated based on the individual scores. This presents an overall
evaluation of city and village life. From Table 4.14 it can be seen that in
general, the evaluation score for city life is higher than that for village life.
The overall score is 1.01 for city life and 0.69 for village life.

For each option – namely, good, normal or bad – an average was made
between all items, and the results are shown in the bottom line of Table
4.14. Corresponding to the overall score, the results indicate that in comparison with village life, there is a higher level of 'good' and 'normal', and
a lower level of 'bad', for city life. On average, 23.1 per cent of the households think that city life is bad, but this figure is 46.6 per cent for village
life.

Corresponding to Table 4.14, the results from the non-migrant households group are shown in Table 4.15. It is seen that generally speaking,
there is no significant difference between the two groups. However, the
score of the non-migrant group is higher than that of the migrant group,
especially for the city life. This suggests that the non-migrant group has a
better impression of city life. Perhaps this is because in comparison with

Table 4.15 Comparison between city and village life, opinions of households without migrant members

	City				Village			
	Good	Normal	Bad		Good	Normal	Bad	
Score of satisfaction	2	1	0	Overall	2	1	0	Overall
Living standards	40.4	52.5	7.1	1.33	16.2	16.2	67.7	0.48
Housing standards	33.3	52.5	14.1	1.19	28.3	52.5	19.2	1.09
Adequate food and dress	44.4	55.6	0.0	1.44	9.1	48.5	42.4	0.67
Medical services	54.5	45.5	0.0	1.55	0.0	15.2	84.8	0.15
Transport	58.6	41.4	0.0	1.59	0.0	37.4	62.6	0.37
Shopping	47.5	52.5	0.0	1.47	3.0	31.3	65.7	0.37
Environmental pollution	18.2	39.4	42.4	0.76	77.8	21.2	1.0	1.77
Family relationships	41.4	58.6	0.0	1.41	37.4	61.6	1.0	1.36
Neighbours	45.5	44.4	10.1	1.35	57.6	38.4	4.0	1.54
Education level	87.9	12.1	0.0	1.88	1.0	8.1	90.9	0.10
Social security	7.1	55.6	37.4	0.70	72.7	27.3	0.0	1.73
Opportunity	33.3	62.6	4.0	1.29	0.0	32.3	67.7	0.32
Social welfare	46.5	43.4	10.1	1.36	3.0	12.1	84.8	0.18
Power using	23.2	41.4	35.4	0.88	8.1	47.5	44.4	0.64
Income	71.7	28.3	0.0	1.72	0.0	32.3	67.7	0.32
Labour intensity	51.5	47.5	1.0	1.51	4.0	50.5	45.5	0.59
Farmer status	0.0	30.3	69.7	0.30	45.5	50.5	4.0	1.41
Power of office	23.2	42.4	34.3	0.89	7.1	53.5	39.4	0.68
Personal motivation	48.5	40.4	11.1	1.37	0.0	35.4	64.6	0.35
Overall	40.9	44.6	14.6	1.26	19.5	35.4	45.1	0.76

the migrant group, the non-migrant group has less experience of the negative aspects of city life.

A more detailed look at the separate items in Tables 4.14 and 4.15 shows that both groups regard peasants' status and environmental pollution as the major bad aspects of city life. Other bad aspects include social security, housing standards, 'power-using' and power of office.[44] For both groups, the good aspects of city life include higher living standards, adequate food and clothing, and the availability of good medical services, transport and education.

For village life, both groups agree that the good aspects are less environmental pollution, better social security and better status for farmers. Many more items are rated as bad aspects, including living standards, housing standards, inadequate food and clothing, medical services, transport, shopping, education level, opportunities, social welfare, power-using, income, power of office, personal motivation, and so on.

The differences between the two groups of households are mainly in how they rate the following aspects: family relationships, relationships between neighbours, and income levels. For these factors, the migrants' households group tended to give city life lower scores. Their opinions about income levels were significantly different between the two groups. Non-migrant households' scores for city and village life are 1.72 and 1.32, respectively, whereas the scores given by the migrants' households are 1.11 and 0.46. Again, this is probably because the group with migrants in the family had a deeper understanding of city life.

Attitudes to life

A series of questions were designed to make comparisons of general attitudes to life (see Appendix). The questions can roughly be divided into two sets, one set negative and the other set positive. Basically, the negative factors are against migration, and the positive factors are more supportive of migration. The questions and the results from households with and without migrants are shown in Table 4.16. For the convenience of comparison, a single score is given for each question by using a weighting system, namely, 5, strongly agree; 4, agree; 2, disagree; 1, strongly disagree. An arithmetic average is then made for both negative and positive factors.

From the table, it is interesting to note that for the negative factors, there is no significant difference between the two groups. This seems to suggest that the two groups of households are all reluctant to leave the villages. For the positive factors, conversely, the migrants' households group's score is 3.92, which is considerably higher than that of the non-migrant group, 3.12. It appears that such attitudes to life do affect the decision whether to migrate. Of course, it is also possible that the attitude of the migrants' households group changed after migration.

Summary

Using the results of the field study, this chapter compares households with and without migrant members, aiming to establish some of the reasons for migration. The current migration situation is also analysed, with a special focus on the social and economic effects of migration on the sending areas. Some major conclusions are summarised below.

Decision as to whether to migrate: a comparison between households with and without migrant members

In the objective aspects, there are considerable differences between households with and without migrant members. The differences in demographic conditions are systematic. In comparison with households with migrant members, for the households without migrants the number of people per household is lower, the percentage of the old people and young children is greater, the overall labour capability is weaker, and the education level is

Table 4.16 General attitude to life: opinion from households with and without migrant. The scales in the table are: 5, strongly agree; 4, agree; 2, disagree; 1, strongly disagree.

		Households with migrant				Households without migrant				
	Weighting scale	5	4	2	1		5	4	2	1
	score					score				
Negative factors										
Village is very poor, but happy to stay	2.24	12	13	29	46	2.77	5	40	35	19
More sons, more happy	3.83	58	17	8	20	3.83	33	44	16	6
Education is less important than money	2.83	31	16	16	40	2.41	10	19	43	27
Home is better than city	4.12	61	25	2	15	3.81	14	69	15	1
The old people are right	2.46	6	25	51	21	2.97	7	44	35	13
Government will help poverty relief	1.62	0	8	40	55	2.21	1	18	62	18
Cadres are powerful	3.93	19	71	13	0	3.80	26	50	23	0
Following others is good	3.95	33	51	19	0	3.70	20	55	22	2
Current social environment is bad	3.65	8	73	22	0	3.35	8	55	36	0
Rich are richer, poor are poorer	4.08	48	40	11	6	3.81	40	30	28	1
Overall score of negative factors	3.27					3.26				
Positive factors										
Moving is positive	4.55	60	42	0	1	3.77	16	64	18	1
Can do better if have a business	3.46	18	50	31	4	2.38	12	10	59	18
Moving reduces poverty	4.35	44	55	4	0	3.20	6	52	38	3
Social environment changing quickly	3.97	16	78	8	1	3.73	7	76	14	2
Try to do one's best	3.28	10	54	33	6	2.53	12	14	61	12
Overall score of positive factors	3.92					3.12				

lower. These are certainly factors impeding migration. As to geographic conditions, it is interesting to note that the households with migrants were further from towns, markets, and train or bus stations. This might be a motivation for migration. In terms of the land quality and quantity, there is no significant difference between the two kinds of household.

In the subjective aspects, there are also considerable differences between the two kinds of household, especially in terms of the decision whether a family member should migrate. On the one hand, households without migrant members are generally not willing to do certain 'low-class' work and are less sensitive to some migration opportunities, less 'brave' when choosing a destination, and less practical in their views on migration. These factors certainly affect migration negatively. On the other hand, households with no migrants tend to overestimate the income of migrants and the living standards of city residents. Correspondingly, they do have a strong desire to work away from the villages. In comparison with households with migrant members, households without migrants say they are more willing to borrow money to learn a skill, or even for migration.

In summary, from the results in this chapter it can be seen that, both subjectively and objectively, there are systematic differences between households with and without migrant members. These have affected their decision-making about migration. However, many households without migrant members do have a desire to work elsewhere, and thus there is a strong likelihood that there may be more migration in the future.

Socio-economic effects of migration on sending areas

The remittances from migrants are normally 2,000–4,000 yuan per year. This is considerably higher than income from agriculture and related areas. The use of remittances is limited to some basic purposes, such as housebuilding or have refurbishing, everyday expenses, and agricultural materials. The vast majority of remittances come from sectors such as coal mining and related industries, as well as construction, manufacturing and service sectors.

Migration has brought marked changes in social and economic activities in the sending villages. Nearly all the households with migrants have surplus money, whereas the corresponding figure is only about 50 per cent for the households from which none has migrated. The labour structure has also been affected. Most women have extra work, both in farming and in domestic labour. Since many households are closely related, this is the case for both kinds of household. Many children in households with migrant members must work after school rather than play or study. There is a trend towards land transfer between households with and without migrant members.

The families of the majority of the migrants studied are still in the villages of origin. The majority of the migrants are working within the province, and many migrants return home quite often. Such a link has certainly affected the social life in the sending areas.

There are various reasons for migrants to return, but having 'earned sufficient money' is not among these. The returned migrants are not in a different economic or social class from other villagers. Most of the returned migrants use their money in housebuilding or house refurbishing, not in investment for rural enterprises. However, many of them have fairly positive plans for their future, which indicates the potential impact of migration.

5   Case study analysis
Destinations

This chapter analyses the questionnaire for migrants (see the Appendix, questionnaire A4). As described in Chapter 3, the two-ended approach was carried out by interviewing 105 migrants from the four villages. Focusing on the current situation for migrants and the social and economic effects, the analysis includes the demographic and social characteristics of migrants, migration channels, relationships between migrants and their sending areas, how migrants find jobs and adjust themselves to an urban environment, their income and working conditions, and their general view of city and village life. Comparison is also made between the region studied and the general situation in China.

Migrants' demographic and social characteristics

This section presents basic data on the migrants interviewed, including their sex, age, educational level, marital status, previous experience, current job sector, and so on.

Sex and age

Of the migrants interviewed, 77.8 per cent are males and 22.2 per cent are females. An important reason for such a male:female ratio is that in Shanxi there are not many female-labour-intensive enterprises like those on the east coast of China.

Figure 5.1 shows the age distribution. Six age groups – 16–25, 26–35, 36–45, 46–55, 56–65 and over 65 – were used. It is seen that the age range 16–35 is dominant, which corresponds with the result in Chapter 4 (see Figure 4.2). A study based on 2,820 households in Sichuan and Anhui also showed that migrants are mainly in this age group (Du and Bai, 1997). In comparison with other Chinese regions, especially south China, a special feature of the region in the present study is that there are fewer young female migrants.

The maximum and minimum ages of the sampled migrants were 65 and 16 for males, and 39 and 22 for females. The oldest and the young migrants

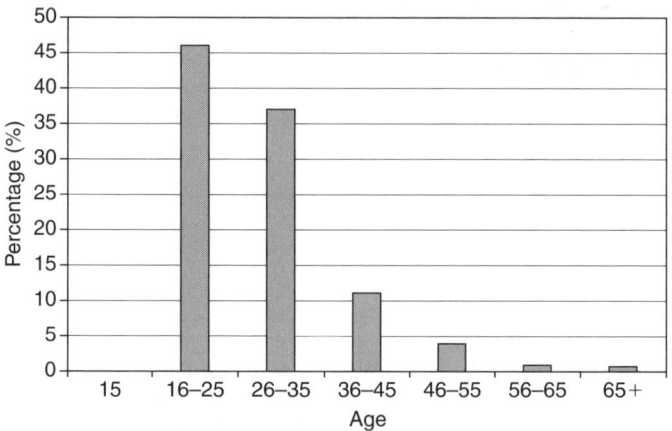

Figure 5.1 Age distribution of the interviewed migrants.

were from the same family: a father and his two sons working in a coal mine. This case is described in more detail later. The youngest female was a waitress in a restaurant in Taiyuan. Her father was the head of a village. She did not know how to do farming work since she was the youngest child in the family and her older brothers did most of farming work for the family. After failing the examination for higher education, she went to her uncle's restaurant in Taiyuan. The oldest female was a wife who went out to join her husband in a coal mine in Datong, and at the time of the study she was running a small shop in the area of the coal mine.

Education

In Chapter 4, it is shown that the average education level of the households with at least one migrant member was higher than that of the households without. Figure 5.2 shows the education level distribution of the sampled migrants. According to the calculation method outlined in Chapter 4 (see p. 75), the average education level of the migrants was 4.57, which is significantly higher than that of other rural residents. This can also be seen by comparing Figures 5.2 and 4.3.

From Figure 5.2 it can be seen that for the migrants, the rate of illiteracy/near-illiteracy is only about 1 per cent, which is significantly less than the average level in their villages, and also much less than Shanxi's provincial level, 10.2 per cent, and the national level, 17.8 per cent (NBSC, 1997). An important reason for this is that since the free compulsory education system was implemented,[1] illiteracy/near-illiteracy rates have been decreasing among the younger generation. It appears that this rate is considerably lower than that in some other developing countries like India

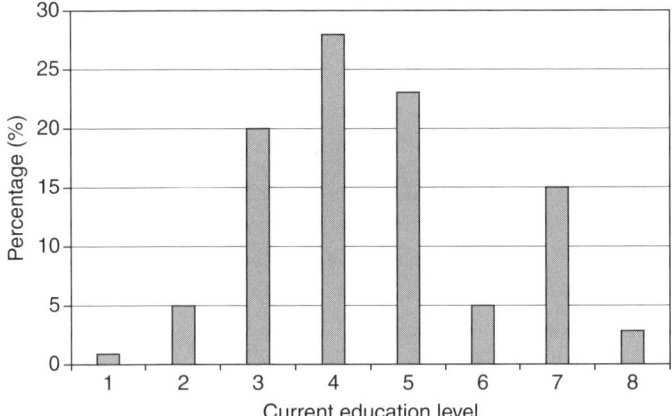

Figure 5.2 Current level of education of the interviewed migrants. 1, illiteracy/ near illiteracy; 2, junior primary school; 3, senior primary school; 4, junior middle school; 5, senior middle school; 6, special secondary school; 7, high school; 8, higher education.

(Breman, 1996). Most of the migrants studied are at levels 3 to 7. In other words, they had completed senior primary school, junior middle school, senior middle school or high school. Three of them had experience of higher education. Two of them had graduated from colleges but they had to pay their own fees.[2] This had changed their *hukou* status. The third migrant at higher education level was trained informally in a college.

Generally speaking, it is hard for migrants to upgrade their educational level after migrating to cities. The interview results show that 96 per cent of the migrants had stayed at the same education level after migration. However, three migrants, as mentioned above, had changed their education level from high school to college. They indicated that this was because they recognised their own capabilities and potentials. A higher education level would increase their self-confidence and enable them to set new targets in the future.

Marriage

It appears that in terms of marital status, there is no significant difference between migrants and other villagers. Of the migrants studied, 55.5 per cent were single, 38.5 per cent were married and 6 per cent divorced. Generally speaking, young and single migrants move further from the sending areas and stay longer than married migrants. Married migrants tend to engage in circular migration between cities and villages, although some couples moved to a city together. Some couples also took their children with them, including children of school age.

Marital status remained unchanged for the majority, but the interview results show that 19 per cent of migrants married after a period of migration. All those migrants returned to marry someone from the village.

Job sector

The whole picture that emerges from many migration studies is of migrants as social pariahs, discriminated against by and excluded from the existing urban institutional environment. Migrants are often seen as poor and undereducated, capable of selling their cheap labour by taking lowly paid jobs that are dirty, difficult, dangerous and tedious, selling vegetables and small household items on streets, or doing repairs and menial work. This study confirms that picture, as can be seen from Table 5.1, which lists the current job sectors of the migrants studied. The jobs are ranked according to their social status. The table also shows the number of migrants in each category.

Migration experience

Based on the interview results, Figure 5.3 shows the year of first migration. It is seen that from about 1990, the number of migrants increased dramatically. This is a significant feature of the region studied. In south China, the 'boom' in migration started earlier.

The results show that 39 per cent of the migrants had come to cities in the past three years, 69 per cent had migrated within the previous six years and 10 per cent of them had been in a city for 10 years. Seventeen per cent of those migrants who had already been living in the city for more than 12 years were mainly the first generation of miners. Among the interviewed migrants, 72 per cent had been in other big cities (such as provincial capitals) before their first migration.

It is interesting to note that the increase of migrants in cities corres-

Table 5.1 Job sectors of the studied migrants. The jobs are arranged according to social status.

Coal and coal industries (43)	Construction (31)	Manufacturing (15)	Others (16)
Miner	Porter	Porter	Catering porter
	Unskilled worker	Unskilled worker	Rubbish collector
Electrician	Semi-skilled worker	Semi-skilled worker	Domestic helper
Plumber	Woodworker	Skilled worker	Waitress and
Gas checker	Bricklayer		waiter
	Plumber		
Contractor[3]	Contractor		Small business owner

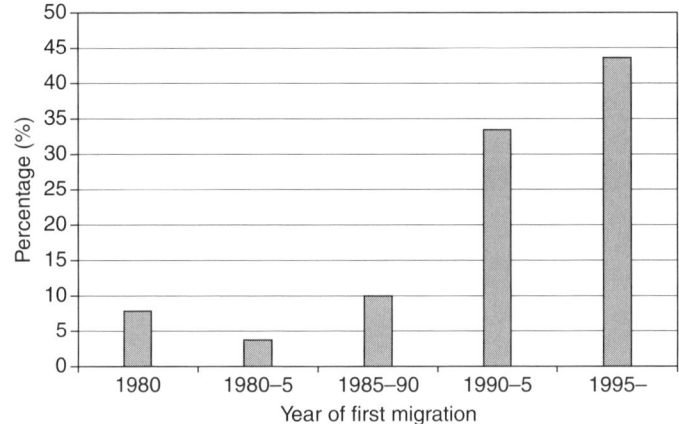

Figure 5.3 Year of first migration of the interviewed migrants.

ponds with the decrease in the number of rural enterprises and their employees in the three sampled counties (see Chapter 3).

Other information

Among the interviewed migrants, 51 per cent of were in Taiyuan (the capital of Shanxi Province) and 42 per cent were in medium-sized cities like Datong and relatively small cities like Changzhi, Yuanping and Xinzhou. Only 7 per cent of them were in Beijing or other provinces. In contrast with migration in the rest of China generally, a significant feature of the studied region is that most migrants have stayed within the province.[3] From the interviews, it appears that the major reason was that many Shanxi people, especially peasants in north Shanxi, were still strongly influenced by the traditional attitude: staying at home is always better than going out. Such a 'closed' migration pattern might be caused by the province's closed geographical condition. It is noteworthy that all the studied migrants in Beijing were working in a hotel owned by the Shanxi government. In other words, they were still in the Shanxi community.

Hukou is another important issue. The majority of the studied migrants had agricultural *hukou*. Two migrants had bought township *hukou* and were planning to move the whole family to the city when they had enough money. Health was sometimes a factor: 90 per cent of the migrants were healthy, but 10 per cent mentioned that they were too old to work in the big cities or had a chronic disease.

During the interviews, it was found that it was easier to talk to those who had had some special experience such as being in the army, or being a cadre. They were keen to talk about broad issues, from the general situation of the cities to government policies. Among the interviewed migrants, six had been in the army and five had been cadres, one at township level, two at village level and two as Communist Party and Communist Youth League officers in the villages.

Migration and feedback channels

This section mainly discusses why and how migrants leave home and their relation to their sending areas.

Reasons for migration

Why people migrate is certainly an important issue, and is briefly discussed in Chapters 2 and 4. In this two-ended approach, reasons (there could be several reasons at once) for working away from one's village were also addressed. Generally speaking, there are three kinds of reasons, namely, objective or material reasons, subjective or ideological reasons, and other factors.

It seems that the objective or material reasons are the most important factors affecting migration. In this case study, the majority of the migrants had left their native villages through to economic necessity. Agricultural income is largely dependent on natural conditions, and in these areas this income is normally not enough to support families. Also, there is very little opportunity for sideline work. When asked why they worked away from the village, sixty-nine per cent of the migrants specified reasons relating to a general need for money, such as there being only limited land and not enough farming work (27 per cent); 22 per cent wanted to have more money; 18 per cent found the income in their village too low; and 2 per cent said they needed money urgently. Other reasons were: learning more about the outside world, 21 per cent; farming work too heavy, 6 per cent; supporting brothers' or sisters' education, 2 per cent; getting money for marriage, 1 per cent; and sent by local government, 1 per cent.

Having limited land is a particularly important factor leading to migration. In Chapters 2 and 3 it is indicated that there is a lack of arable land. With the development of new techniques, such as improved breeds, better chemical fertiliser and mechanisation, this problem is becoming more serious. In the long term, this will speed up the process of urbanisation.

The above reasons all form the 'push' factors for rural–urban migration, especially in Shanxi. Rural–urban migration is also 'pulled' by the job opportunities in cities, especially in coal and related industries, both in big cities like Taiyuan and medium-sized towns like Yuanping.

It is interesting to note that about 20 per cent of the migrants chose subjective or ideological reasons. These included searching for new experience and opportunities, and a desire to see the outside world. This indicates a social aspect of migration.

Interviews revealed some other reasons for migration as well. For example, some migrants do not like farming work or find it is too heavy. Wang, who is from Daixian County and is now working in Yuanping Heavy Coal Manufactory, said:

> 'I like to work in a factory, especially big factories in the cities. Only eight hours' work, and after work, you can do what you want. But in the village it is difficult, there is always so much work to do every day.'

The interviewees were also asked about how they made the decision to migrate. The results show that 63 per cent of the migrants made the decision by themselves, and for 25 per cent of them the decision was made by their parents or relatives. Four per cent of migrants went to cities where friends had already found jobs and 2 per cent obtained work opportunities through local government. It is clear that migration is mainly self-motivated, rather than following governmental arrangements.

Communication and feedback between migrants and sending areas

Migrants in cities send back information, either positive or negative, by oral messages, letters and telephone calls or by coming back personally. The information significantly affects subsequent migration decisions. This kind of feedback can be explained quite simply in terms of stimulus–response behaviour. The feedback process can have one of two effects: it can amplify the difference between villagers by stimulating further migration or it may counteract it by encouraging a return to the initial situation (Mabogunje, 1970).

Communication between migrants and their sending areas

Questions were asked about how the migrants sent back messages, and how often they returned. The general impression is that they keep closely in contact with their villages of origin by continually sending back information and by paying visits regularly. Information about migration normally spreads very quickly in villages. Migrants were asked about their methods of communication with their families in the villages. It was found that letters and oral messages are the major channels, followed by direct phone calls and other methods (e.g. sending messages via relatives' or neighbours' phones, calling local government offices and telegrams). Forty-nine per cent of the migrants use letters as their main way of communicating with their villages. It is interesting to note that about 30 per cent of the migrants still use the traditional method of sending oral messages with friends or relatives returning to the village. Direct phone calls are uncommon; only 7 per cent. Fourteen per cent of interviewed migrants used other methods to contact with their relatives in the villages. Clearly, this reflects the backward local telecommunications system (see Chapter 3).

Personal visits back to their home villages are limited, and migrants are unable to return home more often, not only in view of the extra transport expenses, but also because of the difficulty of getting time off from their work. They normally return when their families have difficulties. However, Chinese New Year is an exception. According to tradition in Shanxi, as in China in general, people who are working away from home ought to come back then whether they are poor or rich. This is a holiday period for most work units. As a result, vast numbers of migrants go back to their villages of origin for New Year, and this causes huge problems for city residents and for the public transport system. The interview results show that during the Chinese New Year period, city residents find many aspects of life very inconvenient since so many migrants go back to their villages. Some milk companies are closed, many small restaurants for breakfast disappear, nearly all children's nannies are not available, and nobody transports coal for those residential areas without gas. The transportation companies are under great pressure. Additional trains and buses are essential to link the most popular sending areas and cities.

The major reasons migrants reported for visiting home are as follows: 1, to celebrate the Chinese New Year; 2, to take a holiday or because work in the city is not busy; 3, because agricultural work in their home village is busy; 4, they had something to deal with at home. Thus the majority of migrants went home either for the Chinese New Year (68 per cent) or when there was a particular need for them to go back, such as busy agricultural work (21 per cent) or when there was something to deal with at home (5 per cent). Only 7 per cent of the migrants went back for a holiday.

One question addressed the frequency of visits per year. Most of the migrants (57 per cent), returned home once a year. Twenty-four per cent of them returned twice a year. Some of them go home very often: three times a year (16 per cent) and four times a year (2 per cent). It is important to note that only 1 per cent of the migrants returned at an interval of more than one year. This indicates the tight link between sending and destination areas. In other words, kinship and locality still play an important role.

Remittance

The interview results showed that 56.7 per cent of the migrants gave money to their family members in the village. It is worth noting that there is no clear boundary between 'giving' money and 'returning' the money that was borrowed from the family for migration. It is unusual to have a contract for such loans, especially between migrants and their parents. The

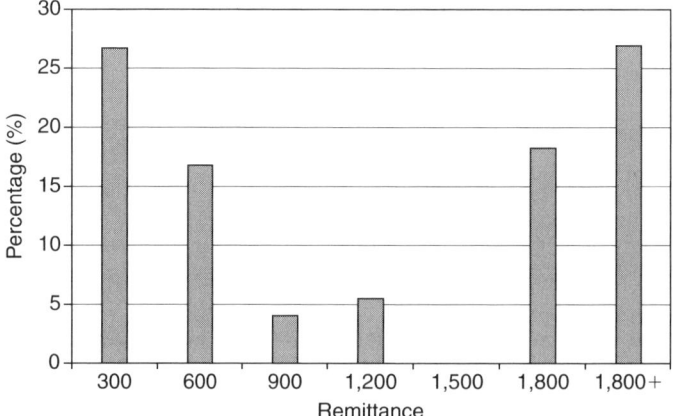

Figure 5.4 Cash remittance (yuan) from each migrant to their family in village
in 1996.

family members who receive money from migrants include spouses and
children, as well as parents on both sides. Migrants are careful to ensure a
balance between the various sides.

About 43 per cent of the migrants did not send money to family
members in their villages. The major reason was that they had not earned
enough money; many of them were still in the initial stage of migration.
For a small number of migrants, the main reason for migration was not to
make more money for their family, and thus they were using the money
for other purposes rather then sending it back to their villages of origin.

The distribution of the value of the remittances is shown in Figure 5.4.[4]
The annual average was 1,221 yuan. In comparison with normal villagers'
income, this amount is a significant addition. It is more than one labourer's
net agricultural income in the villages. Given that the migrants' land in
their native village has not been abandoned and is still maintained by their
family members, the income from migration normally does not negatively
affect the income from farming.[5]

This research shows the ways through which these remittances were
sent home. Usually, local governments calculate how much remittance
income flows into rural villages by using post office records. This research
found that only 46 per cent of remittances were sent through the post and
that a big lump sum, 51 per cent of all remittances, were taken home personally. Unlike in developed countries, bank transfer is still not available
in rural regions in China. Chinese New Year is normally the peak period
for cash remittances.

Another form of remittance is giving presents. Of the interviewed
migrants, 94.8 per cent said that they gave presents to their family,

relatives and friends.[6] As was shown in Chapter 4, most presents are quite basic, namely, food, 42 per cent; clothes, 17 per cent; and items of everyday use, 34 per cent. No jewellery was given and electrical applicances were not common (only 2 per cent). The results are similar to those shown in Chapter 4.

Eighty-five per cent of the migrants spent between 50 and 300 yuan on presents. The average was 73.9 yuan. Giving presents is a very effective way of keeping up social links. However, doing so can be a heavy burden for some migrants – particularly as, since villages are usually small, people tend to be always comparing who has more than who.

Information feedback

Migrants send back not only money and presents, but also information. Migrants who have been successful in getting a secure job send back positive information about the cities. Such positive or favourable feedback can encourage migration and often produces natural migratory flows from particular villages to particular cities. By contrast, migrants who have difficulty getting a job or finding a place to live often send back negative information. The effect of this feedback will slow down further migration from the village to this city.

Urban control system

The urban adjustment mechanism has its own control system, which operates at the opposite end of a migrant's trajectory to encourage or discourage his or her being absorbed into the urban environment. The absorption is of two kinds: occupational and residential. This section analyses how migrants match these two kinds of absorption. The analysis covers ways they find secure jobs, carry out related training, settle in the city environment, documents needed for migrants to stay in the cities, and their plans for the future.

Finding a job

Labour migration is determined by many uncertain factors. A potential migrant expects to find a better job with a larger net income in the cities. Generally speaking, the success of migration is determined by the following three conditions: first, whether or not the potential migrant has basic financial support to move to a city in the first place; second, whether the migrant can find a job there; third, whether the new job fits his or her human capital and personal goals.

When job opportunities are the same, a successful migration will depend on the human capital of a potential migrant, and his or her efforts to find a job. Whether the decision to migrate is based on rough and unspecific information, or on a comparatively stable contract, is quite important. Interviews revealed three main ways of finding city jobs: by oneself, 30 per cent; through relatives and villagers, 25 per cent; and through a labour contractor, 31 per cent. The last two of these can be described as through kinship links, territorial social ties and professional bonds. Other ways of finding the first job are: sent by local government, 14 per cent; recruitment by factory etc., 1 per cent; and others, 3 per cent.

Kinship

Kinship is the fundamental bond uniting the member of the *jia* (*chia*),[7] but it does not confine itself within this group. It extends to a much wider circle and forms the principle of association of larger social groups (Fei, 1939). Kinship includes paternal extension and maternal extension. Members of a kinship group may become economically independent but they are still bound together by various social obligations. In the studied case, one-third of the migrants found their jobs through kinship links. The closer their kinship, the more rapidly they were brought to the cities. For first-time migrants, there are three advantages of this way of finding a city job. First, it does not take a long time and it takes the risk out of finding a job – normally their relatives can find a job for them before they go. Second, it makes it easier to find cheap or free accommodation. Third, the new migrants do not feel like strangers in the cities since they will get support and practical help from their relatives. The following interview extract is a good example:

'The first migrant in our family was my oldest brother. In 1995, he got a chance to work in a construction team in Taiyuan. When I graduated from junior high school in 1996, he gave two bottles of *Fengjiu*[8] to his contractor and secured a place for me as an unskilled labourer. In 1997, he found places for my brother-in-law and my brother-in-law's sister as cooks for the construction team. Their village is 8 km away from ours.'

Sometimes kinship and other effects work together. The following is such a case:

'My father has worked for this coal mine for more than 10 years. At Chinese New Year 1995, he was back from Taiyuan and said that the mine needed new miners, who should be young and reliable, and he would like to introduce me. I joined this mining team that summer. At the same time, another guy, my classmate in middle school, was keen to go with me. However, the head of our mine said that this was a kind of welfare for their old employees rather than for everyone. In 1996, my younger brother enrolled in this coal mine as well.'

Territorial bond

Beside kinship bonds, another fundamental social tie is that of territorial bonds. Those who live near each other find it easy to co-operate in matters of common interest demanding concerted action (Fei, 1939). Here the territorial bond refers to those who live in the same administrative village[9] but who are not related by kinship.[10] Since the introduction of the system of people's communes,[11] administrative villages have become a base unit in the rural areas, along with township or *xiang* in the rural administrative system. Households in it share the same responsibility, carry on the same activities and have an intimate association with each other.

In the cases studied, about 25 per cent of the migrants had found jobs through their fellow villagers. It seems that the territorial bond is less strong than the kinship bond. Note that previous migrants bring their fellow villagers to the cities not only to help these poorer village members but also to enlarge their power or group in the destination cities. Their role is normally merely to give free information rather than to take on the risk of paying transport expenses or providing free accommodation for their newly migrating fellow villagers.

Many migrants believe that it is good to work with their fellow villagers. A male migrant, who was 25 years old and worked at a brick factory said:

'I have worked in this brick factory for three years. During these three years, I introduced seven guys from my village to join this factory. Now I feel much better than when I was here by myself. At that time, some guys were always bullying me and making me do the heavy work or work the night shifts. Now I have a strong group, nobody dares to treat me rough including the team head because we eight work well together and also we could let him down if he gave us too much trouble.'

However, there are also some problems in working with others from the same village. A female migrant, who was 22 years old and worked as a waitress in a restaurant in Taiyuan, said that she would never bring anyone from her village to this city again. This is how she tells the story:

'I cannot say that I do not like my fellow villagers but they always make me seem to come from the middle of nowhere. My neighbour in the village begged my parents many times to ask me to introduce their 16-year-old daughter to this restaurant. I refused, although I knew this restaurant needs waitresses. The main reason is that the girl looks like a typical poor rural peasant. She would have to work with me, live with me and go shopping with me all the time if she worked here. I have got a boyfriend who looks like a city boy. When we go out, nobody recognises that we come from a rural village. I do not want someone here who will always show that I am from a rural village. In addition, last year another villager tried to find a job in this city and could not get it. She stayed here and ate here for three months without paying for anything. When she left, my boss said "Thank goodness, do not let your poor relatives come again." I could not explain that she was not even my relative. Anyhow, I will never bring my fellow villagers here again.'

Professional bonds

The third social-economic tie appears to be professional bonds. Professional bonds are becoming more important nowadays as China develops socially and economically. The representatives are contractors, local labour offices, anti-poverty offices and recruitment teams from some enterprises in cities.

The role of contractors is to recruit migrant labourers and to operate projects which they contract with and can get benefits from. Most contractors come from rural villages. They recruit workers from their native villages as well as from other villages on a voluntary basis. Although they may be related to or come from the same village as their employees, they are operating for profit rather than to help relatives and fellow villagers. The relationship between a contractor and rural migrants is professionally based.

Contractors normally were originally migrant workers themselves. After working as a migrant for some time, some able migrants become contractors. They are respected and powerful in their villages, and in many cases they offer poor villagers the only hope of finding work away from home. Table 5.2 lists some basic characteristics of three contractors studied. According to detailed interviews, it seems that the major characteristics of contractors are:

1 They have broad knowledge about the destination cities because they have been in urban areas for a long time, say 7–17 years.
2 They first went away to work when they were young, say around 20–24 years old.

Table 5.2 Characteristics of three contractors interviewed

No.	Sex	Age	Education	First migrated	Current project	No. of times changed occupation	No. of times moved cities
Q3-78	M	27	Junior high	1990	Construction	4	3
Q3-64	M	34	Junior high	1985	Construction	5	5
Q3-34	M	45	Junior high	1978	Coal mine	2	2

3   They have changed occupation and city very often.
4   They are good at politics, or have close relationships with relevant officials, or have other strong connections in the destination cities.

Since the labour source is the rural villages, contractors use traditional ways of dealing with their teams. For example, they prefer to use their fellow villagers to avoid problems inside a team. One contractor, Wang, mentioned that he was not against people from other nearly villages joining his team, but said that many migrant workers would prefer to have relatives in the team. Contractors are more likely to have an oral agreement concerning payment and living conditions with their workers, instead of formal contracts. Another construction contractor, Liu, said:

> 'The payment is around 20 yuan for skilled workers [*da gong*] and 10 yuan for unskilled workers [*xiao gong*] per day. They are paid at the end of a project if the project gets the money. Food and accommodation are free of charge. If they agree to those conditions, then they can join the team.'

Although there are formal intermediary organisations in cities, contractors seem to play a more important role than those organisations. Contractors control nearly all the job information and they do not publicise this. Formal intermediary organisations in cities usually do not actively make contact with sending areas – at least, in the villages studied, such information is not available.

The role of local government in rural–urban migration

Local governments sometimes arrange for peasants to work away from their villages. There are two ways for local governments to send out peasants. First, city enterprises recruit rural labourers through the local labour bureau. This way reduces the risks of finding a job and saves rural migrants the transport expenses to cities. However, it is often less successful than might be expected, since many city enterprises pay low wages to rural migrants and let them do the heavy work. Also, it takes time for rural migrants to get used to modern or labour-intensive jobs. In the interviewed cases, only two young men got their first job this way, but they quit the factory after a short period. Their experience was as follows:

> 'We were sent to Shanghai Bike Assembly Factory by the County Labour Bureau. We signed a contract before we went. In the contract, it was mentioned that the pay was 450 yuan per month including accommodation and travel between Shanghai and Shanxi. The contract was for six months in the first instance, and we paid 600 yuan in fees and deposit.[12] We went to Shanghai by factory bus. In the first two

months, we got 450 yuan per month, paid 250 yuan for food and saved 200 yuan. From the third month, the factory side said it was time for us to get piece rate wages, with a base wage of 200 yuan. We got around 250 yuan per month from the third month because it was very difficult to match the speed. After six months we came back.'

An officer in Daixiang Labour Bureau said the factory recruited 36 people from Daixiang County in 1995 to work in Shanghai, but all of them came running back within three to six months. In 1996, another unit took 10 men to Beijing as supermarket porters, but after six months only one person remained. The remaining migrant said:

'The work is OK but the wages are low, 450 yuan excluding food and accommodation. It costs 500 yuan to rent a room in the central areas, and I have to share a room with two other people.'

The second way is for local governments to make agreements with city enterprises: fixing the wages, setting insurance policies, and sorting out any problems which may arise between enterprises and migrants. It should be mentioned that the three county governments in this case study regard rural–urban migration as a poverty-alleviation measure. Among the migrants interviewed, 14 were sent by the local anti-poverty offices. The officers said that compared with the huge number of surplus rural labourers, only a tiny number were sent out through the anti-poverty offices. However, these migrants caused many problems for the local anti-poverty offices. For example, 10 construction workers from Wutai County got in a fight with some youngsters in Beijing and were detained by the local police station. In Jingle County, seven migrants broke their contract and went back purely because they did not like the food in south China. Also, in these three counties, several industrial accidents had to be dealt with. The anti-poverty officers think that it is necessary to have an intermediary organisation to deal with job information and the health insurance system, to ensure migrants' rights, and also to provide better preparation for migrants so that they can better adjust themselves to the rules of working and living in cities.

The interviews demonstrate that the peasants have deep faith in the information they received from relatives, villagers and local government about the cities they intended to move into. Also, the peasants are confident about finding jobs in the cities. These findings challenge the widely held view that migrants are guided by nothing but an expectation of finding urban employment and they tend to flow blindly into the cities – a view which implies that migrants are somehow irrational and their movement haphazard. In addition, the findings raise questions for Todaro's expected income model of rural–urban migration, in which job uncertainty is a basic assumption.

Necessary costs and documents for initial rural–urban migration

Rural–urban migration can entail heavy costs – or, in other words, a flow of money out of the village. The initial cost of fares, residence in the cities, purchase of food until an urban job is found, and the cost of qualification and searching for a job can all involve an initial outlay which needs to be met by the village. These initial costs may be quite substantial, and for poor families, present expenditure matters a great deal compared with uncertain benefits later. If risk or borrowing is involved, as it usually is, the very poor can find it almost impossible to migrate.

Documents needed

Generally speaking, urban control can be identified with the city adminis-tration and other sections operating under national laws and statutes. In this way, the urban control system can be represented as the requirement for a series of documents which rural migrants must obtain if they want to work in cities.

Under the *hukou* system, a migrant can neither leave the village nor stay in the city at will. At least three documents from the sending villages are absolutely essential: a 'resident identification card' (*jumin shenfen zheng*);[13] a 'family planning pledge' (*jihua shengyu zheng*),[14] and a 'permit to leave the village to work' (*lixiang zheng*).

Urban governments need to be able to estimate the size of their migrant population and how long the migrants are staying in the cities, and so they try to control migrants' *hukou* registration, employment, room rental and applications for small business licences, and they demand payment of various kinds of fees. At least two documents are needed. One is a 'temporary residence card' (*zhanzhu zheng*), which is valid for one year and has to be renewed each year by showing the resident identifica-tion card. The other one is the 'migrant's work permit' (*wailai renyuan jiuye zheng*) to work in the cities, as analysed in Chapter 2. These sets of documents are essential, and time and money are needed to obtain each document. This may sometimes prevent a migrant getting work.

Table 5.3 shows migrants' responses regarding various documents needed. Note that this is not a complete list of documents. In different cities or different areas of a city, different documents are needed. For example, a migrant may need to buy a formal type of ID card for passing through the main gate of his or her workplace. In some areas, migrants have to pay for street cleaning before they can rent a room. Some migrants have to pay road-repair fees and education fees. It seems that the inten-tion of various city administration units is to control migrants by requiring different documents, and not to help them by providing housing and job information. Having to apply for so many cards and documents is espe-cially resented by migrants, as it seems to emphasise their low social status and the feeling of discrimination from city residents.

Table 5.3 Various documents obtained or not obtained by interviewed migrants

	Yes (%)	No (%)
ID card	98	2
Family planning pledge	81	19
Migration registration card	82	18
Temporary residents card	89	11
Migrant work permit	87	13

All this paperwork involves some payment – fees varied as shown in Table 5.4. It is seen that for most of the documents, the cost is below 100 yuan. Although this is not a big amount of money for salary-earning people, the total amount may well be too high for many would-be migrants, given that the mean income in rural villages is rather low, as seen in Chapter 4. The effect may be to defer migration.

Deposits

When a migrant is offered a job, a deposit payable to the employer is normally needed.[15] In addition, the migrant has to hand over his or her ID card to the employer. Historically, these arrangements were all used to prevent migrants from damaging the working unit, but it seems that they are now becoming a way of controlling migrants. If a migrant resigns, he or she will lose the money. In other words, a migrant cannot run away or change to another job with better income or working conditions within the contract period. For 27 per cent of migrants, the deposit is below 100 yuan; 54 per cent of migrants have to pay around 100–300 yuan for their deposit; and 17 per cent of migrants had paid deposits between 301 and 600 yuan. The highest deposit reported (over 900 yuan) was required for a job as a supermarket porter. The supermarket said that its stock included many valuable goods, and it required a high deposit for security reasons.

The above are just some of the compulsory expenses involved in migration. On top of these, money is needed for temporary accommodation,

Table 5.4 Amount of money (yuan) required for the cards and documents (percentage of respondents who paid these rates)

	Yuan			
	<20	21–50	51–100	>100
ID card	25	53	22	0
Family planning pledge	56	44	0	0
Migration registration card	28	44	22	6
Temporary residential card	0	0	52	48
Migrant work permit	8	17	10	65

travel expenses, and so on. A single ticket from any of the three counties to Taiyuan costs about 30–50 yuan.

Training

A significant feature of the rural–urban migrants interviewed is that they normally do not have special skills and therefore have to earn money by their physical strength. Generally speaking, there are three kinds of training possibilities for migrants, namely, formal training, informal training and training courses. The results of questionnaire A4 showed that 41 per cent of the migrants had formal training, and 59 per cent had informal training or no training.

Need for training

It is often necessary for migrants to have training before starting work. Although there is a cost, training is an investment. This is useful for first-time migrants, and also useful for migrants wanting to change to a better job. The main reasons for having training are as follows:

1   Almost all migrants want to know more about the cities, the jobs and their new lifestyle because they have neither special skills nor the cultural background that city residents have. Also, migrants' experience and knowledge of modern industrial production is less than that of city residents. When asked whether one has more chance if one has a special skill, 63 per cent of the migrants said 'yes', 15 per cent said 'no', and the rest said 'don't know'. This indicates the importance of training.
2   On average, the education level in villages is lower than in cities, although from Figure 4.3 on p. 75 it can be seen that the overall education level of households with a migrant is higher than that of the no-migrant households. Education level tends to affect job hunting. The interviewed migrants were asked about whether a migrant would have better chances of finding a job if his or her education level were higher; 44 per cent answered 'yes', 24 per cent said 'no', and the rest said 'don't know'. Those who come to cities to learn more about the outside world rather than simply getting money rate getting training and learning special skills as more important than some other migrants do.
3   Some recruitment units require a certain education level or formal training for their workers. For example, in 1995, 90 per cent of the city employers set a requirement for a minimum education level (Zhou Q., 1997). Of these, 76.3 per cent required junior high school level and 13.6 per cent required senior high school level or above. Eighty-four per cent of city employers provided formal training or short-term training before migrants started work.

Formal training

In most cases, a formal period of training is organised by employers before or after migrants start work. The Labour Law specifies that it is an employer's responsibility to give employees necessary training in safety awareness and general skills.

Of those 41 per cent of migrants who had formal training, 76.3 per cent of them had had training before they started their first job, 13.2 per cent after, and 4 per cent both before and after. The rate of training found in this study is relatively low in comparison with the general situation in China: 50 per cent of migrants have formal training after they move into cities (Zhou Q., 1997).

The main training organisers for those 41 per cent of migrants who had formal training were their employers (in 83 per cent of cases) or a relevant labour organisation (in 5 per cent of cases). Generally, migrants apply for the jobs first without having the required skills, and then the employers provide essential training related to the migrants' work. In other words, for these migrants, training happens after job hunting.

The result shows that 66 per cent of migrants attended training because it was essential for getting the job. Also, 28 per cent of migrants did so because it was useful for their future. Only 4 per cent of migrants attended training because they were not eligible for an increment or higher position if they did not undergo training.

The influence of training varies. Sixty-two per cent of the migrants did get a job after training; only 5 per cent got more income. For 33 per cent of the migrants, there was no change following training. The situation at national level is slightly different: according to a survey in 1997 (Labour Bureau of China, 1997), trained migrants were paid on average 7.5 per cent more than those who were not trained.

Training courses

Training could also happen before finding a job. There is a tendency for more and more intermediary organisations to provide general training courses to give migrants a basic knowledge about living and finding jobs in the cities. There are also some special courses run by private sources, such as for sewing, cooking, hairdressing, or other skills. However, normally there is no guarantee of a job offer after the course. Some social organisations, such as the Communist Youth League (*gongqingtuan*), Women's Federation (*fulian*) and anti-poverty offices, also provide more opportunities for the rural poor by running training courses, normally free of charge. For example, in Wutai County in 1997, three free training courses were conducted by the above organisations giving an introduction to the process of going to the cities, finding jobs, self-defence and workers' rights, for those who had graduated from junior high school and were contemplating migrating for work.

Informal training

Although 59 per cent of the interviewed migrants had no formal training, many of them had informal training. In other words, they learnt through their work. Informal training is particularly common in small construction teams and small coal mines. Usually, experienced workers show new workers basic skills through their work. No fee is needed for informal training. However, wages may be low and the working hours may be long. Job training without pay is usually beyond the capacity of poor rural households.

It is interesting to note that although there is a lack of training procedures and facilities, some small-scale industries, such as brick factories, coal mines and construction teams, prefer to use workers who are newly arrived in the cities.[16] A brick-factory owner criticised experienced workers as troublemakers because they require higher wages, better working conditions and shorter working hours. He said, 'I do not need experienced workers and no training is necessary for new workers. If a worker comes from a village, he knows how to make bricks using his village experience in traditional methods. What I need are cheap labourers.' In a township-level coal mine, the manger said, 'Neither formal training nor experience is needed for new workers. They have to work under the supervision of their father, uncle or whoever helped him in finding the job.'

The unskilled labour scene is much less uniform than it might seem at first sight, while within each branch of industry the stage of promotion is complex. In a construction team, the contractor said:

> 'At first, young migrants can be helpers in our team. They can get free food and accommodation, but lower pay or no pay for a short period. If I have more projects, they will probably become unskilled workers [*xiao gong*], which means that they can formally join our team.'

It is definitely not profitable for helper-workers to delay ingress into the labour process until they are able to carry out simple tasks repeatedly, perhaps followed by some sort of politicisation that would eventually enable them to cross the threshold into formal-sector employment. This can be an explanation why some migrants have less money than they started with, or even no money, when they return to their village.

Cost-effectiveness of training

The cost of training normally varies from 130 to 500 yuan. Among the migrants in this study who had attended training, 64.1 per cent of them paid the training fees themselves or else their parents paid. This can be regarded as a kind of investment, or a cost for migration. For 20.5 per cent of the migrants, the employers paid the fees. There are also some other ways of paying the training fees, such as fees being partly paid by employees or deducted from initial wages. Both migrant workers and city enterprises consider the costs and benefits of training. City enterprises pay for training and obtain better-qualified labourers. Rural migrants invest in training and, they hope, get higher returns.

Those who had not attended any training were asked their reasons why not. The majority of them thought that training was not useful (54 per cent) or that it could not bring about any change in their current situation (20 per cent). About 21 per cent of them said they did not have time for training. It seems that financial reasons are not the major factor affecting their attitude to learning more skills or knowledge in the cities, because only 3 per cent of them mentioned not having enough money for training fees. In a rare case, one migrant said that he wanted to receive training but his director had not approved.

When the migrants without training were asked whether they would like to pay for training themselves, 88 per cent of them answered 'no'.

Future plans

Since most of the migrants still had peasant *hukou* and did not have a permanent job, it was important for them to consider the future. A question was asked about their short-term future plans. Fifty-two per cent of them wanted to stay in their current job, whereas the rest had various other plans. Nineteen per cent of them were thinking about changing jobs and 18 per cent of them planned to return to their village. Finally, 11 per cent of them did not know what they would do in the short-term future. This means that this sizeable labour group (see Chapter 2) is not stable, and this may well affect urban economic development. The effect may be positive or negative.

The migrants interviewed were asked about their long-term plans. One-third of them wanted to return to their village; of those, about 15 per cent wanted to do business in rural areas and the rest of them had no choice but to return to farming. This means that returning migration has quite strong directivity. This will strongly affect urbanisation in China. On the other hand, fewer than 28 per cent of the migrants chose 'stay in cities'.

It is important to note that 44 per cent of them are not sure about their long-term future. This may suggest that because everything is not that certain, such as policies, work opportunities and development trends, they just do not want to plan. Some of them believe that it could well be the case that today they have a lot of money, but in several years' time their money will be worth nothing.

Staying in the city

Once a migrant has secured employment, his or her city life begins. A number of factors determine the commitment. Among these are wages, expenditure, working environment, welfare, social position, and so on. Based on the statistical results of the questionnaire, these issues are analysed below.

Wages and living expenditure: migrants' economic position

Wages and living expenditure are certainly very important for migrants' economic position. In this study, it was found that wages can be very different in various sectors. Those who work in state coal industries get three or four times more than those in some private-sector jobs. The living expenditure of migrants also varies significantly from city to city. Generally speaking, the bigger a city is, the higher the cost of living.

Wages

Generally speaking, migrants' wages are unstable, are relatively low and vary significantly from job to job. Since wages are often different each month, the migrants studied were asked their highest and lowest incomes per month. The distributions are shown in Figure 5.5. It is seen that for over 60 per cent of the migrants, the monthly income is lower than 600 yuan. About 15 per cent of them get over 1,200 yuan per month. These migrants are normally contractors, or are working in highly profitable state coal industries.

Overall, it seems that migrants' income levels are similar to those of formal workers in state-owned enterprises. In 1997, the average annual income of formal workers in China was 6,280 yuan per capita, and in Shanxi the figure was 5,596 yuan (NBSC, 1997).

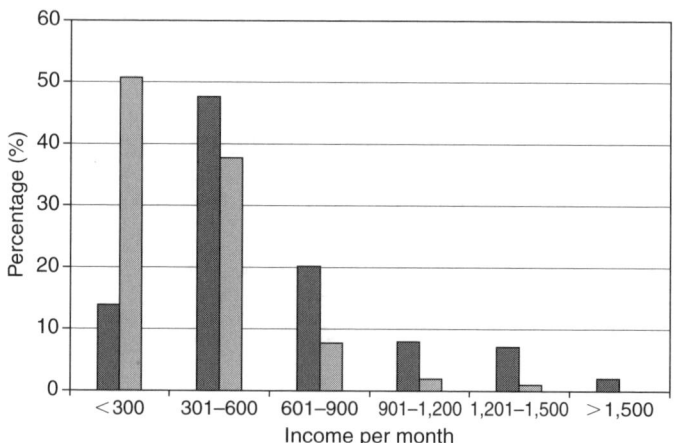

Figure 5.5 Distribution of the highest (■) and lowest (▨) income (yuan) per month for the interviewed migrants.

Coal mining is an important sector in this case study area. The following extract from a migrant's interview gives his description of the wage situation in this sector:

'Generally speaking, in new coal mines, money is needed to build basic structures underground and the transport system. Wages for coal mine workers are therefore low. Wages are also low in some old coal mines, because coal resources are running out. Someone from my village has just moved from an old mine to our mine. This is a relatively new coal mine, but all the basic facilities, both underground and above ground, have been built. Our wages are slightly higher than those in other mines. Our income is around 1,000 yuan per month if there is no accident.[17] It is also possible to get a bonus at Chinese New Year.'

Several migrants in the study are working at Zhaolin brick factory, a star township enterprise with 190 workers, of whom 120 are migrant workers. The director of the factory said that wages for the workers are increasing every year. They rose from 5,900 yuan per capita in 1995 to 6,800 yuan in 1996, and again to 7,200 yuan in 1997. A contractor who was in charge of one team of migrants said that the average income for his team was about 400–500 yuan per month, depending on weather conditions and the power supply. The month before the interview, the migrant workers received only 300 yuan because of power cuts. If there is a power cut, they are normally paid 4 yuan per day towards living expenses.

In some sectors, the situation is very bad. A migrant who is working at a heavy manufacturing factory said that his wages were about 200 yuan a month in the past year, and payment had been delayed for three months. This was mainly caused by the bad economic performance of the factory. Even formal workers were worried about their position. *Xiagang*, namely 'stepping down from one's post' due to redundancy, has become a serious problem in many factories. Consequently, this migrant was ready to go home at any time.

The process of job hunting for a typical migrant as a rational person involves a balance between cost and benefit. The income migrants expect to receive is compared with the income they would get in the village, making allowance for the cost of migrating. In other words, migrants have initial ideas about the wages they expect. According to this study, migrants' expectations were normally higher than their current income, no matter how much their current income was, from 200 to 1,500 yuan.

In addition to the amount of payment, the frequency of payment is also an indication of the type of job. Normally, if a wage is paid monthly, the job is a relatively fixed one. Only about 9 per cent of the interviewed migrants had monthly-paid jobs. Eighty-five per cent of them were paid daily, 2 per cent of them were paid by the week and another 2 per cent

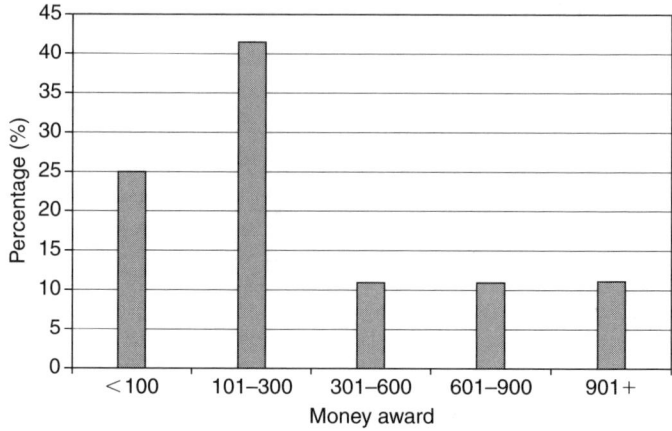

Figure 5.6 Distribution of the money award (yuan) to migrants in 1996, including year-end bonus.

received their payment annually. These kinds of payments indicate that their jobs are fairly unstable.

A common phenomenon in China is the cash bonus.[18] Survey results show that 38 per cent of the migrants studied were given money awards. The amount is shown in Figure 5.6. In addition, 50.5 per cent of the migrants believed that in the year they were interviewed, there would be a year-end bonus.

Although it is illegal to delay payment of workers' wages, late payment is quite a common phenomenon. Even formal employees sometimes cannot obtain their payment on time. This is often due to bottleneck economics and triangle debt,[19] especially in the coal industry. During the interview, the director of a state-owned coal mine said that they had to get enough money to pay migrant workers' wages before Chinese New Year.

Years since migration and income level

One would expect that the longer the period since migration, the higher the migrant's income. To examine the situation in Shanxi, questions were asked relating to the number of years since migration and migrants' wages in each year. In Figures 5.7 and 5.8, the trend line and correlation coefficient between the years since migration and the highest and lowest incomes are shown, respectively. It is noted that there is a very slight tendency that the longer since migration, the higher the wage, but the correlation coefficient is very low for both highest and lowest income. In other words, it appears not to be the case that if migrants stay in a city for a

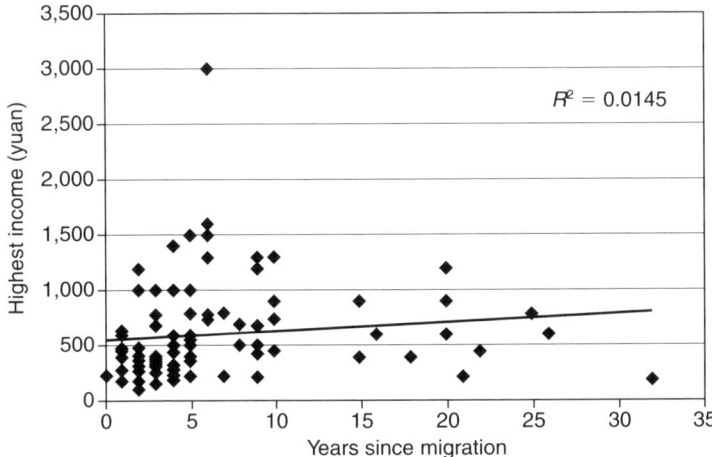

Figure 5.7 Correlation of migration year and current highest income of migrants.

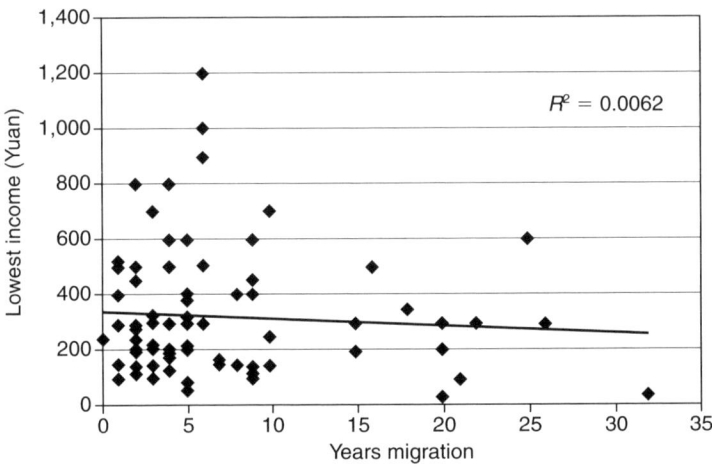

Figure 5.8 Correlation of migration year and current lowest income of migrants.

longer time, they will change jobs several times to get a job with better wage.

This is different from the situation in developed countries, and different too from the former situation in China. One reason for this situation is that migrants are normally treated as temporary workers without tenure. For most of them, wages are determined by job sector, although there are many chances for people to become rich quickly. Another reason is that the type of work migrants are able to obtain is mostly not very technical or completely non-technical. Also, as indicated previously, some employers prefer to employ new migrant workers so that wage levels can be deliberately kept low.

Job change

In the case study, 13 migrants were already in their second jobs, and five had changed their job three times. To investigate the difference in income caused by changing job, Table 5.5 lists the change in the highest and lowest income.

It is interesting to note that changing jobs brings no significant increase in income. The number of migrants with an income decrease is almost the same as the number of migrants with an income increase. Detailed interviews show that for those who changed job, the main reason was that they were formerly on a short-term contract. For those who are satisfied with their current job, there is unlikely to be a change. It is also the case that migrants who have never changed their job may receive higher wages than those who have changed jobs.

Income is not the only reason for changing one's job. Some migrants are trying to work in a better job sector. One migrant mentioned that being a cleaner in a big factory is more respectable and stable than being a cleaner in the catering sector. This indicates that in addition to economic conditions, social position is also an important consideration.

Expenditure

The cost of living in the cities is much higher than that in the villages. Based on the interview results, Figure 5.9 shows the distribution of spending on various items, including accommodation, bills (water, electricity, coal, and so on), food, clothes and travel. It is seen that accommodation and bills were not the major items of expenditure. Most of the migrants needed to pay for these two items, but the amount was only 50 yuan or less per month. Food and clothes were important items of expenditure, and

Table 5.5 Income difference when changing job. The figures shown are the number of people.

Income difference (yuan)	Decreased	100	200	300	400	500	500+
Highest income, job 1 to 2	5	2	2	0	0	1	3
Lowest income, job 1 to 2	5	1	2	0	1	1	3
Highest income, job 2 to 3	2	0	1	1	0	0	1
Lowest income, job 2 to 3	2	1	1	0	0	0	1

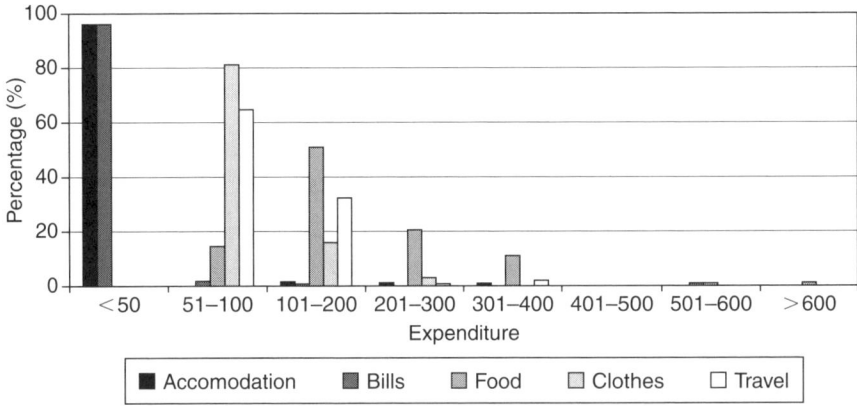

Figure 5.9 Expenditure (yuan) distribution per month on accommodation, bills, food, clothes, and travel.

varied from 100 to 400 yuan. Most of the migrants spent 100–200 yuan in travel home to their village. It seems that this figure is higher than expected. A possible reason is that some migrants also included the cost of presents in this item.

Corresponding to Figure 5.9, the average spending on each item was investigated. The items of expenditure, in descending order, are food (158 yuan), travel (74 yuan), clothes (54 yuan), accommodation (12 yuan), and bills (4 yuan). If an average is made, the total cost would be about 300 yuan per month. Unlike migrants, city residents are given free accommodation (although this does not make much difference), and spend more money on food and clothes.

A migrant's average savings per month were obtained from interviews. It seemed that the amount of savings is 248 yuan, which is quite high. The interviews made it clear that for many migrants, their major or only objective was saving money, and so they kept their expenditure to an absolute minimum. However, this was not the case for all the migrants. About 42 per cent of them did not have any savings at all,[20] mainly because they had not earned enough money. For a small number of migrants, the main reason for migration is not to make more money. If we add up the figures for expenditure and saving, it seems that the average income per month per migrant is about 550 yuan.

Working environment

Migrants as a group tend to be regarded as second-class labour, so their working environment merits particular attention. In this sub-section, the description of the working environment draws on migrants' own accounts of their situation. Their social and political positions were discussed, and welfare issues raised, including the role of the migrants' community in the cities.

Type of employer

Depending on ownership, there are several types of employer unit (*danwei*) in China, including state-owned unit, collective-owned unit,[21] private unit, jointly owned unit, shareholding unit, foreign-invested unit, and Hong Kong- or Taiwan-invested unit. There are many differences between various types of unit, such as in working conditions, welfare, requirement for *hukou* and other documents, contract length, and so on.

It is important to know what kind of unit a migrant is in. Of those interviewed, 46 per cent of the migrants were working in state-owned units (national level). Traditionally these units are more respectable than other kinds of units, especially in the coal-mining sector and related industries. At least in Shanxi, there is a tradition that state-owned coal and related industries recruit people directly from rural areas, partly because rural people normally work hard, and partly because urban people tend to prefer other job sectors. However, it should be noted that the majority of the migrants in the state-owned units are 'contract workers', who are different from 'formal workers'. This situation, with a high percentage of migrants working in state-owned units, is rather different from that in many cities in south China, where many rural migrants work in labour-intensive factories which are private units, jointly owned units, shareholding units, foreign-invested units, and Hong Kong- or Taiwan-invested units.

Collective-owned units in cities are also regarded as quite respectable if the job is on a relatively long-term contract. Thirty-one per cent of the migrants were in this category. However, if the level of the collective is low, say at village level (3 per cent of the migrants were in this category), a unit is a less sought-after employer because the financial resources and management system may not be stable. Nineteen per cent of the migrants were in private-owned units. In this kind of unit, everything is less standard. The wages can be very high or extremely low. For example, one 17-year-old boy worked for a private restaurant for more than 10 hours a day, and he got only 200 yuan per month plus board and lodging. In the same restaurant, another boy did the same job but his wage was 400 yuan per month.

Only one interviewed migrant worked in a foreign-invested unit, and none worked in other kinds of units. Given that the Chinese government strongly encourages investment from overseas, Taiwan, Hong Kong and Macao, especially in the west and central regions, it is expected that there may be more of these kinds of unit in Shanxi in the future.

Contract

With the increased number of migrant workers, legal standards for labour contracts have been introduced, such as the Labour Law of China and the Local Labour Law of Shanxi. According to the Labour Law of China, a written labour contract is needed, and this should include contract-allotted time, details of work, wages and payments, working environment and labour protection, medical insurance and welfare, procedures in the event of a breach of contract, and so on. The interview results showed that the migrants who were in state-owned units all had formal contracts. The contract period varied from one to five years. For the migrants in other kinds of units, some of them had oral contracts with contractors and some of them did not have any contract. For example, one migrant said that neither he nor his employer wanted to sign a contract because both sides are freer without one.

Working hours

The Labour Law of Shanxi stipulates that a working day should not be longer than eight hours and a working week should not be more than six days. Overtime must be on a voluntary basis, and must be paid at 150 per cent of the average daily wage. Also, work done between 11 p.m. to 6 a.m. or during holidays and weekends must be paid at 200 per cent of the average daily wage.

For a large number of migrants who earn their living as unskilled labour, standardised working hours are an unknown luxury (Breman, 1996). Of the migrants interviewed, although 98 per cent of them had fixed daily working hours, many of them worked longer. Fifty-two per cent of them worked 8 hours per day, 7.1 per cent of them worked less than 8 hours per day, and 41.3 per cent of them worked more than 8 hours per day; 8.2 per cent of them even worked more than 12 hours per day. Generally speaking, except in the state-owned units, the use of migrants' physical power is characterised by uncertain working hours per day. Their working time is calculated by day rather than by hours or by physical effort.

On the one hand, it seems that the long working hours in small-scale enterprises such as coal mines or brick factories are typical of employment practices in family workshops. Some employers give migrant workers no choice but to work 12 hours per day. On the other hand, the production methods have the characteristics of modern industry. Everyone is held responsible for his or her own productivity in the piecework system. In these labour-intensive industries, payment for rural migrants is normally based on piecework. A migrant worker who formerly worked in the Shanghai Bike Assembly Factory said that what he did was to keep the machine going. If he could not match the speed, he would lose his bonus.

It is interesting to note that 51.7 per cent of the migrants said they were willing to work longer for more money. They said that they were born to suffer a life of poverty. In fact, most of them were unaware of their rights and the existence of the labour law. The majority of them just tolerated whatever working conditions they had because they did not want to lose their jobs by confronting their employers or complaining to the local labour bureau.

Indeed, keeping the job secure and getting more money are the major reason migrants often work longer than eight hours. To investigate the relationship between working hours and income, a correlation analysis was made, in terms of both the highest and the lowest income. The results are shown in Figures 5.10 and 5.11. It can be seen that there is indeed a tendency for income to increase with increasing working hours. However, the correlation coefficient is very low.

Working environment

Although there are regulations governing the working environment and workers' safety, not every factory takes the regulations seriously. There are regular inspections from the local labour bureau, but the inspection is often ineffective. One reason is that the regular inspection is normally conducted during official working hours, and overtime work and the safety problem during this period are often ignored. Another reason is that some employers show only the positive side to the inspectors by well-prepared presentations.

Among the migrants interviewed, 78 per cent thought that their working environment was not good. This figure is rather high in comparison

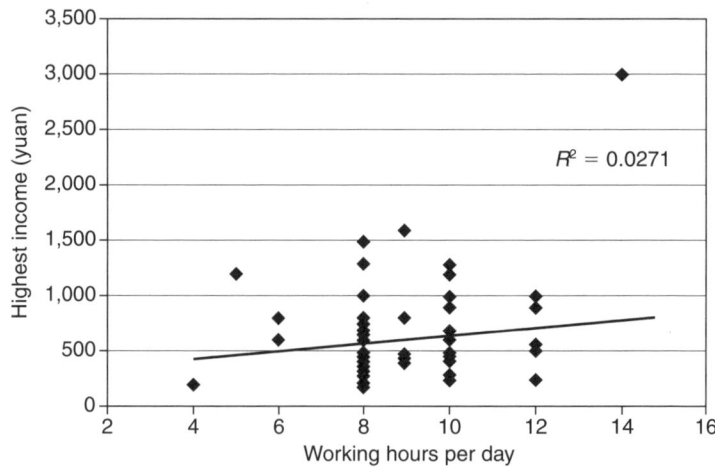

Figure 5.10 Correlation between hours worked per day and the highest income per month.

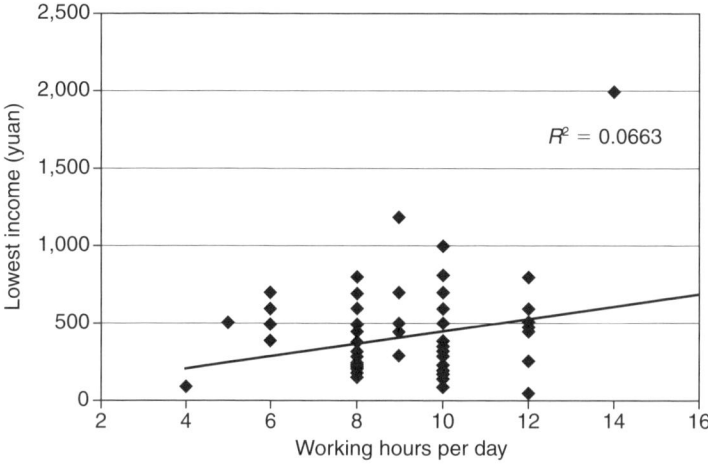

Figure 5.11 Correlation between hours worked per day and the lowest income per month.

with the general figure in China, 62 per cent (Zhou Q., 1997). Reasons given why workplace environment conditions are not considered good are: dangerous, 30 per cent; noisy, 26 per cent; dirty, 14 per cent; and tempera-ture too high or low, 8 per cent. Generally speaking, in the case study, the working environment in state-owned units was better than that in the other units.

Safety in coal mines is an important issue, especially for many migrants in Shanxi. Table 5.6 shows the number and distribution of accidents in coal mines in 1996, both in Shanxi and in China as a whole, and their causes (NBSC, 1997b). It is seen that the majority of accidents happened in collective-owned or private coal mines.

Table 5.6 Number and distribution of accidents in coal mines in 1996 and causes.

Type	Deaths in China	Deaths in Shanxi and causes					
		Total	*Gas*	*Collapse*	*Fire*	*Water*	*Others*
State-owned key coalmines	163	20	13	3	0	0	4
State-owned local coalmines	388	32	5	6	0	14	0
Collective-owned or private coalmines	2,129	183	91	43	14	20	15

Welfare and living conditions

Welfare is certainly an important issue for migrant workers. In China, this normally includes accident injury insurance, medical insurance, accommodation, pension, and so on. Since the socialist system is still dominant in China, formal workers still have their welfare contributions deducted directly from their income, although many workers may not be aware of this deduction. For migrant workers, therefore, the situation may become complicated. Also, welfare is a sign of social position.

Of the migrants interviewed, 37 per cent of them did not have any accident injury insurance, medical insurance or accommodation allowance. Of the rest, 50 per cent did have accident injury insurance, 8 per cent had accommodation allowance and 5 per cent had medical insurance.

Accident injury insurance

About half of the migrants had accident injury insurance, which is vital for some jobs, as mentioned previously. Some employers pay this to insurance companies. If an accident happens, the insurance company will deal with it directly. If no insurance company is involved, normally the employer will pay 50 per cent of the cost if a migrant worker is injured in an industrial accident. If the accident is fatal, the payment will depend on the individual agreement between the migrant and the employer.

Sometimes migrants are asked to pay their accident injury insurance premiums themselves. One migrant explained, 'I hand in 50 yuan per year to my mine for the insurance. I can claim 2,500–3,000 yuan if there is a serious injury, and 5,000 yuan if the injury causes disability.'

Medical insurance

Only 5 per cent of the migrants had medical insurance. This normally covers only serious illness. For those who do not have medical insurance, in some exceptional cases the employers pay a certain proportion of the medical expenses. The proportion varies from 10 per cent to 60 per cent. The proportion, which is negotiable in many cases, may depend on the actual cost. The majority of migrants have to pay for any medical treatment themselves. This could be a very heavy burden if expensive medical treatments are necessary. For example, Huang in Datong was sent to hospital because of a heart attack, and it cost him 2,000 yuan.

It should be mentioned that not every formal worker has full medical insurance either. Somebody working for a not very profitable enterprise may be in a similar situation to that of migrant workers.

Pensions

Only 16 per cent of the migrants had any retirement pension. In most cases, pension schemes can be regarded as a form of forced saving. Some employers deduct 500–1,000 yuan per year from migrant workers' income, and then pay them back when they leave or retire. If the contract is relatively long (*hetonggong*), a migrant may be treated the same as a formal worker in terms of their pension scheme. In this study, the average contract period for such migrants is 7.7 years.

Generally speaking, the pension system in China is changing from being work-unit based to society based. In this way, problems caused by the bad performance of individual work-units can be diminished. It seems that the change will also bring positive changes for migrants.

Accommodation

In China, formal workers normally have free accommodation from the work-unit, although this policy is changing. Only 34 per cent of the migrants interviewed had a right to free accommodation from their employers. For the remainder, their place of residence varied from temporary shed (38 per cent) to private accommodation (21 per cent) and 'others' (7 per cent), including staying with relatives or a fellow villager. This is a relatively new phenomenon, and will certainly affect the housing rental market in cities.

Living conditions are quite bad. Many migrants share a room with others. Among the migrants interviewed, fewer than 30 per cent of them live by themselves or with family. About 30 per cent of the migrants were sharing a room with more than five people.[22] The worst case seen in this study was that of 10 migrants sharing a room. Also, there were three cases of two migrants sharing a bed because they worked different hours.

Social and political position

Traditionally, migrants are portrayed as the lower class in a supposedly two-class urban society where the long-term residents, with urban *hukou*, are the privileged upper class who enjoy security, socialist medicine, almost free housing and heavily subsidised food and urban services. Such urban entitlements are unavailable to peasants, who are depicted as a large but implicitly undifferentiated group with little hope of breaking through the *hukou* barrier (Chan, 1996).

Migrants' community

In addition to their economic position and working conditions, social position is another very important issue for migrants (Solinger, 1993). Before the establishment of the People's Republic of China in 1949, various organisations for *laoxiang*[23] were very common, such as *huiguan* (guild hall), *tongxianghui* (*laoxiang* association) and *lianyihui* (get-together association). These organisations performed multiple functions that affected both state and society. Ever since the Qing Dynasty (1644–1911), Shanxi *tongxianghui* had been very powerful because many migrants from Shanxi had been extremely successful in the business and banking sector. Shanxi *tongxianghui*'s flag can be seen nearly everywhere across the big cities of the county.

Today's picture appears to be different. Rural migrants' networks are loosely structured, lacking any community organisation comparable to the earlier *tongxianghui* and *lianyihui*.[24] Ninety-nine per cent of the migrants interviewed did not belong to any such organisation, and 98 per cent of them indicated that there was no such organisation in the city where they were working. Individuals and small families are connected mainly through kinship, territorial and profession ties, without the support of any wider community. Overall, it seems that the social and political influence of sending areas is much less than that of the destinations.

Today's migrants in urban areas are politically powerless. The only organisation which can 'amplify' the migrants' voice is the workers' union[25] that exists in every working unit. Thirty-three per cent of the migrants interviewed were members of such unions. Unions are sometimes useful for helping with matters like welfare. However, their power and influence are much less than those of trade unions in Western countries. Instead of being independent organisations, unions in China are actually part of the work-unit's administrative infrastructure, and are indirectly led by the unit director.

As a consequence of rural–urban migration, the Chinese city is also taking on some of the features common to other Third World cities. Changes include the formation of migrant communities in both cities and suburbs (Davis *et al.*, 1995).

Who can help

The interviews included a question asking whom a migrant would turn to for help if they had difficulties. Nineteen people said that nobody could help. Only 30 per cent chose their employer. This is very different from the situation in Mao's time. It is also worth noting that only one migrant chose the unions, and none chose the local or home town government. In contrast, 51 people thought that friends are the most helpful.

Self-rating of status in cities

The migrants were asked their views about their social and economic position in comparison with city residents. Fifty people thought that their social position was lower than that of city residents, and 30 people thought that their economic position was lower. Only 36 people thought that they had the same social and economic status as city residents, and a mere 4 people thought they had higher economic status than city residents. Nobody thought that their social status was higher in the cities.

The results indicate that there is still a tendency for migrants to feel they are low-class people in the cities, although the situation is now much better than it was in Mao's time, when a city hukou definitely indicated that a person had a high social position. Certainly, some other factors, such as education level or vocational skills, also contribute to the social position of migrants.

Differences between migrants and formal workers

The interviews included a question about differences between formal workers and migrants. The result was that 28 people thought that there was no difference, but about 33 people thought that formal workers have a higher income and 35 people thought that formal workers have more stable working positions. Ten people thought that there would be a change in their working environment or social position if they became a formal worker. Overall, it seems that the effect of *hukou* status still exists, but is less important than it used to be.

Return to home village

Corresponding to the question put to former migrants who had returned (see Chapter 4), the current migrants were asked about what the opinion of other villagers would be if a migrant were to return to the village. By comparing the result in Chapter 4, it can be seen that current migrants were more positive about their situation if they returned than migrants who already had returned. For example, already returned migrants believed that other villagers thought that they could not find work in the cities, whereas 25 per cent of current migrants believed that other villagers would think they had returned because they had already earned enough money, and 43 per cent of them thought positively that villagers would treat their returning as normal – 'no view'. In contrast, for the current migrants, 20 per cent of them thought that villagers would not understand and 12 per cent of migrants believed that other villagers would think that they could not find a job in the city. These differences seem to suggest that current migrants may need to readjust to village life if they return.

City and village

The rural–urban migration influx has fundamentally changed the social, spatial and economic landscapes of the Chinese cities, making the urban scene much more varied, lively and dynamic, but less safe and orderly than it was during the Maoist era (Davin, 1996b). It is therefore interesting to investigate what migrants think about city and village life. Chapter 4 described the views of households in sending villages; this section analyses migrants' viewpoint.

General comparison between city and village

Table 5.7 shows the results from the migrants and the comparison with the other two groups, namely households with and without migrant members and overall rating of city and village life. Comparing these results with those in Chapter 4 shows that the overall rating of city life from migrants is similar to that from households with migrant members, and is lower than that from the households without migrants. This might be because migrants have more knowledge of the cities, and therefore tend to see more problems. Also, migrants' overall rating of village life is higher than the other groups'. A possible reason is that they miss their home villages.

Looking at the breakdown of detailed items, in comparison with households with migrant members, migrants gave higher scores to cities for shopping, family relationships, social welfare, power using and power of office, and lower scores for housing standards and labour intensity. To villages, migrants gave better scores than village households with migrant members for housing standards, food, family relationships, labour intensity and living standards, and gave lower scores for shopping and farmers' status.

The difference between migrants and the households without migrant members is much greater than that between migrants and the households with migrant members. Generally speaking, households without migrants gave much higher scores to cities in many aspects, such as housing standards, medical services, family relationships, relationships with neighbours, social security, income, labour intensity, and so on. To villages, in comparison with migrants, households without migrants gave lower scores for housing standards, income, labour intensity, personal motivation, and so on. As mentioned previously, an important reason for the difference is that migrants have a relatively deeper understanding of city life, and thus see more problems.

In general, from the migrants' viewpoint there are significant differences between cities and villages in terms of medical services, transport, shopping and education level. In these aspects, they give rather high scores to cities and very low scores to villages.

As to the general attitude to life, the results from migrants are shown in Table 5.8. The scoring system is the same as that in Chapter 4. From Table 5.8 it is seen that for the migrants, the overall score is 3.02 for the negative factors and 3.04 for the positive factors. These scores are considerably lower than those from the other two groups, namely households with and without migrants. Analysing the detailed items suggests that the overall

Table 5.7 Migrants' views on city and village life.[27]

Score of satisfaction	City						Village					
	Good 2	Normal 1	Bad 0	overall	Households with	Households without	Good 2	Normal 1	Bad 0	overall	Households with	Households without
Living standards	40.0	54.0	6.0	1.34	1.48	1.33	6.0	40.0	54.0	0.52	0.36	0.48
Housing standards	8.1	26.3	65.7	0.42	1.09	1.19	61.6	32.3	6.1	1.56	0.84	1.09
Adequate food and dress	30.0	68.0	2.0	1.28	1.39	1.44	13.0	57.0	30.0	0.83	0.30	0.67
Medical services	35.0	63.0	2.0	1.33	1.43	1.55	0.0	23.0	77.0	0.23	0.09	0.15
Transport	69.7	29.3	1.0	1.69	1.53	1.59	5.1	23.2	71.7	0.33	0.38	0.37
Shopping	66.0	33.0	1.0	1.65	1.34	1.47	1.0	19.0	80.0	0.021	0.41	0.37
Environmental pollution	3.0	22.0	75.0	0.28	0.40	0.76	51.0	43.0	6.0	1.45	1.59	1.77
Family relationships	25.0	60.0	15.0	1.10	0.92	1.41	36.0	54.0	10.0	1.26	1.05	1.36
Neighbours	20.0	57.0	23.0	0.97	0.93	1.35	42.0	53.0	5.0	1.37	1.24	1.54
Education level	79.0	20.0	1.0	1.78	1.79	1.88	0.0	19.0	81.0	0.19	0.01	0.10
Social security	8.0	28.0	64.0	0.44	0.30	0.70	61.0	32.0	7.0	1.54	1.61	1.73
Opportunity	37.0	57.0	6.0	1.31	1.33	1.29	4.0	39.0	57.0	0.47	0.51	0.32
Social welfare	38.0	43.0	19.0	1.19	1.03	1.36	2.0	24.0	74.0	0.28	0.20	0.18
Power using	10.0	70.0	20.0	0.90	0.42	0.88	8.0	28.0	64.0	0.44	0.48	0.64
Income	24.0	65.0	11.0	1.13	1.11	1.72	7.0	39.0	54.0	0.53	0.46	0.32
Labour intensity	21.2	47.5	31.3	0.90	1.10	1.51	51.5	33.3	15.2	1.36	0.81	0.59
Farmer status	1.0	29.0	70.0	0.31	0.09	0.30	45.0	50.0	5.0	1.40	1.53	1.41
Power of office	16.0	49.0	35.0	0.81	0.41	0.89	2.0	32.0	66.0	0.36	0.77	0.68
Personal motivation	29.0	61.0	10.0	1.19	1.13	1.37	8.0	44.0	48.0	0.60	0.50	0.35
Overall	29.5	46.4	24.1	1.05	1.01	1.26	21.3	36.0	42.7	0.79	0.69	0.76

Table 5.8 General attitude to life: opinion from migrants. The scales in the table are: 5, strongly agree; 4, agree; 2, disagree; 1, strongly disagree.[28]

	Migrants					*Households with*	*Households without*
Weighting scale	Score	5	4	2	1	Score	Score
Negative factors							
Village is very poor, but happy to stay	2.16	11	15	27	47	2.24	2.77
More sons, more happy	2.85	12	27	56	5	3.83	3.83
Education is less important than money	2.64	14	24	36	26	2.83	2.41
Home is better than city	2.76	20	21	33	26	4.12	3.81
Rhe old people are right	2.68	10	26	50	14	2.46	2.97
Government will help poverty relief	2.12	6	13	49	32	1.62	2.21
Cadres are powerful	4.38	41	53	1	1	3.93	3.80
Following others is good	3.67	28	43	26	3	3.95	3.70
Current social environment is bad	2.98	13	32	50	5	3.65	3.35
Rich are richer, poor are poorer	3.94	52	25	11	12	4.08	3.81
Overall score of negative factors	3.02					3.27	3.26
Positive factors							
Moving is positive	4.15	43	45	8	4	4.55	3.77
Can do better if have a business	2.16	4	13	61	22	3.46	2.38
Moving reduces poverty	3.12	15	35	47	3	4.35	3.20
Social environment changing quickly	3.70	22	53	23	2	3.97	3.73
Try to do one's best	2.06	7	12	42	39	3.28	2.53
Overall score of positive factors	3.04					3.92	3.12

attitude of the migrants tends to be positive, but they also see the negative side of migration through their own bitter experience. For example, most of them strongly agree that moving is positive, but many believe that it is not that effective to do one's best because there are many other factors.

Summary

Based on the results of questionnaires and interviews, a series of analyses has been made of the characteristics and current situation of migrants, as well as the effects of migration on destinations. In the following, the results are summarised.

Migrants in cities

In recent years, there has been a great increase in migrant numbers in Shanxi. Typically, migrants are male, young and single, and their education level is higher than that of other villagers. Generally speaking, migrants tend to find work in certain 'low-class' job sectors.

The migration and feedback channels have been investigated. It has been found that the main reason for migration is to earn money, but also, a considerable proportion of people leave the countryside because they want to learn more about the outside world. The decision to migrate is mostly made by a migrant him- or herself. The migrants have close links with their villages, and the majority of them send back money and information. Nearly all of them go back at least once a year.

Another important aspect is the urban control and adjustment system. Most of the migrants found jobs through friends and relatives. Labour contractors and relevant governmental organisations are also helpful. Government policies and the economic performance of enterprises are also important factors influencing the job market for migrants. A set of documents is required for them to work in cities, and a considerable amount of money is needed for the whole process. This may well affect the course of migration. Training is quite useful for finding and carrying out jobs, but a more efficient system is still needed.

As far as plans for the future go, most of the migrants did not want to go back. If they do go back, most of them do not want to do farming work again.

For most of the migrants, their monthly income was around 550 yuan. This is not bad in comparison with normal city residents. It is interesting to note that there is no high correlation between the length of time since first migrating and income. Changing jobs also does not bring significant increases in income. The main items of expenditure are not accommodation and bills, but food, clothing and travel. About 50 per cent of the migrants have savings, and the average amount saved per month is 280 yuan.

Working conditions are a big issue. Migrants' working hours are normally long and, moreover, longer hours do not necessarily bring in a higher income. The physical environment of the workplace is generally bad.

Welfare provision is not good for migrants. Better systems are needed for insurance, medical services, social security, pensions, and other benefits. About 40 per cent of migrants are living in temporary sheds. Most of them share a room with others.

The social position of migrants is still low in comparison with city residents, although this has improved because of their economic position. It seems that today's migrants have not had the opportunity to establish their permanent roots in the cities or to acquire a more legitimate social status in the cities than that of their predecessors.

The existence of sizeable migrant communities in the cities is still a relatively new phenomenon and their legitimacy there remains uncertain. Few of them are totally optimistic about their future in the cities or have made permanent arrangements to stay, despite the fact that many of them have been in the cities for several years. In fact, they are best seen as long-term sojourners rather than settlers. However, it seems that current migrants might need to make considerable readjustments if they were ever to return to village life.

Migrants do have different views from other villagers regarding general comparisons between city and village life. Migrants tend to give lower satisfaction scores to cities. This might be because they have more direct experience of cities, and therefore tend to see more problems.

The effects of migration on destinations

Rural–urban migration plays an important role in the development of urban areas. Migrants are very important for the construction industry in their receiving areas. They also play an indispensable part in the social services of cities. Without them, most cities cannot move. On the other hand, media reports have tended to see migrants in a negative light, linking them with such problems as increasing crime rates, disorderly (*luan*) street scenes and disregard for family planning (Davin, 1996b).

It should be realised that the selection of jobs and living places by migrants is rational, and once this rationality is accepted, it can be seen that there is a great need for innovation in institutions and socio-economic organisation. Most of the negative aspects of labour migration are the result of distorted policies. The key to turning labour migration into a positive element in economic development lies in whether or not the government can adapt to the inevitable trends in economic development and social structure, meet the requirement for labour migration, guide such migration according to its development, and provide the necessary management and services (Cai, 1998).

The best-known and most influential theoretical model of labour migration, Todaro's model, indicates that the extent and rate of migration vary according to the probability of employment; that is, the more job opportunities a city provides, the larger the scale of rural–urban migration. This appears to be the situation in this study.

6 To what extent can rural–urban migration resolve rural poverty?

Every year, there are enormous numbers of migrants moving from rural to urban areas. This tendency, which started in some provinces in south China, has now extended to other parts of China. There is no doubt that labour mobility is an important factor in the socio-economic development of China. In this study, existing theories and case studies on migration and poverty have been reviewed; the current situation of poverty and internal migration in China has been discussed; and a case study has been carried out in Shanxi, a typical province in central China. Based on the results in the previous chapters, this chapter systematically analyses the causes and effects of rural–urban migration in China, especially Shanxi, as well as the role of rural–urban migration in resolving rural poverty.

Significance of the study

The economic reforms in China have widened the differences between poor and rich, and also stimulated internal migration. Migration has been mainly spontaneous, rather than prompted by government policies. Although there are many different opinions about whether internal migration should be encouraged, controlled or stopped, it seems that the government cannot, and should not, stop internal migration.

The review of previous work in Chapter 2 suggests that although some investigations have been carried out regarding internal migration and poverty in China, it appears that the assessment of the economic and social effects of migration has been insufficient. The effects of internal migration on destination areas, and to what extent rural–urban migration can reduce poverty, are still not clear. Many social problems caused by internal migration and increasing differences between rural and urban areas need to be further investigated. It appears that in some areas, government-provided poverty relief is less helpful in ending poverty than resorting to migration. It would be effective if certain policies could be introduced in combination with anti-poverty projects. In addition to the above, the literature review shows that there has been very limited research on the provinces of central China, where the economic development after the reform has been slower than in many southern provinces, and thus poverty is becoming significant here, particularly in rural areas.

The case study in this research has contributed to the limited research to date. Based on the survey and intensive interviews in three poor counties in a poor region, Shanxi, a detailed analysis has been made of the socio-economic causes and consequences of rural–urban migration. This can be regarded as an important addition to previous investigations into internal migration in China. Moreover, this case study is at a micro-sociological scale, which has not received enough attention in previous research. In addition to the survey carried out in villages from which migrants came, a two-ended approach has been made interviewing migrants in their destination areas. This is evidently the first study of rural–urban migration in China to take an in-depth two-ended approach.

The abundant primary information gathered from the semi-structured interviews not only describes rural–urban migration in some detail, but also delineates the socio-economic consequences of rural–urban migration at a sociological level from different perspectives. The experience of Shanxi not only illustrates the effectiveness and deficiencies of rural–urban migration and to what extent rural–urban migration can resolve rural poverty, but also sheds light on the applicability of various Western migration theories in explaining the development of Shanxi. Most of such first-hand information is unlikely to be revealed either by macro-statistics or by casual observation.

The comprehensive database resulting from the case study will provide a significant resource for basic research and could also influence policy research. It has been used to illustrate the changes in Shanxi's socio-economic development through the development of industries and poverty alleviation. The database is also useful for analysing other effects which may be caused by rural–urban migration, such as the development of infrastructure, the changing nature of production factors, changes in standards of living, the mentality of local people and migrants, and the increasing geographical differentiation of economic growth.

The review of other general investigations of migration and poverty has shown that many of the theories, although developed a number of years ago, and based on case studies of Western countries and some other developing countries, still offer very useful insights into the current situation in China. In this study, these theories have been helpful in looking at the effects of internal migration on economic and social developments from both a panoramic and a historic viewpoint.

Social-economic effects of migration

Effects on sending areas

The results of the village interviews have demonstrated that both subjectively and objectively, there are systematic differences between households with and without migrant members. These have affected decision-making about whether or not to migrate. Objective aspects include demographic and geographic conditions. The former refers to the number of people per household, the percentage of old people and young children in the household, overall labour capability, education level, and so on. The latter includes land quality, distance from towns, markets, train or bus stations, and so on. Subjective aspects include attitudes towards doing 'low-class' work, reasons for choosing a destination, and general views on migration and living standards of city residents. However, it is noted that many households without migrant members would like to be able to send at least one of the family away to work in the cities. This would seem to indicate a tendency towards the likelihood of further migration.

The remittances from migrants are normally 2,000–4,000 yuan (US$245–490) per year. This is considerably higher than incomes from agriculture and related work. The majority of remittances come from coal mining and related industries, as well as from construction, manufacturing and service sectors. The use of remittances is limited to some basic uses, such as housebuilding or house refurbishing, everyday expenses, and agricultural materials. This is different from the situation in some regions in south China, where remittances have played an important role in the development of rural enterprises.

Migration has brought marked changes in social and economic activities in the sending villages. Nearly all the households with migrants have surplus money, whereas only about 50 per cent of the households without migrant members. Labour structure has also been affected. Most women have extra work, in both farming and domestic work. Since many households are closely related, this is the case whether or not a household member has migrated. Many children in households with migrant members must work after school rather than play or study. There is a tendency for the transfer of land between households with and without migrants.

The families of the majority of the migrants in this study are still in their villages of origin. The majority of the migrants are working within the province, and many migrants return home quite often. Such a link has certainly affected social life in the sending areas. It is interesting to note that the returned migrants are not in a different economic or social class from the other villagers. Most of the returned migrants use their money for housebuilding or house refurbishing, not for investment in rural enterprises. This is again different from the situation in some regions in south China. However, many of the returned migrants have positive plans for their future, which indicates the potential impact of migration.

It is important to note that most of the migrants have a higher education level than other villagers. This means that rural–urban migration may cause a 'brain drain' effect in the sending areas. In other words, the average education level may become lower after migration, and this may affect rural development. However, it seems that such effects could be compensated for by the input of migrants returning or visiting, given the close link between the sending and the receiving areas.

Overall, the case study shows that in Shanxi, rural–urban migration has played a positive role in the development of sending areas. However, unlike some regions in south China, migration in Shanxi still has a significant feature of closed poverty. To break this poverty cycle of migration, it appears that it would be helpful to encourage migrants to work in the cities and small towns, although this would be difficult to achieve in the short term.

Effects on destination areas

There is no doubt that rural–urban migrants have caused, and will continue to cause, significant socio-economic changes in their destinations. Through this case study, we now have a clearer picture for Shanxi, a typical province in central China.

Generally speaking, migrants are working in 'low-class' job sectors. The reason for migration is mainly to earn money, but also, considerable numbers of people move to the cities because they want to learn more about the outside world. A set of documents is required for them to work in a city, and considerable amounts of money are needed for the whole process. This may well affect the migration process. Training is quite useful for finding work, but a more efficient system is still needed.

The monthly income is around 550 yuan (US$68) for most of the migrants. This is not bad in comparison with normal city residents. About 50 per cent of the migrants have savings, and the average amount saved is 280 yuan (US$34) per month. Their working hours are normally long; however, the long working hours do not necessarily bring in a higher income. The physical environment of the workplace is generally bad. Welfare provision is not good for migrants. Better systems for insurance, medical services, social security, pensions and other benefits are needed. About 40 per cent of them are living in temporary sheds. Most of them share a room with others.

The social position of migrants is still low in comparison with city residents, although this has improved because of their economic position. It seems that today's migrants have not had the opportunity to establish their permanent roots in the cities or to acquire a more legitimate social status in the cities than their predecessors. The existence of suitable migrant communities in the cities is still a relatively new phenomenon and their legitimacy there remains uncertain. They are best seen as long-term sojourners rather than settlers.

Hukou is certainly an important issue for migrants. It is an important reason for their low social position in their destinations, and their weak position in competing for jobs with city residents. The future of migrants in the cities depends primarily on the *hukou* system no matter whether they are temporary, long-term or circular migrants. It is possible that the tightly controlled *hukou* system may be abolished in the near future. Instead, a new household registration law has been discussed by the State Council, and such a system would allow qualified peasants to move to the built-up areas of county-level cities and designated towns, where they will be registered as urban residents. Nevertheless, migration to big cities like Beijing, Tianjin and Shanghai will continue to be strictly controlled. This study suggests that the current *hukou* system does not significantly affect the volume of rural migrants in Shanxi, since most of the migrants are working in coal mines and construction teams in Taiyuan and some small and county-level cities in the surrounding areas. There is a trend towards a slowdown in the rate of increase of numbers of migrants to the big cities because of saturation of employment and administrative restrictions, whereas the rate is forecast to become higher in smaller cities.

Although media reports have tended to see migrants in a negative light, rural–urban migration does play an important role in the development of destination areas. Migrants are very important for the construction industry in their receiving areas. They also play an indispensable part in the social services of cities. Without them, most cities cannot run. It seems that most of the negative aspects of labour migration are the result of distorted policies. As indicated by Cai (1998), the key to turning labour migration into a positive element in socio-economic development lies in whether or not the government can adapt to the inevitable trend in economic development and social structure, and provide the necessary management and services.

The Todaro model indicates that the extent and rate of migration vary according to the probability of employment – that is, the more job opportunities a city provides, the larger the scale of rural–urban migration. This appears to be the situation in this study. However, an important phenomenon in current Chinese cities is the 'job suspension'[1] of many state-owned enterprises, and this certainly affects rural–urban migration. On the one hand, this will affect the income level of migrants, because these 'suspended' workers' income is often used as a reference level. On the other hand, the 'suspended' workers are encouraged to find other jobs, and some of them tend to go to the job sectors formerly dominated by migrants.

It appears that the pressure on urban unemployment is mounting. The country's registered unemployed figure stands at 6.8 million, 4.5 per cent of the urban labour force (Ministry of Labour and Social Security, 2002). Since many suspended workers are not included among the unemployed, some labour researchers have estimated that the country's real urban jobless rate may have hit the alarming level of 7 to 10 per cent and may continue to rise. This oversupply of labourers is expected to peak in the next few years, with 12–13 million people entering the job market each year and only about 8 million job opportunities created annually. Perhaps if China maintains its current economic growth rate at above 7 per cent, the central government will be able to keep the registered urban jobless rate within 5 per cent until 2005. The service sector, small and medium-sized companies, and collectively and privately owned businesses have been called upon to play major roles in creating jobs by the government. Clearly, this situation will affect the volume of rural–urban migration.

The Chinese government has invested a large amount of financial support in improving the unemployment insurance system[2] and, at the same time, strengthening the system of a minimum cost of living for urban residents. The aim is that all eligible poor urban residents will have their essential needs met. The implementation of a minimum cost of living for urban residents may lead to a slowing down of the flow of rural–urban migrants seeking to settle down in small cities and towns, since local governments may need to provide financial support to those new rural–urban migrants whose incomes are below the new urban minimum cost of living, to enable them to become urban residents.

More importantly, observers have noted an increasingly impoverished urban population, and large number of rural–urban migrants might pose a serious potential threat to social stability, a thorny issue that calls for more painstaking efforts to deal with it properly.

To what extent can migration resolve rural poverty

Migration has an enormous impact on some villages and urban areas. Moreover, migration tells us about important components of development and welfare. Many migrants move in response to changes in conditions, either in their village of origin or at the place of destination. Most such relevant conditions concern the level, reward and duration of agricultural income – earning opportunities, the intra-village distribution of land and the main source of such opportunities. Compared with other economic activities, the reduction of rural–urban inequality and intra-rural inequality are probably a better cure for rural poverty.

There are two major issues preventing the development of rural areas of China. One is the urgent need to find jobs for rural surplus labour and the other is the slowness of the rise of farmers' income.

According to the case study and the analysis of China's circumstances in general, it seems that surplus labour in rural areas will be a long-term phenomenon. The country had a total of 482 million rural labourers at the end of 2001, with 328 million of them engaged in agricultural production. That number is expected to increase by over 8 million a year over the next five years. It is estimated that about one-third of China's rural labourers – 150 million surplus rural labourers – are not fully employed, and from 2001 to 2010 there will be 63.5 million new rural labourers. In addition, joining the World Trade Organization (WTO) will result in the loss at least 20 million jobs in agriculture. Major grain-, cotton- and oil-producing areas will be the worst affected because all of these are sectors with a large concentration of rural labour. This will be an important challenge for the government.

There are three major options for absorbing rural surplus labour: the agricultural sector in rural areas, the non-agricultural sector in rural areas, and the urban areas.

In the agricultural sector, adjusting agriculture is now one of the government's most pressing tasks. The policy readjustment is set to focus on improving agricultural and rural economic structures and increasing the income of farmers, while sharpening the market competitiveness of the country's farm produce. In the short term, it would be unrealistic to underestimate the negative effects on rural employment and the incomes of Chinese farmers of the country's entry to the WTO. However, in a five-year period after China's accession to the WTO, the agricultural sector will trim a large number of jobs. The major reasons will be competition on prices and competition on the quality of agricultural products.

China has no comparative advantages in grain production because of higher costs and low quality. Both the production costs and retail prices of China's grain and the majority of other agricultural products are higher than the average in the world market, and during the next two decades they are likely to stay at this relatively expensive level. In improving productivity and quality, China has shifted the focus from quantity to quality agricultural products and made marked progress in optimising its agricultural structure. In response to emerging market opportunities, the acreage reserved for cash and fodder crops increased by 30.6 per cent (6 million hectares) in 2000, compared to 1998. An area of 16.7 million hectares of the country's rice paddies – more than half of the country's total – are producing top-grade strains. However, it will take a long time for China to collect its small landholdings together to build a large-scale agricultural economy. For the foreseeable future, the majority of Chinese farmers will continue to concentrate their efforts on getting relatively high yields from plots of lands. Labour-intensive agricultural products, such as vegetables and horticultural products, may fare somewhat better in the short term, but will face equally difficult challenges in the long term. Currently, the government plans to fully exploit labour-intensive industries such as animal husbandry and aquaculture to create more job opportunities for farmers and to increase their income. Overall, joining the WTO will bring structural changes to agriculture and many other business sectors based on agriculture.

Guaranteeing the steady growth of jobs in rural enterprises is very important. The nation's village and township enterprises currently employ 128 million rural workers and are expected to provide about 10 million job openings for the country's rural surplus labourers between 2001 and 2005. The 10th Five-Year Development Plan for Township Enterprises states that the number of employees in the country's township enterprises is expected to hit 135 million by 2005, with annual increases of 2 million. The rapid development of township enterprises, which contribute up to 30 per cent of China's gross domestic product (GDP), has been an important force in solving two tricky issues for China: the slowness of the rise of farmers' income and the need to find jobs for the excess rural labour force.

Farmers' net income from township and village enterprises was 29.9 per cent of the average net income per capita in 1996, and this figure increased significantly to about 34 per cent in 1999 (Ministry of Agriculture, 2001).

However, the future of rural enterprises is uncertain. The development of village and township enterprises is hampered by poor product quality, outmoded technology, serious pollution problems, difficulty in getting loans, and illicit fees levied against them. In accordance with China's industrial and environmental protection policies, a large number of small-township steel mills, coal mines and cement plants are being shut down. Furthermore, many rural enterprises are still not able to compete with state-owned enterprises on an equal footing. Government should consolidate input into township enterprises, while the enterprises should speed up their industrial adjustment, branch out into the service sector, optimise and improve secondary industry, and speed up the development of primary industry.

Small cities and towns are developing quickly, along with the Chinese government's positive policy on accelerating urbanisation. Urbanisation could play a decisive role in stimulating economic growth and domestic demand. A 1 per cent increase in urbanisation annually usually adds three percentage points to economic growth. It is forecast that urbanisation levels will reach 45 per cent by 2010. Furthermore, the construction of small cities and towns is very important for providing job opportunities for surplus labourers from poor regions, allowing more rural labourers to move from traditional agricultural production to manufacturing and the tertiary sector. The tertiary sector, including service industries, now accounts for only 32 per cent of China's GDP, compared with 60–70 per cent in developed countries. The development of small cities and towns would be an important step in the structural reform of rural employment. In the future, China needs to get more people out of the countryside and into big cities like Beijing and Shanghai. This is a fundamental way to increase farmers' incomes.

This study suggests that rural–urban migration offers the most potential in trying to resolve the problem of rural surplus labour and results in a rapid increase in farmers' cash income all over the country. It has been reported that from 1997 to 2000, the annual average income from agricultural production decreased from 1092 yuan to 600 yuan per capita. Meanwhile, the average annual income from rural migrants working in the cities increased from 512 yuan to 700 yuan per capita (NBSC, 2002a).

This study also suggests that the pressure on the whole ecological system can be diminished if the consumption of resources needed for basic agricultural production is transferred out of the villages. It has been predicted that if 200 million farmers left their farms to live and work in cities and towns, 1.2 million hectares of farmland could be saved (NBSC, 2002a). The country's sustainable development strategy in poor regions will significantly benefit from rural–urban migration. Furthermore, rural–urban migration could help to reduce rural population growth rates, while increasing incomes and consumption rates, and improving farmers' living standards. It is calculated that in next 15 years, a 30 per cent reduction in the rural population alone could enhance rural incomes per capita by 30 per cent (NBSC, 1999).

The case study shows that a high level of emigration from a village is intimately associated with unequal distribution of resources, such as quality of land and availability of drinking water. As to the effect of land, it seems that any single-factor analysis of land-based determinants of migration is inadequate. Moreover, because landholdings have become individualised and codified in tenured systems, even for those who have migrated to small cities and towns, land distribution can be a particularly potent force in explaining migration patterns. As to the type of migrants, it seems that the migration flow tends to consist of both rich, educated villagers and poor people. However, usually it is the poor but not the very poorest who move out from the villages.

Central China is a very important region in terms of the relationship between migration and poverty. Taking the central province of Shanxi as an example, this study reveals the significance of rural–urban migration for poverty alleviation. Rural–urban migration is a direct and quick method of alleviating poverty:

1   By reducing surplus labour in the villages, the efficiency of agricultural production can be increased, and thus, overall incomes become higher.
2   Migrants bring back money as well as increased knowledge, alternative techniques and new attitudes. This is also important for poverty alleviation.

Unlike in some regions in southern China, in Shanxi the effects of migration are still at an initial stage, mainly in terms of some basic requirements like housing and everyday expenses. The major reasons are:

1   The income from migrants is relatively lower in Shanxi than elsewhere in China because migration takes place predominantly within the province rather than to the east coast.
2   This wave of migration in Shanxi began about five to ten years later than that in some other regions in south China, and a certain housebuilding development period is required.

3   Shanxi is relatively enclosed geographically and thus offers fewer opportunities for the development of rural enterprises and businesses.

The study of Shanxi also suggests that the work by the local governments on helping and supporting rural–urban migration has been insufficient. The government should promote training to expand farmers' work skills and their ability to adapt to the market economy, and should also help in the establishment of intermediate agencies to help farmers find jobs in the service sector in the cities. The following recommendations for action summarise what the study found would be useful, indeed necessary, developments in government poverty alleviation work:

1   Local governments should investigate the working sector, regional distribution and general situation of current migrants so that better guidance can be given to future migrants.
2   They should establish a labour database, including the number of surplus labourers, the sex ratio, education level, job opportunities, and so on. This would be useful for potential employers.
3   As a general rule, it is more efficient to find a suitable (easy to enter) rather than the best (in terms of payment) market for rural surplus labour. Also, it would be useful to develop and improve the existing 'labour base' for rural surplus labour.
4   Greater attention must be paid to welfare provision.

In conclusion, this study indicates that in China's poor regions, rural–urban migration is an effective way of resolving rural poverty, especially as a way of quickly increasing peasants' cash income. Together with other strategies such as cutting agricultural taxes and various fees, developing rural enterprises and applying administrative decentralisation, rural–urban migration will positively affect the economic and social development in the sending areas and destination areas.

Appendix

Questionnaires and discussion outlines used in the case study (English version)

A.1 Questionnaire for households with migrant members

_____ Province _____ County _____ Village
Household number _____ Name of interviewee _____ Date of interview

I Descriptive data concerning study households

1 Household members

Name	Relationship to household head	Sex	Age	Marital status	Education level	Occupation	Current place of residence	Physical labour capability		
								Strong	Weak	None

2 Landholdings

Type of land	From collective	Transferred out	Transferred in	Duration of use	Soil quality			
					Very good	Good	Not good	Poor
Cultivated land (*mu*)								
Forestry land (*mu*)								
Uncultivated land (*mu*)								
Water (*mu*)								

3 Agricultural and other income in the previous year

Source of income	Total income (yuan)	Income within the township (yuan)
Farming		
Husbandry and forestry		
Labour output (hire)		
Others		

4 Agricultural and other expenditure in the previous year

Expenditure item	Total expenditure (yuan)	Expenditure within the township (yuan)
Farming		
Husbandry and forestry		
Hiring in contract labour		
Others		

5 Income from migrant member(s)'s wages in the previous year

Sector	Income (yuan)			
	Within township	Within county	Within province	Outside province
Coal				
Manufacturing				
Construction				
Transport				
Trading				
Services				
Other non-agricultural				

6 Other income last year

Item	Poverty relief fund	Collective bonus	Friends and relatives	Others
Income (yuan)				

7 Loans last year

Source	Loan (yuan)
Bank	
Village collective	
Private	
Others	

8 Which children are the most important?

	Importance	Reasons			
		Family name	Labour	Education	Others
Sons					
Daughters					
All					

II Migration details

1 Situation when the migrant left the village:
   (1) Alone; (2) couple; (3) whole family; (4) others.
2 Reason for choosing the migrant:
   (1) Sex; (2) age; (3) marriage status; (4) educational level; (5) experience (in army or business); (6) experience in migration; (7) others.
3 Reason for choosing the current destination:
   (1) More opportunities; (2) with relatives or friends; (3) organised by local government; (4) organised by labour contractor; (5) factory recruitment; (6) others.
4 Total remittances last year (cash plus presents, sent and brought back)_____ yuan.

5   Presents they gave to the family last year:
(1) Food; (2) clothes; (3) jewellery; (4) electrical applicances; (5) goods for everyday use; (6) others.

6   How did the migrant send back cash and presents?
(1) By post; (2) by him/herself; (3) brought back by friends; (4) others.

7   How do you spend the remittances?
(1) Building or refurbishing house; (2) buying production materials, such as chemical fertiliser; (3) everyday expenses; (4) investment for factory or business; (5) children's education; (6) others.

8   Migrants' income in comparison with that of normal villagers:
(1) Higher; (2) same; (3) lower; (4) don't know.

9   Communication methods with migrants:
(1) Telephone; (2) letter; (3) oral message by friends; (4) others.

10 The migrant(s) come home every _____ months, and normally during:
(1) Holiday (spring festival not included); (2) when work in the city is not busy; (3) when there is something to deal with at home; (4) agricultural work is busy.

11 In which situation would you not want the migrant work away from the village again?
(1) Earned sufficient money; (2) having difficulties away from home village; (3) need labour at home; (4) Miss each other; (6) others.

12 Is there any change in land use rights after migration?
(1) No; (2) yes, if so, what change? _____.

13 Is there more work after migration?
(1) Yes; (2) no.

14 Change in life after migration:
(1) Higher living standards; (2) more information; (3) better education for children; (4) everybody has work to do; (5) more work for women and the old; (6) lack of people to look after children.

15 Changes relating to agricultural labour structure after migration:
(1) Similar to the co-operation in the old-style production team; (2) co-operation between friends and relatives; (3) hiring labour; (4) transferring land; (5) others.

16 Change in living standards after migration:
(1) Much better; (2) slightly better; (3) slightly worse; (4) much worse; (5) no change.

17 Is there any work that cannot be done because of migration?
(1) No; (2) yes, if so, what? _____.

III *Attitudes to migration*

18 How many markets do you go to regularly? _____
How far is the farthest one? _____ km
How far is the nearest one? _____ km

19 Distance from the nearest bus or train station. _____ km

20 What is your opinion of the migrants who come here to work from south China in comparison with local people?
(1) Bear hardships; (2) more migration experience; (3) brave; (4) more stratagems; (5) don't know.

21 What would you do if there were a factory nearby?
(1) Try to work there; (2) go there to have a shower, see film or see doctor, if possible; (3) do some small-capital business; (4) try to send son or daughter to work there.

22 If there were an opportunity for you to go to the cities to be a pedlar, roadside shoe-repairer, rubbish collector, domestic help worker, what would you think?
(1) Don't want to do it; (2) dare not go because not familiar with cities; (3) yes, if no skill is needed; (4) yes, if more income; (5) it may be difficult because there are already too many people.

23 Where do you get information about agricultural products, prices etc.?
(1) Televison, radio and newspaper; (2) local friends and relatives; (3) friends and relatives in cities; (4) local officials; (5) get information by oneself.

24 Do you have any surplus money?
(1) Yes; (2) no.

25 If you have surplus money, how do you spend it?
(1) Save it in the bank; (2) build and refurbish house; (3) children's education; (4) marriage; (5) business; (6) others.

26 Are you willing to borrow money to extend your family economy?
(1) No;
(2) If yes, maximum amount: 500–1,000 yuan
                              1,001–2,000 yuan
                              2,001–3,000 yuan
                              over 3,000 yuan.

27 Are you willing to spend money to learn a skill?
(1) No;
(2) If yes, maximum amount below 500 yuan
500–1,000 yuan
over 1,000 yuan.

IV Satisfaction with city and village life

	City			Village		
	good	normal	bad	good	normal	bad
Living standards						
Housing standards						
Adequate food and clothing						
Medical services						
Transport						
Shopping						
Environmental pollution						
Family relationships						
Neighbours						
Education level						
Social security						
Opportunity for further education and jobs						
Social welfare						
Power using (i.e. official corruption or officials' misuse of power)						
Income level						
Labour intensity						
Farmer status						
Power of office (i.e. administrative control)						
Environment for personal motivation						

V General attitude to life[1]

(The following are some people's view of life. Please indicate your opinion.)

	Strongly agree	Agree	Disagree	Strongly disagree
We are very poor here, but we are quite happy.				
Moving a tree will kill it, but moving people is always positive.				
More sons, more happiness.				
School education is not important if one can make money.				
Even though the standard of living is higher in cities, home is better.				
If I had an opportunity to run a business, I could do it well.				
You will have trouble if you don't listen to the old people.				
If there is a migrant in the household, the whole family will not be poor.				
Poverty is not a problem. The government will help, anyway.				
The world is changing so quickly that I cannot follow the changes.				
I will try even if I fail.				
Officials are very powerful.				
It is always correct to follow others.				
The social environment is becoming worse nowadays.				
The rich are becoming richer, and the poor are becoming poorer.				

VI *Questions for women and children*

28 (Women) Do you have more farming and domestic work to do since many migrants left the village?
(1) Yes. There is more (a) farming work; (b) domestic work; (c) looking after children and elderly; (d) others.
(2) No. The work is being done by (a) parents and other family members; (b) relatives and friends; (c) hired labour; (d) others.

29 (Women) Who can help when you have difficulties?
(1) Parents; (2) husband's parents; (3) relatives and friends; (4) government; (5) others.

30 (Children) What do you do after school?
Before migration: (1) play; (2) study; (3) work; (4) others.
After migration: (1) play; (2) study; (3) work; (4) others.

31 (Children) Do you want to go to the city where the migrant in your family is working?
(1) Yes, because: (a) good food; (b) good school; (c) others.
(2) No, because: (a) fear of city people; (b) don't think the city is good; (c) others.

31 (Children whose parents are working) Do your parents pay the person(s) who are looking after you while they are away from the village?
(1) Yes. _____ yuan per year.
(2) No, because _____.

A.2 Questionnaire for households without migrant members

_____ Province _____ County _____ Village
Household number _____ Name of interviewee _____
Data of interview

I *Descriptive data of study households*

Same as A.1.I.

II *Migration situation*

1 Do you have relatives or neighbours who are working away from the village?
(1) Yes; (2) no (go to question 6).

2 Reason for their choosing the migrant:
(1) Sex; (2) age; (3) marital status; (4) educational level; (5) experience (in army or business); (6) experience in migration; (7) others.

3 Reason for their choosing the current destination:
(1) More opportunities; (2) with relatives or friends; (3) organised by local government; (4) organised by labour contractor; (5) factory recruitment; (6) others.

4 As far as you know, their decision for migration was affected and made by:
(1) Themself; (2) relatives and friends; (3) parents; (4) local government; (5) factory recruitment; (6) others.

5 As far as you know, they found their first job through:
(1) Themselves; (2) relatives and villagers; (3) through labour contractor; (4) sent by local government; (5) recruitment by factory, etc; (6) others.

6 Migrants' income in comparison with that of normal villagers:
(1) Higher; (2) same; (3) lower; (4) don't know.

7 Your income in comparison with that of households with migrant members:
(1) Higher; (2) same; (3) lower; (4) don't know.

8 Reasons for not working away from the village
(1) No money for going out; (2) need to look after parents or children; (3) busy in farming work; (4) no opportunities; (5) too old; (6) others.

9 Have there been any changes in land-use rights after migration?
(1) No; (2) yes. If yes, what changes? _____.

10 Is there any land transformation between your household and migrant households?
(1) Yes, which is _____ mu. We can still do another _____ mu.
(2) No.

11 Changes relating to agricultural labour structure after migration:
(1) Similar to the cooperation in the old-style production teams; (2) co-operation between friends and relatives; (3) hiring labour; (4) transferring land; (5) others.

12 Is there any work that cannot be done because of a shortage of labour?
(1) No; (2) yes, which is _____.

13 Change in life after migration:
(1) Higher living standards; (2) more information; (3) better education for children; (4) everybody has work to do; (5) more work for women and the old; (6) lack of people to look after children.

III Attitudes to migration

14 How many markets do you go to regularly? _____
How far is the farthest one? _____ km
How far is the nearest one? _____ km

15 Distance from the nearest bus or train station. _____ km

16 What is your opinion of the migrants who come here to work from south China in comparison with local people?
(1) Bear hardships; (2) more migration experience; (3) brave; (4) more stratagems; (5) don't know.

17 What would you do if there were a factory nearby?
(1) Try to work there; (2) go there to have a shower, see film or see doctor, if possible; (3) do some small-capital business; (4) try to send son or daughter to work there.

18 If there were an opportunity for you to go to cities to be a pedlar, roadside shoe-repairer, rubbish collector, domestic help worker, what would you think?
(1) Don't want to do it; (2) not dare to go because not familiar with cities; (3) yes if no skill is needed; (4) yes if more income; (5) it may be difficult because there are already too many people.

19 Where do you get information about agricultural products, prices, etc.?
(1) Televison, radio and newspaper; (2) local friends and relatives; (3) friends and relatives in cities; (4) from local officials; (5) get information by oneself.

20 Do you have any surplus money?
(1) Yes; (2) no.

21 If you have surplus money, how do you spend it?
(1) Save it in the bank; (2) build and refurbish house; (3) children's education; (4) marriage; (5) business; (6) others.

22 Are you willing to borrow money to extend your family economy?
(1) If yes, maximum amount: 500–1,000 yuan
1,001–2,000 yuan
2,001–3,000 yuan
over 3,000 yuan;
(2) No.

23 Are you willing to borrow money to work away from the village?
(1) If yes, maximum amount: 500–1,000 yuan
1,001–2,000 yuan
2,001–3,000 yuan
over 3,000 yuan;
(2) No.

24 Are you willing to spend money to learn a skill?
(1) If yes, maximum amount: below 500 yuan
500–1,000 yuan
over 1,000 yuan;
(2) No.

IV Satisfaction with city and village life

Same as A.IV.

V General attitude to life

Same as A.V.

VI Questions for women and children

25 (Women) Do you have more farming and domestic work to do since many migrants left the village?
(1) Yes. There is more (a) farming work; (b) domestic work; (c) looking after children and elderly; (d) others.
(2) No.
26 (Women) Who can help when you have difficulties?
(1) Parents; (2) husband's parents; (3) relatives and friends; (4) government (5) others.
27 (Children) What do you do after school?
(1) Play; (2) study; (3) work; (4) others.
28 (Children) Do you want to go to the cities?
(1) Yes, because: (a) good food; (b) good school; (c) others.
(2) No, because: (a) fear of city people; (b) don't think city is good; (c) others.

A.3 Extra questions for returned migrants

_____ Province _____ County _____ Village
Number _____ Name of interviewee _____ Data of interview

1 Reasons for returning to village.
(1) End of contract; (2) not enough income for family; (3) health reasons or getting old; (4) cannot find a job; (5) lack of necessary expenses in the cities; (6) earned enough money; 7, others.
2 The way of using remittance money:
(1) Building or refurbishing house; (2) investment for business or small factory; (3) children's education; (4) saving in bank; (5) others.
3 Currently what do you do in the village?
(1) Farming; (2) business or establishing a rural enterprise; (3) working in a rural enterprise; (4) others.
4 In comparison with your migration income, is your current income:
(1) Higher; (2) lower; (3) same.
5 What do the other villagers think of you?
(1) Got sufficient money; (2) cannot find a job in the city; (3) return is normal, no view; (4) don't understand; (5) others.
6 Your future plan is:
(1) Migrating again; (2) staying in agriculture; (3) exploring other opportunities; (4) don't know.

A.4 Questionnaire for migrants

_____ City _____ County   Name of interviewee
_____No. _____ Data of interview

I Personal information

1 Migrant

Sex	Age	Age first left village	Education level	Education level when first left village	Marital status	Marital status when first left village	Heath status

If the spouse is with the migrant, please fill the following:

Sex	Age	Age first left village	Education level	Education level when first left village	Marital status	Marital status when first left village	Heath situation

2   Have you ever been in the army?
    (1) Yes; (2) no.
3   Do you have experience of being a cadre?
    (1) Yes, which was (a) at township level or above; (b) at village level;
    (c) as a cadre of the Communist Party, or the Women's Federation, or
    Communist Youth League.
    (2) No.
4   Had you ever been in a big city before you migrated?
    (1) Yes; (2) no.
5   What kind of *hukou* do you hold?
    (1) Village; (2) city; (3) others (please specify).

II Basic situation in the destination

1 Your work experience (starting from the first job)

Date	Workplace	Job type	Highest pay	Lowest pay	Any workers' union?

If the spouse is also working in the destination, please fill the following:

Date	Workplace	Job type	Highest pay	Lowest pay	Any workers' union?

2 Do you have a work contract with the employer?
  (1) If yes, what kind of contract? (a) oral agreement; (b) written contact.
  (2) If no, the reason is: (a) the employer didn't mention it, I also didn't mention it;
  (b) I would like one, but the employer didn't want a contract;
  (c) it is rather strict, so I don't want to have a contract;
  (d) it is not flexible if I sign a contract;
  (e) I don't know why.
3 Have you paid a deposit to the employer?
  (1) Yes, which is _____ yuan.
  (2) No.
4 Do you have any of the following identification documents?
  (1) ID card: (a) Yes, which costs _____ yuan.
        (b) No.
  (2) Family planning pledge: (a) Yes, which costs _____ yuan.
        (b) No.
  (2) Migrant registration card: (a) Yes, which costs _____ yuan. It was issued by:

                                        (i)   local labour office;
                                        (ii) labour office in the destina-
                                              tion;
                                        (iii) private channel or through
                                              agents.
                                  (b) No, because:
                                        (i)   didn't know this was neces-
                                              sary;
                                        (ii) expensive and time-consum-
                                              ing;
                                        (iii) no problem if you don't have
                                              one;
                                        (iv) no use.
(3) Temporary residential card: (a) Yes, costs _____ yuan, valid for
                                      __ years.
                                  (b) No.
(4) Migrant work permit: (a) Yes, costs _____ yuan, valid for __
                               years, and issued by
                                        (i)   employer;
                                        (ii) labour office in the destination;
                                        (iii) private channel or through
                                              agents.
                                  (b) No.

5   Have you attended any sort of training?
    (1) Yes, the training is: (a) formal training course;
                                (b) informal training.
    (2) No. [Please go to question 11]
6   When was your training?
    (1) Before finding a job; (2) after finding a job.
7   Who organised the training?
    (1) Relevant labour organisation; (2) Communist Youth League,
    Women's Federation, anti-poverty organisation, etc.; (3) employers;
    (4) others.
8   Who paid your training expenses?
    (1) Myself; (2) employers; (3) others.
9   Why did you attend the training?
    (1) No offer of job if no training; (2) no increment or higher position if
    no training; (3) useful for the future; (4) Others.
10 Difference made by the training:
    (1) Found a job; (2) increment or promotion; (3) no change.
11 Why didn't you attend a training course?
    (1) Not enough money for training fees; (2) training has no effect on
    job finding or income; (3) training is not useful; (4) too busy; (5) not
    approved by employer; (6) others.
12 Are you willing to attend training at your own expense?

(1) Yes; (2) no; (3) depends on the amount of money needed.

13 Do you have the right to have free accommodation from your employer?
(1) Yes; (2) no.

14 Currently you are staying in:
(1) Normal accommodation supplied by the work place; (2) temporary shed; (3) private; (4) others.

15 Do you share a room with other person(s)?
(1) Yes, with _____ person(s); (2) no.

16 Is there any pension for your current work?
(1) Yes; (2) no.

17 What type of firm do you currently work for?
(1) State owned; (2) foreign investment; (3) Hong Kong or Taiwan invested; (4) invested jointly by Chinese and overseas sources; (5) county level; (6) village level; (7) private.

18 Are you paid:
(1) Daily; (2) weekly; (3) monthly; (4) annually; (5) others.

19 Are your working hours fixed?
(1) Yes, _____ hours every day; (2) no, about _____ hours per day.

20 Do you want to extend your working hours to get extra pay?
(1) Yes; (2) no.

21 How is your working environment?
(1) Good;
(2) Not good, because it is: (a) too dirty;
(b) too noisy;
(c) dangerous;
(d) temperature too high or too low;
(e) others.

22 Do you have the following?
(1) Accident injury insurance; (2) accommodation allowance; (3) child benefit; (4) medical insurance.

23 Did you get a bonus last year?
(1) Yes, which was _____ yuan; (2) no.

24 Will you get a bonus this year?
(1) Yes, because _____; (2) no, because _____.

III Attitude of migrants to migration

1 Why you are working away from the village?
(1) Sent by local government; (2) limited land and not enough farming work; (3) need money urgently; (4) the income in the village is too low; (5) farming work is too heavy; (6) learning more about outside world; (7) want to have more money; (8) have to support brothers' or sisters' education; (9) get money for marriage.

2   Who decided that you would migrate?
(1) Local goveronment; (2) parents or relatives; (3) yourself; (4) friend who had aready migrated; (5) others.

3   You found your first job through:
(1) Yourself; (2) relatives and villagers; (3) labour contractor; (4) sent by local government; (5) recruitment by factory, etc; (6) others.

4   Your expenditure:
(1) Rent _____ yuan; (2) water, electricity and coal _____ yuan; (3) food _____ yuan; (4) clothes and everyday expenses _____ yuan; (5) travel ____ yuan.

5   Do you have surplus money each month?
(1) Yes, which is about _____ yuan; (2) no.

6   How do you communicate with your family in the village?
(1) Telephone; (2) letters; (3) oral messages; (4) others _____.

7   How often do you go home?
_____ times each year.

8   When do you go home?
(1) Spring festival; (2) when the work in the city is not busy; (3) when agricultural work is busy; (4) when there is something to deal with at home; (5) others ____.

9   Do you give money to your family in the village?
(1) Yes, which was _____ yuan last year; (2) no.

10   How do you send money or presents back?
(1) By post; (2) by myself; (3) brought back by friends; (4) others.

11   Do you give relatives and friends presents when you go home?
(1) Yes, which were worth about _____ yuan last time; (2) no.

12   The presents are normally
(1) Food; (2) clothes; (3) jewellery; (4) electical applicances; (5) goods for everyday use; (6) others.

13   Do you belong to a *tongxianghui*?[2]
(1) Yes; (2) no.

14   List other *tongxianghui* you are aware of in this city.
(1) _____; (2) _____.

15   What do you think about your social and economic position in comparison with city residents?
(1) Same; (2) better economic position; (3) worse economic position; (4) worse social position.

16   Do you think you could find a better job if your education level were higher?
(1) Yes; (2) no; (3) not necessarily.

17   Do you think you could find a better job if you had a skill?
(1) Yes; (2) no; (3) not necessarily.

18   What would the difference be if you were a formal worker?
(1) No change; (2) higher salary; (3) stable job; (4) better working condition; (5) better social position.

19 Who will help if you have difficulties?
(1) Nobody; (2) employer; (3) local trade union, Women's Federation or Communist Youth League; (4) local government; (5) government in hometown; (6) friends from same village or region (*laoxiang*).

20 Your plan for the near future is:
(1) To stay in the current job; (2) to change job or change city; (3) go back to village; (4) don't know.

21 Your long-term future plan is:
(1) To return to village to do farming work when enough money earned; (2) return to village to do some business; (3) stay in city; (4) don't know.

22 If you go back, what do you think the villagers' view would be?
(1) Got sufficient money; (2) cannot find a job in cities; (3) return is normal, no view; (4) don't understand; (5) others.

IV Satisfaction with city and village life

Same as A.IV.

V General attitude to life

Same as A.V.

VI What should the government do for migrants?

A.5 Questionnaire for local officials and village cadres

Name _____ Village _____

I Demographic information concerning the village (1995/1996/1997)

1 Population
2 Number of labourers:
Male
Female
3 Number of households
4 Migrants:
Male
Female

II Industry and environment

1 Are there rural enterprises in your village? If so, please give details for

each enterprise, including date of establishment, source of the capital, source of the workers, and ratio of men:women employed.

2 What is the role of rural enterprises in the economic development of your village.
3 How many households have electricity?
4 How many households have running water?
5 Has there been any shortage of water in your village?
6 Is it difficult for villagers to see a doctor?
7 Can villagers get medicines?
8 Is there a village school? If yes, how many pupils at each level?
9 What is the literacy rate in your village?
10 How many shops are there in your village?

III Migration

1 When did migration start in your village?
2 What are the occupations of the migrants?
3 Where do they migrate to?
4 How many migrants are there in your village?
5 Does the local government have formal or informal policies for migrants' land use rights?
6 How many migrants have returned in the last three years?
7 What do villagers think about the returned migrants?
8 Does the local government have formal or informal policies for migration?

IV Poverty

1 What was the villagers' average income in the last three years?
2 Have there been anti-poverty public works in your village in the last three years?
3 Has your village received poverty-relief funds from government or other sources?
4 If there are rural enterprises in your village, what is the average wage of the workers?

A.6 Outline for informal discussion

1 Is rural–urban migration an alternative way to reduce poverty?
2 Has rural–urban migration played a positive role in rural development?
3 If rural–urban migration has reduced the labour force in the village, what are the solutions for agricultural work?

4 To what extent has rural–urban migration influenced the attitude of young people in rural areas?
5 Have living standards changed since there began to be large numbers of migrants?
6 What is the future of rural–urban migration?

Notes

Introduction

1 US$100 = 827.68 yuan and £100 = 1,289.74 yuan (*People's Daily*, 18 March 2002).
2 See Chapter 2 for a detailed discussion on the poverty line.
3 It was shown by a quite separate report two years after the census that 150 million rural surplus labourers are flooding to cities for jobs (*China Daily*, 2002).
4 This refers to labour movement during the less busy agricultural seasons.
5 The estimate appears to be accurate, although no exact figure has been obtained.

2 Poverty and internal migration in China

1 In 1996, the population in the provinces was: Inner Mongolia, 23.07 million; Shanxi, 31.09 million; Shaanxi, 35.43 million; Ningxia, 5.21 million; Gansu, 24.67 million; Qinghai, 4.88 million; Xinjiang, 16.89 million; Yunnan, 40.42 million; Sichuan, 114.30 million; Hebei, 64.84 million; Henan, 91.72 million; Guangxi, 45.89 million; Guizhou, 35.55 million; Jilin, 26.10 million, and Heilongjiang, 37.28 million (NBSC, 1997).
2 The international subsistence level is 1,800 kcal.
3 Since the UN divided the Engels coefficient into four levels, with values above 60 per cent indicating poverty, Chinese government set the Engels coefficient for poor households at 63.6 per cent in 1989. Another three levels – 50–60 per cent, 40–50 per cent and below 40 per cent – indicate development, beyond subsistence and better off respectively.
4 This is mainly through the growth of output and income. A large-scale campaign launched from the highest level of central government also played an important role.
5 From 1986 to 1998, the alleviation fund from the central government was over 1,100 billion yuan. Local governments provided an additional one-third of the amount given by central government. Donations from city residents amounted to over 30 billion yuan.
6 In the late 1980s, the Grameen Bank introduced its GB model, loaning peasants small sums at low interest rates. These were first implemented in China in 1994.
7 Singh and Tabatabai (1993) described some policies in Mao's time: 'Mao's essential point was that forced-draft industrialisation, which neglects agriculture and standards of living of the people, would be counter-productive. He

still believed heavy industry to be essential for the long-term industrialisation of the country, but he thought that better results would be achieved in this sphere if agriculture were put on a secure foundation and consumption levels of the peasantry improved. Otherwise the peasantry would feel exploited; and not only would that mean lower motivation, but it would destroy the worker/peasant alliance which had been the cornerstone of the Chinese revolution, with serious consequences for long run development.'

8 The 'real' difference may be different from the figures in Table 2.2, especially when taking into account price differentials and their changes.

9 White-collar and blue-collar workers.

10 Some of these have been stopped in recent years.

11 Both market towns and designated towns but not county capitals.

12 *Hukou* regulations were passed in 1958 but their systematic enforcement actually began in 1960. More detailed explanation of this system can be found in a later section.

13 There was a slowdown between 1989 and 1991 corresponding to national belt-tightening which curtailed urban construction.

14 General speaking, migrant workers are not offered the same benefits as urban workers, such as almost free accommodation, an allowance for medical fees and a pension.

15 The total populations of Sichuan and Shanxi were 112.14 and 30.45 million in 1998 (NBSC), respectively.

16 The total populations of Zhejiang and Hunan were 42.84 and 63.55 million in 1998 (NBSC), respectively.

17 *Laoxiang* means people from the same origin, which could be a village, a township, a county or a province.

18 For various economic reasons, many firms are reducing the number of employees. Currently about 10 million people have 'lost' their job, partly or wholly, although they still belong to their firm in theory.

19 The term *xiao-kang* became popular in China after the economic reform in the early 1980s.

20 The reasons include accommodation, security, transportation, and so on.

21 Some of those people keep moving back to their traditional home places.

22 If the baby is born at its mother's temporary residence, the registration of birth can wait until the mother returns to her permanent abode.

23 Directive of the State Council of the People's Republic of China no. 87, 25 July 1991, Beijing.

3 Case study region and methodology

1 The population was 30,090,000 in 1997 (NBSC, 1997).

2 This figure had increased to 1,956 yuan by 2001 (NBSC, 2002b).

3 It was 1,222 yuan in 2001 (NBSC, 2000b).

4 The national population growth rate for the years between 1986 and 1990 was 1.426 per cent, 1.557 per cent, 1.661 per cent, 1.573 per cent and 1.439 per cent, respectively.

5 The speed of development of agriculture and industry in Shanxi is lower than the national level. The increase of GDP from 1993 to 1995 was 8 per cent. By considering the effects of new technology, it was predicted that the rate of increase in 1996–2000, 2001–5, and 2006–15 would be 10.7 per cent, 8.5 per cent, and 8 per cent, respectively (Chang, 1995).

6 Curve extension based on the increase/decrease ratios between 1990 and 1999.

7 In Shanxi, rural surplus labour is often caused by poor land and limited rural

enterprises. Seasonal rural surplus labour is also an important phenomenon in northern China. In winter, many peasants stay at home.

8 In Wutai, one additional village was sampled for the case study.

9 Township, or *xiang*, is an administrative level between county and village. It consists of a number of villages and sometimes also one or more small towns.

10 During the Cultural Revolution period (1966–76), many students who had graduated from senior high school in the cities were sent to the countryside for 're-education'.

11 Some local governments sold township *hukou* in order to increase their revenue. In 1997, each *hukou* cost about 3,000 yuan. Once they had acquired a township *hukou*, rural people could buy a house, send their children to the schools and open small businesses in towns.

12 According to a young cadre, Liu, who has worked there for several years, the population in this *xiang* dropped from 598 in 1995 to 502 in 1997.

13 Net income of rural households refers to the total income of the permanent residents of rural households during a year after the deduction of expenses for productive and non-productive business operation, the payment of taxes, and the payment to collective units for their contracted tasks. The net income may be spent on investments in productive and non-productive construction, used for daily living expenses or kept as savings deposits. It is a comprehensive indicator to show the actual level of income of a peasant household. Note that the net income of a rural household includes not only the income from the productive and non-productive business operations, but also the income from non-business operations, such as remittances by migrants, government relief payments and various subsidies.

14 Field study database.

15 Roads which can be used by cars.

16 In Beijing, one in two high school students can go to university or college.

17 Washing coal and injecting water. The water consumption is about 1 tonne coal:1 tonne water.

18 1 *mu* = 6.67 acres = 0.1647 acre.

19 See note 8 for a definition of rural surplus labour.

20 This increase also includes the effect of inflation.

21 Note: another reason for the enormous decrease in the number of rural enterprises is that the statistical definition of rural enterprises became slightly different from 1995 to 1997. Some very small businesses were not included in 1997.

22 State ownership or collective ownership.

23 The interview scripts and relevant documents resulting from this case study weighed over 20 kg.

24 Final version after the pilot study; see later section.

25 Chinese Academy of Social Sciences, Beijing University, NBSC, etc.

26 Daixian, Mr K. Wang; Jingle, Mr G. Zhou; Wutai, Mr H. Liu.

27 Some of them were too far away to follow. For example, two migrants were in Guangdong, and one in Wuhan, Jiangsu Province.

4 Case study analysis: sending areas

1 The capital city of Shanxi Province, and the second biggest city in Shanxi, respectively.

2 In a number of cases, distance from towns or roads has been shown to be positively related to migration. A study in India suggests that there is a threshold distance around a town, within which the rate of migration from villages is inversely proportional to distance (Connell *et al.*, 1976). Lea and Weinand

(1971) found a positive relation between the distance from a main road and migration in New Guinea.

3 Note: the villages studied are administrative villages, which normally consist of a number of natural villages.

4 A county near the three counties studied.

5 A famous tourist site.

6 Those concerned were single with no family.

7 In south China, where there are more job opportunities for females, some households prefer to send out young females, as females tend to be more conscientious in sending back remittances than males in their early period in the cities.

8 Figures are 1997 rates. Meals and accommodation are free for the workers.

9 In China, every student in high school learns this theory, but not many people can remember it, and apply it in real life.

10 People who have already moved to the cities and are now in a position to help others to migrate.

11 For university graduates in China, a job is normally guaranteed by the government, and they will automatically get a city *hukou*.

12 In some of Shanxi's neighbouring provinces, the coal industry is also quite strong.

13 The sum of the percentages is over 100 per cent. This is because there are multiple choices for this question.

14 Considering that some peasants might not want to give this figure, during the interview I gave some ranges and they were asked to choose one.

15 There are two types of land, consumption and responsibility land. The regulations are slightly different for the two kinds. Peasants have more decision-making power on the former, and the latter is more related to the requirements of the state. Normally the responsibility land is several times bigger than the consumption land.

16 During 1979–83, the collectively owned land was distributed to individual farm households, creating a nation of family farms. Each household was granted the right to use land to organise independent agricultural production, though land ownership remained with the collective. The distributed cropland was typically contracted to individual households on an egalitarian basis. Each household received an amount of land proportionate to family size.

17 The five basic provisions are as follows. 1. Encourage peasants to make investments in land, to make land more fertile, and to continually increase agricultural productivity. 2. Peasants have only use rights, not ownership, of the land they contract. They must manage and use the land well. The land cannot be wasted for other use, soil from the land cannot be taken away, and the land cannot be rented or sold. 3. Peasants can use this land for a long time. It can be readjusted by the collective after consultation with the peasant who contracts the land. 4. Peasants will get reasonable compensation for investment if during the contract period the peasant makes active investments which upgrade the land. 5. In terms of current infrastructure and engineering projects on the land, the infrastructure and projects will go with the land when it is transferred (Prosterman *et al.*, 1999).

18 The 30 years policy applies nation-wide, including here.

19 In many parts of Africa, male migrants may be absent for a long period without affecting agricultural production (Miracle, 1967). Harris (1972) states that in Papua New Guinea, output per capita will not fall until over a third of young men are absent. Barber (1961) estimated that a subsistence agricultural system will not be harmed until more than 50 per cent of the male labour force is absent.

20 Some peasants in the villages studied go to other, richer counties to help with farming work during busy seasons. It is a long-standing tradition that amounts to a form of seasonal short-range migration in rural areas.

21 For example, because of repeated drought, the yield of major farm crops dropped in 1997–8.

22 Such as those who have children or elderly parents to look after or those who take the positions of village cadres.

23 The form of organised co-operation in agricultural production used during Mao's time.

24 The following are the reasons that those households do not have any migrant members: Household 1: small children aged 3 and 7; Household 2: too old (aged 64 and 66); Household 3: village doctor; Household 4: village cadre; Household 5: shop-owner, lives with parents; Household 6: parents are too old; Household 7: no other skills except farming.

25 For example, in 1996 the yield of major farm cereals per hectare was 3,750 kg in Shanxi, 5,841 kg in Liaoning, 5,517 kg in Zhejiang and 5,233 kg in Jiangxi (NBSC, 1997).

26 A similar phenomenon was also observed in another country by Bedford (1973).

27 This pattern is also widely seen in the central and western parts of China (Zhang, 1999), where rural enterprises are not highly developed and rural poverty forces men to move out to seek jobs.

28 Especially since 1949, the year the People's Republic of China was established.

29 The overall rise in labour intensity was also discussed by Marx (1970).

30 The change of women's role appears to correspond with Marx's (1973) discussion on the labour process – labour power as capital.

31 'Labourers-in-themselves' means labourers who are lacking in subject consciousness. 'Labourers-for-themselves' refers to labourers who have subject consciousness (Meng, 1996).

32 Including interviews with schoolteachers.

33 This seems to be different from the situation in some other countries. It was reported that there were systematic links between the educational status of children in the West Usambaras and the access of their parents to land – it was apparent that child labour was a critical component of the total supply of tea-plucking labour and that the children involved were unlikely to be regular or consistent school attenders (Sender and Smith, 1990).

34 See the previous section.

35 Chinese New Year is not included.

36 For returned migrants, over 45 may mean 'getting old'. It seems that this is also the case in Africa (Byerlee, 1972).

37 Information from the Shanxi Anti-poverty Office.

38 I.e. by land transfer. As mentioned in the previous section, the cost of acquiring transferred land is normally rather low in the region studied.

39 I did ask a government officer whether it is legal to get so much transferred land. He said that this is an excellent example of 'returning innovation' in Shanxi, and this is more important than other issues.

40 Caldwell (1969) indicated that many migrants use their money to retire to a better house and think of their urban skill as something that has achieved its purpose.

41 Caldwell (1969) showed that in Africa, return to the village was much more prevalent and occured at a younger age in villages closer to the coastal towns because: (1) Their skills can often be employed to some extent in the villages. (2) They are not entirely leaving the cash economy or more modernised society. (3) The decision is not so final or difficult to implement, since the dis-

tances are not great. In the studied villages in Shanxi, some migrants who retired from Taiyuan or Datong coal mines were working in towns near the villages and coming back weekly or even more frequently.

42 Comprehensive statistical results have been obtained from this section of the questionnaire, as presented in the three tables that follow. However, to focus on the mainstream of this study, only a brief analysis of the results has been carried out. More detailed analysis will be made in a separate future work.

43 Meaning 'OK'.

44 Power-using (i.e. official corruption or officials' misuse of power) measures how officials use their power. Power of office (i.e. administrative control) measures how powerful the administrative units are.

5 Case study analysis: destinations

1 The system was introduced in the 1960s to 1970s, and became widely and practically effective in the 1980s.

2 Higher education is normally free in China. However, some universities and colleges accept a small number of students whose scores in the national admission examination are slightly lower than the basic line for admission, but those students must pay the fees themselves.

3 Two migrants were in Guangdong, and one in Wuhan, Jiangsu Province. Also see note 27, Chapter 3.

4 The results from household interview are shown in Chapter 4. Note: in Figure 5.4, only cash is included, but in Chapter 4, presents are also included.

5 More detailed discussion of the effects of migration on sending areas is given in Chapter 4.

6 Note: this figure refers not only to their family. That is why it is different from that in Chapter 4, where 46.7 per cent people said 'no present'.

7 *Jia* (*chia*) is defined as the basic social group in the village, an extended family. The members of this group share common property, keep a common budget and co-operate to pursue a common living through division of labour. A *jia* (*chia*) is essentially a family but it sometimes includes children even when they have grown and married. Sometimes it also includes some relatively remote matrilineal kin.

8 A famous and rather expensive liquor.

9 It may include several natural villages and have a relatively large population.

10 Generally taken to mean not within the past five generations.

11 The former people's communes are called *xiang* now.

12 See p. 133 for a more detailed discussion regarding deposits.

13 All residents, including rural residents and city residents, have to have a resident ID card, which was introduced in 1985. This card has contributed to greater spatial mobility. It can be used to seek employment, register at hotels, apply for a business licence, and to register as a temporary urban resident in the cities.

14 No matter whether a migrant is single or married, with or without children, he or she has to have a family planning pledge in order to get a migration registration card from the local labour bureau.

15 It seems that in some other countries, such as India, such a deposit system is not common (Breman, 1996; Connell *et al.*, 1976).

16 Say, with less than three years' experience.

17 Coal-mining accidents have been, and still are, a major concern for many migrants and their families (see Table 5.6), although mining techniques have improved, especially in the state-owned coal mines, and many regulations have

been introduced. Health damage is another concern. However, many migrants still seek work in this sector because there are more job opportunities, and incomes are relatively high.

18 There are two kinds of money award, the normal money award and the year-end bonus. Migrants' income per month or per week normally consists of two parts, a fixed amount and a money award. The amount of money awarded depends on the performance of the firm as well as the performance of the migrant. At the end of each year (just before the Chinese New Year), there is usually a larger money award. Such a system is also quite common for ordinary workers in cities.

19 Sometimes firms buy coal but do not have enough money to pay for it because other firms have bought their products with delayed payment.

20 This figure corresponds to the percentage of migrants who do not send money to their family members in the village. See p. 124

21 This can be in cities or rural areas, and at any level, such as county level, township level or village level.

22 In China, sharing a room is not uncommon. For example, in universities, normally four to six students live in a room of 12–18 square metres in area.

23 *Laoxiang* means people from the same origin, which could be a village, a township, a county or a province.

24 In the draft version of the questionnaire, a series of questions were designed to gather information on this aspect of migrants' social organisation, but the pre-testing of the questionnaire suggested that there are no such organisations as *huiguan*, *tongxianghui* or *lianyihui*.

25 Or other similar unions like the Women's Federation and the Communist Youth League.

6 To what extent can rural–urban migration resolve rural poverty?

1 Or unemployment, see Chapter 2.

2 In the government budget report in 2002, a total of 86 billion yuan (more than US$1 billion) for social security programmes will be earmarked in the central budget, up 28 per cent from the previous year. To solve the problem of basic living allowances for the urban needy, the government decided to increase subsidies from the central budget to the minimum cost of living from 2.3 billion yuan (US$277 million) in 2001 to 4.6 billion yuan (US$554 million) in 2002. Furthermore, a total of 51.2 billion yuan (US$6.17 billion) from the central budget will be allocated to subsidise pensions for retirees of state-owned enterprises and living allowances of their laid-off workers in 2002. The input is unprecedented. In fact, the number of the urban needy covered by the system of minimum cost of living grew from more than 4 million in early 2001 to over 11.2 million at the end of the year. Expenditure from the central government on social security programmes in 2001 was 5.18 times the figure for 1998.

Appendix

1 Note: the order of the items has been adjusted in the analysis in Chapter 4.

2 A *laoxiang* association or, in other words, a union of people sharing a common origin.

Bibliography

Adepoju, A. (1983) 'Patterns of migration by sex in West Africa', in C. Oppong (ed.) *Female and Male in West Africa*, London: Allen and Unwin.

Adepoju, A. (1984) 'Migration and female employment in south west Nigeria', *African Urban Studies*, vol. 8.

Adepoju, A. (1988) 'An overview of rural migration and agricultural labour force structure in Africa', *African Population Studies*, no. 1.

Ahiauyo-Akakpo, A. (1974) 'L'impact de la migration sur la société villageoise: approche sociologique', in S. Amin (ed.) *Modern Migration in Western Africa*, London: Oxford University Press.

Anderson, J. A. (1972) 'Social strategies in population change: village data from central Luzon', Paper 15, South Asia Development Advisory Group, New York Asia Society.

Bai, Nansheng (1998) 'Laodongli waichu dui nongye de yingxiang' (The effects of rural urban migration on agriculture), to be published.

Baines, D. (1991) *Emigration from Europe, 1815–1930*, Basingstoke: Macmillan.

Bao, Ji (1995) *Shanxi lishi* (History of Shanxi), Taiyuan: Shanxi daxue chubanshe (Taiyuan: Shanxi University Press).

Barber, W. (1961) *The Economics of British Central Africa*, Manchester: University of Manchester Press.

Bassett, K. and Short, J. R. (1980) *Housing and Residential Structure*, London: Routledge and Kegan Paul.

Beaujeau-Garnier, J. (1966) *Geography of Population*, London: Longman.

Bedford, R. D. (1973) *New Hebridean Mobility*: A study of circular migration, Research School of Pacific Studies, Australian National University, Canberra.

Beijing Youth Daily (*Beijing Qingnianbao*) 21 April 1999, p. 1.

Berg, E. (1965) 'The economics of the migrant labour system', in H. Kuper (ed.) *Urbanisation and Migration in West Africa*, Los Angeles: University of California Press.

Berliner, J. S. (1977) 'Internal migration: a comparative disciplinary view', in A. A. Brown and E. Neuberger (eds) *Internal Migration: A Comparative Perspective*, New York: Academic Press.

Bogue, D. J. (1969) *Principles of Demography*, New York: Wiley.

Breman, J. (1996) *Footloose Labour*, Cambridge: Cambridge University Press.

Byerlee, D. (1972) 'Research on migration in Africa: past, present and future', Rural Employment Paper 2, Department of Agricultural Economic, Michigan State University, East Lansing.

Cai, Fang (1998) 'Economic reasons for migration, the organisation of labour force and selection of jobs', *Social Sciences in China*, Spring.

Caldwell, J. C. (1969) *Africa Rural–Urban Migration: The Movement to Ghana's Towns*, Canberra: Australian National University Press.

Centre of Human Resources Development of West Region (1995) Internal report for the World Bank on migration.

Cerase, F. P. (1974) 'Migration and social change: expectations and reality – a case study of return migration from the United States to southern Italy', *International Migration Review*, vol. 8.

Chan, Kam Wing (1996) 'Post-Mao China: a two-class urban society in the market', *International Journal of Urban and Regional Research*, no. 1.

Chang, Jianyu (1995) 'Shanxi jiuye qingkuang' (Investigation of the employment in Shanxi), *Shanxi Tongji* (Shanxi statistics), no. 1.

Chen, Hong (1996) 'Woguo nongcun waichu wugong yu nongye fazhan' (Rural out-migration and rural development in China), *Renkou Yanjiu* (Population research), vol. 20, no. 4.

Chen, Jiyuan and Yu, Dechang (eds) (1993) '*Zhongguo nongye laodongli de zhuanyi*' (The transformation of China's agricultural labour), Beijing: Renmin chubanshe.

Chen, Kang (1982) 'Gongye yu nongye shengchan de jiandaocha' (The scissors price differential between industrial and agricultural products), *Zhongguo Shehui Kexue* (Social sciences in China), Spring, Beijing.

Chen, Y. (1989) 'The temporal and spatial variation of erosion and sediment yield on the Loess Plateau', in M. Lucian *et al.* (eds) *Taming the Yellow River: Silt and Flood*, Dordrecht: Kluwer Academic Publishers.

Cheng, T. and Selden, M. (1994) 'The origin and social consequences of China's *hukou* system', *China Quarterly*, no. 139.

Clyde-Mitchell, J. (1959) 'The cause of labour migration', *Bulletin of Inter-African Labour Institute*.

Cohen, A. (1972) *Arab Border Villages in Israel*, Manchester: Manchester University Press.

Connell, J. (1973) 'Social network in urban society', in B. D. Clark and M. B. Gleave (eds) *Social Patterns in Cities*, Special Publication 5, London: Institute of British Geographers.

Connell, J., Dasgupta, B., Laishley, R. and Lipton, M. (1976) *Migration from Rural Areas*, Delhi: Oxford University Press.

Croll, E. J. and Huang, Ping (1996) 'Migration for and against agriculture', *Research report*, SOAS (School of Oriental and Africa Studies), University of London.

Dahya, B. (1973) 'Pakistanis in Britain: transient or settlers', *Race*, vol. 14, no. 3.

Davin, D. (1996a) 'Migration and rural women in China: a look at the gender impact of large-scale migration', *Journal of International Development*, September–October.

Davin, D. (1996b) 'Images of the migrant in the Chinese media', Paper presented at the workshop on European–Chinese and Chinese domestic migration, Oxford.

Davis, D. S., Kraus, R., Naughton, B. and Perry, E. J. (eds) (1995) *Urban Space in Contemporary China: The Potential for Autonomy and Community in Post-Mao China*, New York: Cambridge University Press.

Day, L. H. and Ma, Xia (eds) (1994) *Migration and Urbanisation in China*, Armonk, NY: Sharpe.

Diehl, W. D. (1966) 'Farm–no farm migration in the South-East: a costs–returns analysis', *Journal of Farm Economics*, special issue, 48ii.

Du, Ying and Bai, Nansheng (1997) *Zouchu xiangcun* (Out of the villages), Beijing: Jingji Kexue Chubanshe (Beijing: Economic Science Press).

Elkan, W. (1973) *An Introduction to Development Economics*, London: Tavistock.

Fei, H. T. (1939) *Peasant Life in China*, London: Routledge and Kegan Paul.

Fei, J. and Rainis, G. (1961) 'A theory of economic development', *American Economic Review*, 60, no. 4.

Findley, S. E. and Williams, L. (1990) 'Women who go and women who stay: reflections of family migration processes in a changing world', *Working Paper Series*, Geneva: International Labour Organisation.

Friendland, A. B. (1971) 'An ethnographic study of San Mateo Almonoloa, a Mexican peasant village', Ph.D. thesis, University of California, Los Angeles.

Galbraith, J. K. (1979) *The Nature of Mass Poverty*, Harmondsworth: Penguin.

Gao, Hongbin (2001) 'Fupin yu fazhan' (Poverty alleviation and development), Internal report, State Council, Beijing.

Goldstein, S. and Goldstein, A. (1990) 'Migration in China: data, policies, and patterns', in C. B. Nam, W. J. Serow and D. F. Sly (eds) *International Handbook on Internal Migration*, Westport, CT: Greenwood Press.

Goldstein, S. and Guo, S. (1991) 'Temporary migration in Shanghai households', *Demography*, no. 2.

Gu, Sheng and Li, Chang (1995) 'Woguo renkou liudong he chengshihua de lilun sikao he zhengce yanjiu' (Population movement and urbanisation in China: theoretical consideration and policy options), *Renkou yanjiu* (Population research), vol. 20.

Gugler, J. (1968) 'The impact of migration on society and economy in sub-Saharan Africa', *Africa Social Research*, vol. 6.

Guo, Zemin (1995) 'Woguo de chengshihua shuipin' (On the real urbanisation level in China), *Renkou yu jingji* (Population and economics), vol. 92.

Haddon, A. C. (1919) *The Wandering of People*, Cambridge: Cambridge University Press.

Harris, G. T. (1972) 'Labour supply and economic development in the south highland of Papua New Guinea', *Oceania*, vol. 43.

Harris, J. R. and Todaro, M. P. (1970) 'Migration, unemployment and development: a two sector analysis', *American Economic Review*, vol. 60.

Hart, D. V. (1971) 'Philippine rural–urban migration: a view from Caticugan, a Bisayan village', *Behavioural Science Notes*.

Hawthorn, G. (ed.) (1978) *Population and Development*, London: Frank Cass.

Herberle, R. (1938) 'The causes of the rural–urban migrations: a survey of German theories', *American Journal of Sociology*, vol. 43.

Herbst, P. G. (1964) 'Organisational commitment: a decision model', *Acta Sociology*, vol. 7.

Hirschman, A. O. (1957) 'Investment policies', *American Economic Review*, vol. 47.

Houston, C. J. (1979) 'Administrative control of migration to Moscow, 1959–75', *Canadian Geographer*, vol. 23.

Huang, P. C. C. (1985) *The Peasant Economy and Social Change in North China*. Stanford, CA: Stanford University Press.

Huang, Ping (ed.) (1997) *Xunzhao shengcun-dangdai zhongguo nongcun waichu renkou de chehuixue yanjiu* (In search for survival: A sociological study of rural urban migration), Kunming: Yunnan Renmin Press (Kunming: Yunnan People's Publishing House).

Inkeles, A. (1983) *Exploring Individual Modernity*, New York: Columbia University Press.

Inkeles, A. and Smith, H. (1974) *Becoming Modern*, London: Heinemann.

Jahiel, A. R. (1997) 'The contradictory impact of reform and environmental protection', *China Quarterly*, no. 194 (March).

Jahiel, A. R. (1998) 'The organisation of environmental protection in China', *China Quarterly*, no. 156 (December).

Ji, Dangsheng and Shao, Qin (eds) (1995) *Zhongguo renkou liudong de shitai yu guanli* (The situation and management of Chinese population movement), Beijing: Zhongguo Renkou Kexue Chubanshe (Beijing: China Population Press).

Ji, Ping; Zhang, Kai and Liu, Dongliang (1985) 'Beijing jiaoqu de hunyin qianyi (An analysis of marital migration among residents of Beijing suburbs)', *Zhongguo Shehui Kexue* (Social sciences in China), Spring, Beijing.

Jia, Daming (1999) 'Guanyu xiangzhen qiye' (China's rural industries), *Zhongguo Guoqing Guoli* (China's national conditions and strengths), vol. 74.

Jiang, Zemin (1997) '2000 nian xiaochu pinkun' (End of poverty by 2000). Government report, *Renmin Ribao* (*People's Daily*), 6 January.

Johnson, G. E. and Whitelaw, W. E. (1972) 'Urban–rural income transfers in Kenya: an estimated remittance function', Communications paper, University of Nairobi Institute for Development Studies.

Kang, Xiaoguang (1996) *Pinkun yu fan pinkun lilun* (The theory of poverty and strategy of anti-poverty public works in China), Beijing: Kexue Chubanshe (Beijing: The Science Press).

Keith, G. and Zhao, R. (eds) (1993) *The distribution of income in China*, New York: St Martin's Press.

Knight, J. and Song, L. (1993) 'How far can migration of rural labour alleviate poverty in rural China?', Paper prepared for the International Conference on China's Rural Reform and Development in the 1990s, Beijing.

Kolars, J. F. (1963) 'Tradition, season and change in a Turkish village', Occasional paper, University of Chicago.

Labour Bureau of China (1997) 'Survey of 4,000 Households in Eight Provinces, 3,000 migrants in four cities', Internal report.

Lavely, W. (1991) 'Marriage and mobility under rural collectivisation', In R. Watson and P. Ebrey (eds) *Marriage and Inequality in Chinese Society*, Berkeley: University of California Press.

Lea, D. A. M. (1964) 'Abelam land and sustenance: swidden horticulture in an area of high population density', Ph.D. thesis, Australian National University.

Lea, D. A. M. and Weinand, H. C. (1971) 'Some consequences of population growth in the Wosera area, East Spik District', in M. W. Ward (ed.) *Population Growth and Socio-economic Change*, New Guinea Bulletin 42, Australian National University.

Lee, E. S. (1966) 'A theory of migration', *Demography*, vol. 3.

Lewis, G. J. (1982) *Human Migration*, London: Croom Helm.

Lewis, R. K. (1967) 'Hadchite: A study of emigration in Lebanese village', Ph.D. thesis, Columbia University.

Lewis, W. A. (1954) 'Economic development with unlimited supplies of labour', *Manchester School of Economic and Social Studies*, vol. 23.

Li, Rongshi (1996) 'Dangqian renkou liudong de yixie yanjiu' (Some considerations on the floating population in contemporary China), *Renkou Yanjiu* (Population research), no. 1.

Li, Shi (1994) 'Bashi niandai de diqu fazhan he renkou liudong' (A study on the development of regional economy and population migration in the 1980s in China), *Renkou Yu Jingji* (Population and economics), vol. 94.

Li, Sizeng (1996) 'Sheng nei liudong yu shehui jingji fazhan' (Inter-provincial migration and socio-economic development), *Renkou Yu Jingji* (Population and economics), vol. 98.

Lipton, M. (1977) *Why Poor People Stay Poor: A Study of Urban Bias in World Development*, London: Temple Smith.

Liu, Chuan (1995) 'Pinkun diqu de renkou ziyuan yu shehui jingji fazhan' (Population, resources and socio-economic development in China's poor areas), *Renkou Yu Jingji* (Population and economics), vol. 94.

Liu, Fuhe (2000) 'Poverty alleviation and development', internal report, State Council, Beijing.

Lo, C. W. H. and Leung, S. W. (2000) 'Environmental agency and public opinion in Guangzhou: the limits of a popular approach to environmental governance', *China Quarterly*, no. 163.

Ma, L. and Xiang, Biao (1998) 'Native place, migration and emergence of peasant enclaves in Beijing', *China Quarterly*, September.

Ma, Laurence and Fan, Ming (1994) 'Jiangsu xiao chengzhen' (Urbanisation from below: the growth of towns in Jiangsu), *Zhongguo Chengshi Yanjiu* (China urban studies), no. 10.

Mabogunje, A. L. (1970) 'Systems approach to a theory of rural–urban migration', *Geographical Analysis*, vol. 2.

Mallee, H. (1996) 'In defence of migration: recent Chinese studies of rural population mobility', *China Information*, vol. 10, Winter 1995–Spring 1996.

Mallee, H. (1997) 'Rural household dynamics and spatial mobility in China', in T. Scharping (ed.) *Floating Population and Migration in China*, Hamburg: Institut für Asienkunde.

Mallee, H. (1998) 'Rural population mobility in seven Chinese provinces', in F. Christiansen and Zhang Junzuo (eds) *Village Inc.: Chinese Rural Society in the 1990s*, London: Curzon.

Marx, K. (1970) *Capital*, vol. 1, London: Lawrence and Wishart.

Marx, K. (1973) *Grundrisse – Foundations of the Critique of Political Economy* (rough draft), London: Allen Lane.

Meier, G. M. (1975) *Leading Issues in Economic Development*, London: Oxford University Press.

Meng, Xianfang (1996) 'Men in non-agricultural occupations and women on the land and development of women', *Social Sciences in China*, vol. 7, no. 1.

Miller, S. M. and Roby, P. (1970) 'Poverty: changing social stratification', in P. Townsend (ed.) *The Concept of Poverty: Working Papers on Methods of Investigation and Life-Styles of the Poor in Different Countries*, London: Heinemann Educational.

Ministry of Agriculture (2000) *Chengshi Renkou* (Urban population), internal report.

Ministry of Labour and Social Security (2002) White Paper on Labour and Social Security in China.

Ministry of Village Affairs (MVA) (1965–8) *Koy Evanter Etudierine Gore*, Ankara, Turkey.

Miracle, M. P. (1967) *Agriculture in the Congo Basin: Tradition and Change in African Rural Economics*, Madison: University of Wisconsin Press.

Murphy, R. (1999) 'Returning migrants', Ph.D. thesis, University of Cambridge.

Myrdal, G. (1957) *Economic Theory and Under-developed Regions*, London: Duckworth.

NBSC (National Bureau of Statistics of China) (1985–2000) *Zhongguo Tongji Nianjian* (China statistical yearbook), Beijing.

NBSC (1992b) *Zhongguo Nongcun Tongji Nianjian* (China Yearbook of Rural Household), Beijing.

NBSC (1996b) 'One per cent sample of population census in 1995', internal report.

NBSC (1997b) *Zhongguo Meitan Gongye Tongji Nianjian* (Statistical Yearbook of Chinese Coal Industry), Beijing.

NBSC (1998b) 'Result of sample survey in 226 cities and counties', internal report.

NBSC (1999) 'The speed of urbanisation in China', internal report.

NBSC (2001) *Zhongguo Nongcun Tongji Nianjian* (China yearbook of rural household), Beijing.

NBSC (2002a) 'Result of the Fifth Census', internal report.

NBSC (2002b) *Shanxi Tongji Gongbao* (Statistical Bulletin of Shanxi).

Nolan, P. H. (1979) 'Inequality of income between town and countryside in the People's Republic of China in the mid-1950's', *World Development*, vol. 7, Oxford: Pergamon.

Nolan, P. H. (1993) 'Economic reform: poverty and migration in China', *Economic and Political Weekly*, 26 June.

Pei, Jian (1994) 'Sichuan laodongli bianji qianguo' (Sichuan's labour force felt across China), *Renmin Ribao* (*People's Daily*), 27 November–3 December.

People's Daily (*Renmin Ribao*) (2000) 'Zengjia shiyi fupinkuan' (Central government added 10 billion yuan poverty alleviation funds), 2 February.

People's Daily (*Renmin Ribao*) (2000) 'Shangdong 16 wan ren qianli huanghe tanqu' (160 thousand peasants have moved out from Yellow River flooding areas), 13 February.

People's Daily (*Renmin Ribao*) (2000) 'Jin nian wo guo cheng zhen shiyelu' (The rate of unemployment in cities), 24 February.

People's Daily (*Renmin Ribao*) (2000) 'Wai hui hui lu' (Exchange rates), 18 March.

People's Daily (*Renmin Ribao*) (2000) 'Kaifa xibu' (Poverty alleviation in western China), 17 May.

Pieke, F. N. and Mallee, H. (eds) (1999) *Internal and International Migration: Chinese Perspectives*, London: Curzon.

Pittin, R. (1984) 'Migration of women in Nigeria: the Hausa case', *International Migration Review*, Special issue: Women in Migration, vol. 18.

Prosterman, R. L., Hanstad, T. and Li Ping (1999) 'Land reform in China: the two-field system experiment in Pingdu', *Social Sciences in China*, Spring.

Ravenstein, E. G. (1885) 'The laws of migration', *Journal of the Royal Statistical Society*, vol. 52, no. 2.

Ravenstein, E. G. (1889) 'The laws of migration', *Journal of the Royal Statistical Society*, June.

Research Group on Peasant Workers (1994) 'A survey of migrant workers in 149 factories in the Pearl River Delta region', *Social Sciences in China*, vol. 3.

Richmond, A. H. (1969) 'Sociology of migration in industrial and post-industrial societies', in J. A. Jackson (ed.) *Internal Migration*, London: Sage.

Riddell, J. C. (1970) 'Labour migration and rural agriculture among the Gbannah Mano of Liberia', Ph.D. thesis, University of Oregon, Eugene.

Rochin, R. I. (1972) 'Inter-relationships between farm environment, off-farm migration and rates of adoption: dwarf wheat on irrigated small-holdings in Pakistan', Paper for the workshop on empirical studies of small-farm agriculture in developing nations, Purdue University, West Lafayette, IN.

Rowntree, B. S. (1941) *Poverty and Progress: a Second Social Survey of York*, London: Longmans.

Rowntree, B. S. (1980) *Poverty: A Study of Town Life*, London: Garland.

Sabin, L. (1994) 'New bosses in the workers' state: the growth of non-state sector employment in China', *China Quarterly*, no. 140.

Scharping, T. (1987) 'Urbanisation in China since 1949: a comment', *China Quarterly*, no. 109.

Scharping, T. (ed.) (1997) *Floating Population and Migration in China*, Hamburg: Institut für Asienkunde.

Selassie, S. G. (1986) 'Patterns of women's employment in Africa', in JASPER (Jobs and Skills Programme for Africa of the International Labour Organisation), *The Challenge of Employment and Basic Needs in Africa*, Nairobi: Oxford University Press.

Sen, A. (1981) *Poverty and Famines*, Oxford: Clarendon Press.

Sender, J. and Smith, S. (1990) *Poverty, Class, and Gender in Rural Africa: A Tanzanian Case Study*, London: Routledge.

Shaw, R. P. (1974) 'Land tenure and the rural exodus in Latin America', *Economic Development and Cultural Change*, vol. 23.

Shaw, R. P. (1975) 'A note on cost-relative calculations and decisions to migrate', *Population Studies*, vol. 28.

Sheng, Yuming (1993) *Intersectoral Resource Flows and China's Economic Development*, Basingstoke: Macmillan.

Singh, A. and Tabatabai, H. (eds) (1993) *Economic Crisis and Third World Agriculture*, Cambridge: Cambridge University Press.

Sjaastad, L. A. (1962) 'Cost and return of human migration', *Journal of Political Economy*, supplement, October, part 2.

Skinner, E. P. (1965) 'Labor migration among the Mossi of Upper Volta', in H. Kuper (ed.) *Urbanization and Migration in West Africa*, Berkeley: University of California Press.

Skinner, G. W. (1977) *The City in Late Imperial China*, Stanford, CA: Stanford University Press.

Solinger, D. J. (1993) 'China's transients and the state: a form of civil society?', *Politics and Society*, vol. 21, no. 1.

Solinger, D. J. (1997) 'Migrant petty entrepreneurs and a dual labour market?', in T. Scharping (ed.) *Floating Population and Migration in China*, Hamburg: Institut für Asienkunde.

Song, Lina (1995) 'The situation and policies of rural–urban migration', *Social Sciences in China*, no. 4.

Speare, A. (1971) 'Urbanization and migration in Taiwan', University of Michigan, Population Studies Center, Working Paper 11.

Stamp, P. (1989) 'Technology, gender and power in Africa', Technical Study, International Development Research Centre, Ottawa.

State Council (1984) 'Guowuyuan guanyu nongmin dinju xiaochengshi de zhishi' (Circular of the State Council concerning the question of peasants entering market towns for settlement), Government report, no. 26, Beijing.

State Council (1991) 'Quanmin suoyouzhi qiye zhaoyong nongmin hetongzhi gongren de guiding' (Issue of hiring peasant workers by state-owned enterprises), Government report, no. 23, Beijing.

State Council (1995) 'Yi gong dai zhen xiaochu pinkun' (The situation of public works and poverty alleviation), Government report, no. 8, Beijing.

State Council (1998) 'Nongcun pinkun renkou' (Report on the rural poor population), Government report, no. 18, Beijing.

State Council (2001) *Nongain Fazan Baipishu* (White Paper on the development of rural China), Government report, Beijing

State Council Development and Research Centre (2001) *Nongmingong Xianzhuang* (The development of peasant workers), survey report, Beijing.

Stouffer, S. A. (1940) 'Intervening opportunities: a theory relating mobility and distance', *American Sociological Review*, vol. 5.

Tang. S. Y., Cheung, K. C. and Lo, C. W. H. (1997) 'Institutional constraints on environment governance in urban China: the case of Guangzhou and Shanghai', *China Quarterly*, no. 152.

Tawney, R. H. (1932) *Land and Labour in China*, London: George Allen and Unwin.

Thomas, R. (1954) *Migration and Economic Growth. A Study of Great Britain and Atlantic Economy*, Cambridge: Cambridge University Press.

Tienda, M. and Booth, K. (1988) 'Migration, gender and social change: a review and reformulation', Paper given at Conference on Women's Position and Demographic Change in the Course of Development, Oslo, Liège, IUSSP.

Todaro, M. (1969) 'A model of labour migration and urban unemployment in LDCs', *American Economic Review*, vol. 59.

Todaro, M. (1976) *Internal Migration in Developing Countries*, Geneva: International Labour Organisation.

Todaro, M. and Rampel, H. (1972) 'Reply to comment on labour migration in less developed countries', *Manpower and Unemployment Research in Africa*, no. 2.

Tong, Xing and Lin, Mingang (1992) *Daxue Renkou Yanjiu* (University research and training in demography), Beijing: Beijing daxue chubanshe (Beijing: Beijing University Press).

Tong, Xing and Lin, Mingang (1995) 'Pinkunxian de yanjiu' (A study of poverty lines in rural areas), *Social Sciences in China*, vol. 16, no. 2.

Townsend, P. (ed.) (1970) *The Concept of Poverty: Working Papers on Methods of Investigation and Life-Styles of the Poor in Different Countries*, London: Heinemann Educational.

Townsend, P. (ed.) (1979) *Poverty in the United Kingdom: A Survey of Household Resources and Standards of Living*, Harmondsworth: Penguin.

Walsh, A. C. and Trlin, A. D. (1973) 'Niuean migration: Niue social-economic background characteristics of migrants and settlement in Auckland', *Journal of Polynesian Society*, vol. 82, no. 1.

Wang, Gin (1996) 'Wo guo renkou liudong he diqu fazhan' (Population migration and regional economic development in China), *Renkou Yanjiu* (Population research), vol. 6.

Wang, X. and Bai, N. (1987) *The Poverty of Plenty*, London: Macmillan.

Wang, Youzhao (1994) 'Anhui sheng zhengyan shi baogao' (Policy research office of Anhui provincial committee), Local government report, Anhui.

Wang, Yuzhao (2000) 'Fupin jijin' (Fund to help poor farmers), Local government report, Guizhou.

Wiseman, R. F. and Roseman, C. C. (1979) 'A typology of elderly migration based on the decision-making process', *Economic Geography*, vol. 55.

Wolpert, J. (1964) 'The decision process in perspective', *Annals of the Association of American Geography*, vol. 54.

Wolpert, J. (1965) 'Behavioural aspects of the decision to migrate', *Paper and Proceedings of the Regional Science Association*, vol. 15.

Wolpert, J. (1966) 'Migration as an adjustment to environmental stress', *Journal of Social Issues*, vol. 22.

World Bank (1988) *World Bank Country Study: Growth and Development in Gansu Province*, Washington, DC.

World Bank (1992) *China: Strategies for Reducing Poverty in the 1990s*, Washington, DC.

World Bank (2000) *World Development Report 2000/2001: Attacking Poverty*, Washington, DC.

Wu, H. (1994) 'Rural to urban migration in the People's Republic of China', *China Quarterly*, no. 139.

Xinhua News (2001) 'China set to ease restrictions on migrant labour', 17 September.

Xu, Yuan (1982) *Shehuizhuyi De Jiage Zhidu* (Price issues under socialism), Beijing: Caizheng Jingji Chubanshe (Beijing: Finance and Economic Press).

Yan, R. (1988) *Zhongguo Nongye Chanpin De Jiandaocha* (The price scissors of the agricultural products in China), Beijing: Beijing Renmin Daxue Chubanshe (Beijing: China People's University Press).

Yang, Xueling (1995) 'Wo guo de laodongli liudong he nongcun jingji fazhan' (Labour mobility and urban and rural economic development in China), *Renkou Yu Yanjiu* (Population and Economics), vol. 92.

Yang, Z. and Xiao, Z. (1996) 'Liudong renkou he chengshihua' (Flowing population and urbanisation), *Renkou Yu Yanjiu* (Population and economics), vol. 98.

Yin, Zijinag and Yu, Qinhong (1997) *Zhongguo Huji Zhidu De Biange* (Reforming China's household registration system), Beijing: Zhongguozhengfa Daxue Chubanshe (Beijing: China Political Science and Law University Press).

Young, E. C. (1928) 'The movement of farm population', *Bulletin of the Cornell Agricultural Experiment Station*.

Zhan, Rong (1994) 'Ruhe dundai nongcun shengyu laodongli de wenti' (Problems and treatments of surplus labour in rural areas), *Zhen Xi Zhi You* (Bulletin of the Shanxi political consultation), no. 5.

Zhang, L. and Zhao, S. (1998) 'Re-examining China's "urban" concept and the level of urbanisation', *China Quarterly*, vol. 54.

Zhang, Mei (1999) 'Rural privatisation and women's labour: property rights and gender concepts in inner Mongolia and Xinjiang', in J. West, Zhao Minghau, Chang Xiaqun and Cheng Yuan (eds) *Women of China: Economic and Social Transformation*, London: Macmillan.

Zhao, Minliang (1995) 'Shanghai gongye zhong nongmingong de diaocha' (Investigation of migrant workers in some industries in Shanghai), *Zhongguo Renkou Kexue* (Chinese population science), no. 3.

Zhao, Ying (2000) 'Wo guo chengshi jumin shenghuo shunpin yousuo tigao' (The living standard of city residents is improving), Results of a survey from the Mainland Marketing Research Centre. To be published.

Zheng, Ping (1999) *Zhongguo Dili-zhiran, Jingji, Renwen* (China's geography: natural conditions, regional economics, cultural features). Beijing: Wuzhou Chubanshe (Beijing: China Intercontinental Press).

Zheng, Sheng (1996) *Qian-Jin* (Shanxi government report), vol. 5.

Zhou, Qiren (1997) 'Jihui yu nengli' (Chances and capabilities), internal report, State Labour Bureau, China.

Zhou, Xinwen (ed.) (1999) *Zhongguo Shishi Yu Shuzi* (China: Facts and figures), Beijing: New Star Publishers.

Zhu, Ling (1994) 'Bianqian zhong de fupin gongzuo he nuxin fazhan' (Poverty alleviation and women's development in China's transition), research report, Chinese Academy of Social Sciences.

Zhu, Ling (1996) 'Fu pin dai kuan' (Poverty alleviation loan), *Poverty Alleviation by Credit*, vol. 2.

Zhu, Qingfang (2000) 'Gei di shouru zhe jixu jia xing' (Pay more to lower-income employers), *Renmin Ribao* (*People's Daily*), 8 May.

Zou, Lanchun (1996) *Beijing De Liudong Renkou* (Beijing's floating population), Beijing: China Population Press.

Index